0013047

Books are to be returned on or before
the last date below.

B27407

SCREENING FOR CHILDREN WITH SPECIAL NEEDS

SCREENING FOR CHILDREN WITH SPECIAL NEEDS

Multidisciplinary Approaches

Edited by Geoff Lindsay

CROOM HELM
London & Sydney

© 1984 Geoff Lindsay
Croom Helm Ltd, Provident House, Burrell Row,
Beckenham, Kent BR3 1AT
Croom Helm Australia Pty Ltd, First Floor,
139 King Street, Sydney, NSW 2001, Australia

British Library Cataloguing in Publication Data

Screening for children with special needs
    1. Children – Research
    I. Lindsay, Geoff
   362.7'95   HQ768.8
   ISBN 0-7099-1636-1

Printed and bound in Great Britain by
Biddles Ltd, Guildford and King's Lynn

CONTENTS

List of Figures

List of Tables

Preface

Acknowledgements

1. Introduction *Geoff Lindsay*	1
2. Medical Screening and Surveillance *Ruth M. Powell*	12
3. The Role of the Health Visitor *Kathleen Jennings*	43
4. Audiological Screening and Assessment *Anna MacCarthy and Judith Connell*	63
5. The Speech Therapist and Language Disorders *Kath Thompson*	86
6. Looking for Trouble: A Teacher's Point of View *Mary Jane Drummond*	98
7. The Role of the Educational Psychologist *Geoff Lindsay*	116
8. The Social Worker: Front Line and Last Ditch *Bryan Craig*	134
9. The 1981 Education Act and its Implications *Geoff Lindsay*	153
10. Overview *Geoff Lindsay*	167
Bibliography	188
Notes on Contributors	199
Index	200

To my parents

LIST OF FIGURES

4.1 Example of an Audiogram   78
10.1 Compensatory Interaction   177

LIST OF TABLES

1.1 Placement by Disability   8

1.2 Prevalence of Physical Disorders, Intellectual and Educational Retardation in 10- to 12-year-old Children   9

3.1 Example of Health Visitors' Screening Tests of Development   56

4.1 Stages of Hearing Assessment and Intervention   64

5.1 Summary of the Results of a National Survey of Speech Therapy Provision   89

5.2 Percentage of Children rated at the lowest part of the Infant Rating Scale Level I, Expressive Language Items (N = 1342)   93

7.1 Frequencies of Children in Categories, expressed as percentages   127

7.2 Percentage Efficiency of IRS Level I scores in predicting Reading Failure at 7 years   129

10.1 The Accuracy of a Screening Test's Prediction of the Existence of a Specified Problem   174

10.2 Variation of IQ Over Time   175

PREFACE

The early years are a time of great importance in determining the chances that a child will have for his or her later life. During this period, major developmental changes will occur. The child will learn to communicate linguistically and socially, to walk, run and climb and to develop a large number of cognitive skills. But it is also a time of susceptibility to potentially hazardous experiences. Before the baby is born the mother's own health and her receipt of injuries may have an effect on the baby. Smoking, for example, is known to affect the growth of the fetus. The birth itself may result in trauma for the baby, with short- and long-term adverse consequences. Then there are the normal hazards of everyday life – common childhood illnesses, accidents, family trauma and environmental disadvantage.

Over the past twenty years or so there has been growing interest in the early identification of difficulties suffered by children. The rationale is simple: the sooner we can identify such problems the sooner we can take action. This action might be curative or ameliorative. But the range of possible problems that could be identified and the large number of children involved has led to the development of simple and quick methods of identification. The general term for such a procedure is *screening*.

There are now screening programmes being carried out at various stages from before conception to the 7-plus age level. These are concerned with physical, psychological, linguistic and social development of children. They are conducted by a range of professionals from different services, using a variety of methods. In addition each service will have other methods of identifying children's difficulties, and of liaising with other services. Such arrangements are often peculiar to a particular locality, and indeed may not be the same for all agencies within one locality. In Sheffield, for example, social work, education and medical services are based upon different geographical divisions of the city. Despite attempts to improve communication between the agencies, this is still far from perfect. Each area has similar difficulties.

All of these factors can make a bewildering situation for the parents of a child with special needs – and for the professionals themselves. Many such children require assistance from more than one agency and parents can often be confused by the succession of 'experts' they are asked to consult. Similarly professionals often have only limited know-ledge of the work of other workers with young children, and of the constraints upon their work.

This book has two purposes. First it is intended to describe the work, training and general situation of the main professionals who work with young children. Second, the practices of identifying children with special needs, in particular the use of screening procedures, will be described and critically evaluated. These discussions will be placed within the context of the 1981 Education Act which became operative in 1983.

ACKNOWLEDGEMENTS

I would like to express my thanks to Gordon Mitchell, Education Officer of the National Deaf Children's Society for the results of an unpublished review of research into the identification of hearing impairment, and to Emeritus Professor Ronald Illingworth and colleagues for comments on Chapter 2, 'Medical Screening and Surveillance'. I am also grateful for the excellent services of Lynne Clark who painstakingly typed the several drafts of this book.

1 INTRODUCTION

Geoff Lindsay

This book is concerned with the early identification of special needs in young children, a process which has gained in popularity over recent years. It is hoped that by early identification of a problem, prevention of a more serious problem can be averted. For example, certain cancers can be identified at an early stage of development, treatment can be provided, and a major illness, or even death, can be averted. Our concern is with young children, mainly in the 0 to 6 years age range, but many of the same ideas, and indeed problems, are common to all forms of identification.

Identifying problems in young children is not always an easy task. In fact, as we will show, it is far more difficult than earlier optimistic endeavours suggested. However, it is clearly a worthwhile aim of prevention if more serious difficulties can occur. There have been many advances in this area over recent years and many children have had lives which have been made easier and more fulfilling as a result of these developments. An example is treatment of the metabolic disorder phenylketonuria (PKU) which previously resulted in children suffering mental retardation. A highly successful screening programme (see Chapter 2 for details) has resulted in children suffering from this disorder having much better life chances. Those identified shortly after birth can be put on a special diet, and research which has followed up these children has shown that, although they still suffer some difficulties, as a group they are much less affected than those for whom no special diet was provided. For example, mean IQ of the children studied by Berry, O'Grady, Perlmutter and Bofinger (1979) who received early treatment was 98, compared with 83 for all those who were treated late or not at all. The treatment of children with PKU is an example of a most satisfactory programme where highly accurate identification is followed by effective treatment. Unfortunately, as we shall show, most programmes of identification are not so straightforward.

Identification

The purpose of identification of problems is action. Unless some action can follow there is little point in undertaking the programme of identification. For example, it is possible to screen all seven-year-old children and identify those whose reading development is retarded. But unless it is intended to provide for these children either extra or different resources or teaching, little has been achieved. Indeed such an initiative could be criticised on ethical grounds if no intervention follows.

In this context it is important to distinguish two related, but different processes: a survey on the one hand and screening on the other.

The essential difference between these two processes is one of specificity. For a survey, what is required is an overall picture. For example, the number of children in a certain area of a city who are under five; or the range of percentages of children in secondary schools whose reading is below a normal 10-year level (which might be anything from 2 to 20 per cent). For this process it is not necessary to know which children are affected.

A local authority may wish to know how many children under the age of five live in a certain area in order to plan the allocation of resources. Alternatively a Local Education Authority (LEA) may decide to compare schools on, say, reading achievement in order to allocate extra support or remedial teachers. In such cases a *survey* might be undertaken.

In contrast, a District Health Authority (DHA) will wish to identify all those children with hearing difficulties, or an LEA might decide to identify which children require special educational provision owing to learning difficulties. Here a *screening* process will be suitable. We want to know whether any particular individual has a problem of development.

There are implications of this distinction which are largely concerned with scale and accuracy. A city like Sheffield with about 91,000 school children (1983 figures) could achieve accurate results for any survey using a sampling technique. For example, to determine what proportion of eight-year-olds were poor readers (however defined) it would be possible to test not the 6,000 children of that age, but perhaps a 10 per cent sample, that is 600. The savings in time and money are obvious. Clearly this is not possible when individual children's difficulties are at issue: all must then be investigated.

Secondly, there is the issue of accuracy. No measurement process is entirely accurate. In some cases the instruments used are subject to inconsistent results, while in addition there is the 'human element' – intruments may be misread, results recorded incorrectly, or judgements of less objective measures may vary between people. In later chapters these issues will be taken up with respect to various identification techniques used to examine children with developmental problems. But it is worth mentioning here that even such apparently simple processes as measuring height and weight can be problematic. Rutter, Tizard and Whitmore (1970) report that children in their sample of 9 to 10-year-olds on the Isle of Wight were tested and then retested four weeks later for both height and weight. In each case the measurements were carried out by the health visitor/school nurse. However, the correlation coefficient between the two testings was only 0.91 (n = 99) for height and 0.94 (n = 72) for weight. In 8 of the 99 cases the heights recorded varied by 5 cm or more, and in one case by as much as 12 cm!

Screening and assessment are processes which are both concerned with the examination of individual children. However they are distinct, though related, activities and it is important to distinguish those attributes which are common and those which are discrepant if each is to be fully understood.

Screening

Acceptability

Any investigation of a child's development must be of a form which is acceptable to both the child and the parents. Unpleasant and painful experiences, for example, are clearly to be avoided. This aspect is probably more important with screening. Where there is a likelihood of a disorder a child may require an examination which is unpleasant in some way. It may be justified to undertake this in such cases, but not at the level of screening when most children will not have the problem sought. For example, a pin prick to obtain blood for testing neonates is acceptable for screening; lumbar punctures and brain scans are not.

Specificity

Any particular screening process should be aimed at a specific problem. These can, however, vary in the degree of specificity; for example, screening for PKU is highly specific, screening for learning difficulties is not. In general psychoeducational difficulties are subject to lower degrees of specificity which are partly the result of the nature of these problems, and partly a result of the varying link between the problem and cause. For example, PKU can be traced to a specific problem with the body's processing of an amino acid, phenylalanine. Failure to learn to read, however, has multifactorial causes.

Sensitivity

Any screening procedure must be sensitive, i.e. accurate. To discover that half of those children thought to have learning problems are in fact normal is at best wasteful, and at worse damaging, in that those children might then have been given inappropriate help. In later chapters we will show how accuracy is highly variable, with psychoeducational screening once again being less susceptible to accurate results than many screenings of physical conditions.

Cost-effectiveness

Screening should be simple and quick. If this is achieved it can also be cheap. If in addition the screening is highly accurate it will be cost-effective. For example, screening by health visitors is quick and relatively cheap, but measurement of cost-effectiveness is hampered by insufficient evidence on accuracy (see Chapter 3).

Pass/Fail Result

The end of the screening process for any child should be a simple categorical statement. Ideally this should be pass/fail although many screening processes would also have an intermediate stage of 'doubtful', or similar category. In the former case, provided the screening is accurate, action is easy to determine. In the latter, a further decision must be made with regard to the 'doubtful' children. This will be determined, in part at least, by the numbers of children in such a category. Should they all be retested immediately, or followed up a year later? Unfortunately it is rarely possible to avoid having such a category. As Ruth Powell argues (see page 22), even screening of PKU has been found to be more problematic than once considered as there are borderline children who require repeated monitoring to ensure that they do not subsequently suffer damage owing to raised levels of phenylalanine.

Resources

It has already been stated that screening without resource allocation is to be avoided. Surveys can be used to determine a need, and their results be used to put pressure on authorities, but this is not the purpose of screening programmes.

Early Identification

Implicit in all screening procedures with children is the idea that 'the earlier the better'. Clearly if a problem can be identified at a stage when its effects on the child's development are slight this is to be welcomed. Screening for sensory impairment is a good example where early identification can lead to appropriate intervention. When this does not occur we know that such affected children may have their development seriously affected.

But 'early' in this phase actually refers to two different issues. First, identification should be early in the development of the disorder or problem. In this context identification could occur at any chronological age. For example, Ruth Powell shows (page 28) that children's visual ability often deteriorates in later childhood. 'Early' in this case, will be at Junior or Secondary school age. Other problems may not occur until much later in life. Some psychological problems do not occur until early adolescence and it is not uncommon for youngsters to change from a pattern of normal adjustment, to one giving rise to concern, after transfer to secondary school (Lindsay, 1983).

Second, 'early' may refer to chronological age. In some cases early identification may take place before the baby is born, particularly with genetic and chromosomal abnormalities such as Downs Syndrome. In other cases 'early' may refer to the perinatal period. With hearing impairment the most obvious time for early identification, at this time, is the second half of the first year of life. The Bullock Report (DES, 1975) urged that problems with reading and language generally be identified not at 7 to 8 years, as was the practice in the early 1970s, but at 5 to 6 years, before the child had the added burden of a sense of failure.

'At Risk' Screening

Unfortunately these two different aspects of early identification are sometimes not fully appreciated and programmes have been instituted which have not succeeded. This is particularly the case with the history of 'at risk' screening when the purpose is to identify children who are likely to develop a particular problem. For example, children may be tested at 7 years to see if they have reading difficulties, but attempts have been made to screen them at 5 years to identify those children who will later have problems with reading. Such screening involves an appraisal not of the ability or condition itself, but of some other ability or condition which correlates, and is thought likely to relate causally with the target ability (see page 176).

Assessment

Assessment refers to the detailed appraisal of an individual child on specific dimensions. It will differ from professional to professional and with the nature of the problem. For example, a psychologist will give a different assessment of a child exhibiting behaviour problems compared with one who has learning difficulties.

Assessment has many of the attributes outlined above in common with screening. The main differences concern scale. Children will often be assessed following some form of screening procedure. This might be a formal process, whereby all children are screened, and those who fail the test are passed on for assessment (e.g. with hearing problems). Alternatively, children might be referred for assessment following intervention by another professional, or concern expressed by a parent (e.g. many psychological problems).

Assessment is normally carried out by professionals who are more highly trained with respect to the problem at hand. Thus audiologists will assess children with suspected hearing impairment, speech therapists will assess those with speech and language problems, while health visitors will screen for both. Consequently assessment differs also in terms of depth and extensiveness. Language functioning, for example, will be examined over a longer session and in much greater depth by a speech therapist. On the other hand, such a process thereby becomes more expensive than the screening procedure in both terms of time and cost of personnel and resources.

The results of an assessment will not be a simple pass/fail distinction, but should contain a detailed appraisal of the child's areas of strengths and weaknesses. The advice section of the Statement of special educational needs under the 1981 Education Act is an example of this (see Chapter 9). In addition, clear advice on resource allocation should be possible following an assessment.

One problem with assessment, however, is that it is often conceptualised in the same terms for all areas of functioning. In some cases, particularly with organic disorders, it is useful to have a diagnosis. However, with all social and psychological problems, and the psychological or educational implications of organic disorders, such diagnoses are often at best irrelevant, and at worse distinctly unhelpful. A good example is that group of children who have severe difficulties with written language, despite otherwise normal abilities and functioning. Such children have been diagnosed 'dyslexic', by medical practitioners. Even now there are still major debates in the press and within professions about the usefulness of the concept — whereas what the children need is a careful appraisal of their needs, and appropriate intervention.

In general there appears now to be a move away from a labelling or categorising process to one of describing strengths, weaknesses and needs. In our view this is much welcomed.

Young Children with Special Needs

The preceding discussion has considered the processes of identifying children with special needs. But who exactly are these children? How many are there? The subsequent chapters will report on specific groups of children as they come to the attention of different professionals, but for the present it is necessary to give an overview of this issue.

Definition

There are a number of terms which have often been used interchangeably — e.g. handicap, disability, defect, disadvantage. A defect may be considered a fault in the child's physical make-up, which often gives rise to a disability. For example, the absence of a limb will impair the child's ability to do certain things. Whether this constitutes a handicap depends on both the task and the compensatory resources that can be brought to bear. For example, a child with no strength in the lower limbs will be handicapped with respect to certain sports, but not necessarily with respect to academic subjects. Disadvantage is now more commonly reserved for discussions of socially disabling conditions — e.g. poor housing, reduced finances.

The Warnock Report (Department of Education and Science, 1978) recommended that a more useful term was 'special educational needs', and this has started to replace terms such as 'handicap'. This change is not, however, merely semantic. It represents a change in emphasis moving from what is wrong with the child and on to what the child needs in order to have optimal development. Also, the terms 'impairment' and 'disability' will be used here in preference to 'handicap' when the actual 'within-child' problem is being considered (see Heron and Myers, 1983, for a discussion).

Incidence

Studies of special educational needs are, however, only just beginning and in general statistical data are derived from surveys using older systems of categorisation. For example, the Isle of Wight study (Rutter *et al*, 1970) describes the prevalence of psychiatric disorders, intellectual and educational retardation and physical disorders. The results of this and the National Child Development Study led the Warnock Committee to suggest that about one in five children (20 per cent) would have special educational needs at some stage in their school lives, while about one in six would have such needs at any one time.

Studies of incidence are, of course, subject to differing interpretations depending upon the original definitions. Another way of assessing prevalence rates is to use administrative criteria. Thus, in 1977 it could be claimed that 1.8 per cent of children were handicapped (in administrative terms) in that they were attending special schools or special classes designated as such by LEAs or similar provision.

Data produced by the Sheffield LEA present a similar picture. For 1983, 2.13 per cent of its pupils were in special schools or special units. An examination of the referral of children to these schools and units in 1982 is presented in the LEA's Education Statistics handbook for 1983 and reproduced in Table 1.1. Two points will be made about this information. First, it makes use of categories of handicap. Second, it refers only to those children placed in special provision. It does not include those children who are integrated into ordinary schools, but who may have comparable disabling conditions.

Table 1.1: Placement by Disability

	Boys	Girls	Total
Mild Learning Difficulties	62	17	79
Moderate Learning Difficulties	31	25	56
Severe Learning Difficulties	9	6	15
Delicate	14	6	20
Maladjusted	21	10	31
Moderate Learning Diff./Maladjusted	2	3	5
Physical Handicap	6	7	13
Deaf	4	2	6
Blind	9	—	9
Partial Hearing	2	2	4
Partial Sight	—	1	1
Speech Disorder	3	—	3
Short Term Support	32	10	42
Special Nursery	10	5	15
	205	94	299

Source: Education Statistics, 1983; City of Sheffield

Table 1.2: Prevalence of Physical Disorders, Intellectual and Educational Retardation in 10- to 12-year-old Children

Disorder	% of age group
All physical disorders	5.7
Asthma	2.3
Uncomplicated epilepsy	0.6
Cerebral palsy	0.5
Deafness	0.2
Blindness	<0.1
Mental subnormality	0.4
Intellectual retardation	2.5
Reading backwardness	6.6
Specific reading retardation	3.7

Source: Rutter *et al* (1970).

The Isle of Wight study (Rutter *et al*, 1970) presents prevalence rates for a large number of developmental problems including physical disorders (e.g. cerebral palsy and deafness) and educational and intellectual retardation. A sample of these is presented in Table 1.2. As discussed above, the exact meaning of such data is dependent upon the original definition of the terms, and the table uses the classification used by the authors. In many cases, children in fact suffered from more than one disabling condition.

It is apparent from data such as these that while about 20 per cent of children may have special educational needs, less than about 2 per cent are catered for within the special school system. It is likely that this percentage will drop still further as the move towards integration increases in pace. In addition, the prevalence of problems and impairments varies. Severe hearing or visual impairment is rare, compared with those who have specific reading retardation. But, as was suggested above, while the first is a relatively straightforward 'within-child' impairment, a reading problem may be caused by a number of factors, not all of which are 'within-child'.

This may be even more of an issue with maladjustment, yet so-called maladjusted children form a sizeable percentage of those in special schools, and their numbers have been increasing over the years. The Sheffield data show this group of children to make up about 10 per cent of referrals into special education. Hegarty and Pocklington (1981) report that the number of schools for the maladjusted increased by almost half, from 142 to 208 between 1972 and 1980.

When considering prevalence rates, therefore, it is important to bear in mind that their 'purity' will be variable. Severe and profound developmental disabilities may be classified relatively simply, but a problem such as maladjustment (or behaviour problems) will depend not only on the child but the family, school or pre-school provision, community resources and other factors, especially definition.

Professionals

The identification of problems experienced by children in the age range 0 to 6 years is largely the task of the parents and a number of professionals who work with young children. In this book the work of these professionals will be considered in some detail.

Each professional has a role to play in the identification of special needs. In some cases they are involved in routine screening of children, while in others their role is directed more towards a detailed assessment of a child already identified by others as causing concern. The procedures used in early identification by each professional will be discussed, including an evaluation of their effectiveness.

Collaboration

Because of the large number of professionals there is, inevitably, a certain amount of confusion and lack of understanding which is a potential hazard. Parents may not appreciate the differences between one worker and another, or the legitimate boundaries of their advice. They may not know, for example, who recommends which school would best meet the child's needs. But parents are not alone in this. The professionals themselves often have a less than clear idea of what their colleagues do. Teachers and social workers, for example, often have stereotyped ideas of each other (see Chapter 8). Often one may come across a worker who has little idea of how many health visitors there are in the same area, or of the workload of speech therapists. The types of training received by each professional are also rarely appreciated. Consequently we shall present for each worker a description of the type of work done and general information on training, workload and patterns of working (e.g. methods of referral).

Conclusion

If children with difficulties are to receive the best help available, their problems should be identified as soon as possible. Futhermore effective help should be provided, and professionals involved with the child should work together closely. Finally, it must be remembered that throughout all this the significant role of parents must be recognised. Although this is not a book *about* parents, it is certainly one *for* parents.

2 MEDICAL SCREENING AND SURVEILLANCE

Ruth M. Powell

Introduction

Medical practitioners, or 'doctors' as they are commonly known, are concerned with the detection of developmental difficulties from the antenatal period right through to adolescence. Different types of medical practitioner will be involved at different stages, including paediatricians in hospitals, clinical medical officers in well-baby and school clinics, and general practitioners. All of these have the same basic training, to become fully qualified, and so be registered as a medical practitioner, but then enter different branches of medicine usually undertaking further training.

It is difficult to separate medical screening from surveillance. These are closely linked and aim to identify, by selective tests or examinations, any defects of the body structure or function which may lead to disability or handicap. It is important that the different types of medical practitioners mentioned above integrate their work in order that a coherent medical screening and surveillance system is implemented. There is also a need to work closely with other professionals in the health services, including nursing and laboratory staff, as well as those in the education and social services.

Training for Medical Practitioners

There are approximately 4,000 medical students in each year of training in Britain at present. The basic training period may be for either five or six years. At the end of this time the student qualifies for a medical degree but must spend a year gaining further clinical experience before becoming fully registered as a medical practitioner. The medical courses are intended to give the students a thorough understanding of the normal structure and function of the body and of the ways in which disease and disorders of function can affect the body.

When studying paediatrics the student will be expected to gain a picture of the child in health and in sickness, considering the factors leading to normal development and those which place the child at risk.

The pre-registration year in hospital gives experience in general medicine and surgery. This is followed by more specialised work for short periods of 4-6 months, during which time examinations are taken. These may be for diplomas – e.g. DCH: Diploma in Child Health or for further degrees; MRCP: Membership of the Royal College of Physicians. Doctors wishing to work in Community Child Health will be expected to have had hospital paediatric experience.

At present, doctors involved with developmental screening in the Community Child Health Service can expect to be given further training in the procedures used in developmental assessments. They may also be sent on courses run by the various University Departments of Paediatrics across the country. These vary from a short course of less than a week to day release every week during the three terms of the academic year. A few doctors have higher degrees, but a well-planned training programme with a proper career structure has yet to be established.

The Joint Committee for Higher Medical Training is presently considering the training programme for doctors who wish to pursue a paediatric career in the community.

Hospital Consultant Paediatricians are required to have had four years of experience at Senior Registrar level. A similar period would be expected of a Community Paediatrician and experience before this would need to reflect his or her role in the future – e.g. child psychiatry, general practice, obstetrics, paediatric research. The MRCP will be essential.

Senior Clinical Medical Officers already in a post may be offered individual consideration, with account being taken of their experience and their post-graduate qualifications.

Health Provision for Children

There are two main types of health provision for children: preventative services within the community and treatment services provided by the hospitals and primary care team. Ideally, as recommended in the Court Report (Department of Health and Social Security, 1976) they should be integrated with the care of the child being of top priority. We are gradually moving towards this in the preventative side of paediatrics. Family doctors are doing developmental testing in both their own clinics and those run by the Health Authorities. Consultant appointments are being made with the paediatrician having a definite commitment to work in the community not only with the family doctor but also with the Clinical Medical Officers. More junior appointments are being arranged so that doctors can spend half their time working in the hospitals and half in the community. This seems particularly successful where the hospital work entails assessment of the handicapped, treatment of accident and emergency patients, research into the cause of death in the very young or family planning and marital counselling.

Reorganisation (1982) has resulted in the replacement of Area Health Authorities by District Health Authorities. Clinical Medical Officers are accountable to the District Medical Officers, but they are responsible for their own clinical judgement. The District Medical Officer now works with a team of Specialists in Community Medicine. Each specialist may have more than one field of responsibility and may work in more than one district; the latter depends on the size of the district. Sheffield is one of the largest single district authorities and covers the same geographical area as the old AHA. Difficulties may arise where a large Education Authority has to work with more than one Health Authority.

The doctors who are Specialists in Community Medicine (SCM) are gradually being replaced on retirement by doctors with limited child health experience. These doctors will be trained in management, planning and epidemiology and will have gained the MFCM, the Membership of the Faculty of Community Medicine. The responsibility for the reorganisation of Child Health Services in the community is gradually moving to Senior Clinical Medical Officers with Specialists in Community Medicine retaining the planning role, e.g. SCM (Child Health and Social Services) and SCM (Environmental Health).

In addition to their clinical duties, the Senior Clinical Medical Officers are expected to be involved with management, to develop a special interest and to supervise the Registers, i.e. non-accidental injury and handicap. Many have a teaching responsibility towards medical students, nurses being trained as health visitors and post-graduate doctors.

Community Health Councils aim to reflect the public's concern in health services. They have a right to visit all hospitals, health centres and clinics and must be consulted if a District Health Authority wishes to develop or reduce the service provided. They meet those who are responsible for planning services and provide views and information gained from regular contact with the general public through surveys and research.

Screening Procedures

Screening is a deliberate search for diseases in their earliest stages. It is not practical to screen for diseases where there is no treatment available. Apart from this there are more than thirty different conditions that can be diagnosed ante-natally, but because most of them are very rare, total screening of the population would be too expensive.

Screening throughout the country tends to vary according to the resources available; the medical screening tests are limited at present and are likely to remain so. When considering the introduction of new tests to the total population the criteria recommended by Wilson and Junger (1982) for the World Health Organisation in 1968 still apply, and the following questions must be answered:

(a) Is the test sensitive and specific for a particular disorder?
(b) Is it possible for it to be performed quickly and cheaply?
(c) Does it give a simple pass/fail result?
(d) Are the resources available for the early treatment of the disorder with the prospect of positively influencing the course of the disorder?

If the disorder is not likely to cause undue stress or inconvenience, or if leaving the disorder to proceed through its natural course and arranging treatment when it becomes appropriate is satisfactory, screening for the disorder may not be acceptable for personal and financial reasons. If the specificity of a test is good the number of false positives will be at a minimum. If not, resources will be taken up with the provision of facilities for further investigations, which may be costly and perhaps hazardous.

If the child's developmental ability is questioned unnecessarily anxiety may be generated which may affect the child's performance during subsequent assessment, or the parents may become overprotective.

The sensitivity of a test should be good enough to ensure the minimum of false negatives so that we are not given a false sense of security.

These and other hazards related to screening programmes are well documented in a report from a World Health Organisation working group (WHO, 1980).

Antenatal Screening Procedures

Blood Tests

At present, blood is taken from all pregnant women when they book into the antenatal clinic, whether it is run by the family doctor or the community health service.

(1) The *haemoglobin level* is estimated to see if there is anaemia and tests are done for certain diseases known to affect the unborn child, e.g. syphilis.

(2) The mother's *immunity to rubella* (German Measles) is checked: the number of babies at risk from congenital rubella syndrome should fall as the vaccination programme for 12-13 year old girls proceeds. The greatest risk to the fetus is from infection occurring during the first 8 weeks of pregnancy. The damage to the fetus can vary considerably from severe illness in the newborn period, associated with defects of the eye or heart, to deafness which may be diagnosed later in infancy. If a mother has no immunity to rubella, she should be vaccinated as soon as possible after the birth of her baby, thus removing the risk factor for future pregnancies.

(3) *Blood group* must be checked. The mother and baby may have different blood groups; if there is marked incompatibility between their blood groups the baby may be jaundiced at birth. The severity of the condition, known as haemolytic disease of the newborn, depends on the degree of the incompatibility. The commonest form is due to ABO incompatibility but this is usually mild; the Rhesus factor is much more of a problem. Most of us have a positive Rhesus blood factor, but if a mother is Rhesus negative and she has had a Rhesus positive baby or miscarried a Rhesus positive fetus she may have developed antibodies to Rhesus positive blood. These antibodies will cross the placental barrier in future pregnancies and cause damage to the fetal red cells. The level of the antibodies in the mother's blood is checked regularly, but does not always accurately reflect the degree to which the baby is affected. Tests must be done on the amniotic fluid surrounding the baby as well. A severely affected pregnancy may be managed by delivering the baby at 34 weeks and then giving the baby an exchange transfusion. Small amounts of the baby's blood are replaced by healthy Rhesus negative blood. This process removes the affected cells with the antibody causing the disease.

If the baby is so immature that it would not be safe to deliver it by a Caesarian birth, it may be given a blood transfusion while still in the uterus.

The transfer of the baby's blood to the mother's circulation mainly takes place during the birth and as the build up of antibodies takes several weeks, it is possible to prevent this happening by giving her an injection of anti-Rhesus immunoglobulin within 72 hours of delivery. Fetal red cells which have entered her circulation will be destroyed, protecting any future Rhesus positive babies she may have. The amount of immunoglobulin given will depend on the fetal cell count in a sample of maternal blood. First babies are thought to be rarely affected, but it is now recognised that such a fetal cell count should follow any episode where the development of antibodies may be provoked – e.g. threatened abortion, antepartum haemorrhage or amniocentesis.

(4) In many parts of the country the maternal *blood level of alpha-feto protein* (AFP) is measured. This protein is raised from the 13th week of pregnancy when a woman is carrying a baby with an open neural tube defect – i.e. the nervous tissue which is normally covered by membranes, spine and surface tissues may be partially or completely exposed. The defect may be high, resulting in the absence of essential brain tissue as in anencephaly. A lower defect affecting the spinal cord is known as spina bifida. The defect may be a minor one perhaps only recognisable on X-ray; on the other hand the nervous tissue when exposed gives raised levels of AFP in the amniotic fluid and in the maternal blood.

A raised maternal AFP can be associated with fetal defects other than those previously mentioned. However, the usual reason for a high result is that the date of the last menstrual period is inaccurate, e.g. because of bleeding after the pregnancy has commenced, or because there are twins, giving a false positive result. Conversely, if the length of the pregnancy is over-estimated the level may seem normal when it is really raised, i.e. a false negative.

A high level of AFP in the maternal blood will indicate the need to repeat the test and if this also shows a high level, further tests to estimate the true length of the pregnancy and to obtain a sample of the amniotic fluid which surrounds the baby should be considered.

Amniocentesis

Amniocentesis is preceded by an ultrasound examination. Waves from a source outside the body are passed through the mother's abdominal wall to the contents of the uterus and are reflected back to the machine. The echo is converted into an electrical signal and a picture can be built up showing the size and shape of the baby, and the position of the placenta.

Amniocentesis involves passing a needle into the sac that contains the baby, within the uterus, avoiding the baby and the placenta, but drawing off some of the amniotic fluid which surrounds the baby. An ultrasound information display helps with the procedure. Biochemical analysis of a sample of cell-free amniotic fluid makes it possible to determine whether a defect is likely to be present.

Amniocentesis is ideally performed at 16 weeks. It is offered to women who are at risk of bearing a child with abnormalities. This group should include those with a personal or family history of physical defects such as spina bifida, or mental retardation as occurs in Down's Syndrome. All women over the age of 35 years should also be considered.

It is said that significant defects only occur in 2–3 per cent of all births. If a mother does not come into one of these groups the risks of doing the procedure must be considered carefully, and she should always receive appropriate counselling. Both parents should know that the tests cannot ensure that the result of the pregnancy will be a normal baby and there is the possibility of a termination to be considered if the results indicate that the fetus appears likely to have a defect. Counselling before amniocentesis is always to be recommended.

Amniocentesis should be carried out between 16 and 20 weeks if it is to be a safe procedure: there is always a small risk. Around one per cent of all amniocenteses are said to be followed by spontaneous abortion, but it must be remembered that some of these pregnancies would have been the ones likely to end prematurely anyway. Research continues on the risk to the fetus.

Tests on the sample of fluid obtained include:

(1) Biochemical analysis of a sample of cell-free amniotic fluid to determine the level of alpha-feto protein (AFP).

(2) Culture of fetal cells which have been taken from the amniotic fluid. Examination of these cells, called fibroblasts, will show the sex of the fetus and will indicate whether there is a chromosomal abnormality affecting the whole body, such as Down's Syndrome (often called Mongolism), or affecting one aspect of the body function such as the production of haemoglobin. Mistakes occasionally occur if the sample of cells includes some cells from the mother. If this happens there is a chance that a girl will be predicted, but a boy will be born.

The importance of that will be realised when considering the concern of a wife who is a carrier of Duchenne Muscular Dystrophy. The couple may be unable to comtemplate having a baby boy who would have a 50:50 chance of inheriting this severe muscle disorder, which inevitably leads to progressive weakness and death in early adult life. A girl would be unaffected but she would carry the gene.

(3) Biochemical tests can also be done to determine whether other handicapping conditions are likely to be present, such as those arising from inborn errors of metabolism. The lack of certain enzymes may

result in unwanted material being stored in the tissues of the body. An example of such a storage is Tay-Sach disease. It is common in certain Jewish races and the material, a lipoid, is stored mainly in the nervous tissue. It affects the brain and leads to progressive blindness and dementia. The disorder is carried by recessive inheritance and will only appear if two people carrying the same type of genetic material have a child.

(4) Estimation of the fetal bilirubin level, as this will be raised if there has been destruction of the fetal red cells.

(5) Estimation of the level of antibodies to maternal Rhesus negative blood, if this is appropriate.

Ultrasound Diagnosis

It is now possible to detect a wide variety of defects ranging from abnormalities of the central nervous system to those of the kidney, heart and limbs. Ultrasound can give accurate dating of all pregnancies and identify babies who are not growing properly.

It may be possible using ultrasound to reduce the number of women requiring amniocentesis before deciding whether or not to continue with the pregnancy. But the cost of doing these examinations more frequently than at present must not be under-estimated. Personnel, equipment and accommodation would need to be provided.

All women having ultrasound examination should have the technique explained to them and should be aware that they may find that their unborn child is not normal. Conversely, if a mother has previously had a child with a congenital defect, the reassurance that this baby appears normal and that it is alive and moving within her, can be of great comfort.

Fetoscopy

This is the examination of the fetus by means of a narrow tube or telescope. The image obtained can be magnified and the external appearance of the fetus can be viewed for abnormalities. The umbilical cord can be visualised enabling a sample of fetal blood to be obtained. At present this investigation remains a research procedure, the risks to the fetus, the placenta and the possibility of a subsequent abortion have to be evaluated.

Apart from viewing the fetus, analysis of the blood sample offers the chance to make a diagnosis in such inherited disorders as thalassaemia and sickle cell disease. It might soon provide the prenatal diagnosis of Duchenne Muscular Dystrophy and haemophilia. Ultrasound scanning is used before and during the examination to ensure that the procedure is done as safely as possible.

The value of a small fragment of fetal material obtained very early in pregnancy has led to research for a safe technique for obtaining this by passing a similar 'viewing' tube into the uterus through the cervix. As the developing ovum becomes embedded, villi grow into the lining of the uterus. A small sample of villus could be used to provide information about inherited disorders, much earlier in pregnancy, when abortion would be much safer and more acceptable.

Radiology

Radiology is mentioned because it is occasionally necessary to take a radiograph in pregnancy, when the need to obtain diagnostic information exceeds the risks of the examination. If ultrasound scanning suggests that the fetus is affected by a serious skeletal disorder — for example marked shortening or absence of the limbs, a single radiograph at 20 weeks to confirm the diagnosis can be helpful when discussing the problem with the parents. This can be particularly important if the skeletal disorder is known to be associated with other congenital defects or there is a strong possibility of a still birth. As ultrasound is increasingly used as a diagnostic measure the use of radiographs during pregnancy may cease to be necessary for this purpose.

The Need for Counselling

It is important to realise the implications of prenatal tests if they may result in the parents' having to consider whether to keep the pregnancy or not.

Earle (1981) recommends supportive counselling from the earliest stages, when the first tests are done; the family practitioner should be kept informed so that help can be given if a decision whether or not to proceed with further investigations is necessary. Stress itself can affect the pregnancy and may lead to increased smoking or drinking alcohol.

The feelings of many women, particularly those of the Asian cultures, prevent them from allowing the termination of pregnancy even when a deformity or disorder is confirmed. Sympathetic counselling during the pregnancy with referral to the appropriate supportive agencies will be essential during this period and after the birth. In Sheffield two medical social workers have been appointed specifically to help such families during the stressful early period when the baby is small.

In November 1982, Weatherall reviewed recent medical practices aimed at reducing the number of children born with congenital abnormalities: 'In the field of birth defects, prevention is to be preferred to procedures of pre-natal diagnosis with their sensitive consequence of termination of pregnancy.'

Neonatal Screening

Phenylketonuria (PKU) and Congenital Hypothyroidism

Incidence of phenylketonuria: 1 in 15,000
Incidence of hypothyroidism: 1 in 4,000–6,000

These are two disorders which can be identified in the newborn period and where the criteria for screening can be met. Both can be treated successfully.

Congenital hypothyroidism may be present at birth with no clinical features to be found on examination. Untreated, the child will be short, intellectually impaired and have a coarse, dry skin and little hair.

A person with PKU is unable to break down the amino acid phenylalanine in the normal way and therefore it accumulates in the body. If PKU is not recognised, intellectual impairment is inevitable. When the diagnosis has been confirmed, a special diet is recommended. This should be continued during childhood under medical supervision.

The DHSS now recommends that all babies have tests for both conditions. A sample of blood is obtained by the midwife from the baby's heel on the 6th day of life. The drops of blood are collected on a piece of absorbent paper and are sent to a laboratory for testing.

As PKU screening is a good example of an effective screening programme it will be described in more detail. The evidence available suggests that PKU screening is highly efficient. In the MRC/DHSS Phenylketonuria Register, Newsletter 7, (1980) it is reported that there were only four false negatives during the period 1974–8.

In 1964 routine screening for phenylketonuria was introduced. A national register was set up to examine the effectiveness of phenylalanine diet. In 1968 the national screening programme for phenylketonuria was re-organised. Previously a urine test was recommended for all neonates, but a substantial number were missed. The new programme recommended a heel prick between the 6th and 14th day of life to provide a blood sample for analysis at certain laboratories.

Between 1964 and 1974 there was a steady increase in the number of infants diagnosed as having PKU. This was due to the increase in the number being screened, but also to the smaller number of false negative results with the blood test.

By 1974 only 1–2 per cent surviving infants were not being tested

(Medical Research Council Steering Committee, 1981). Then it was realised that patients with a persistent accumulation of phenylalanine could be suffering from a wide range of disorders nearly all due to the lack of phenylalanine hydroxylase. Thus, PKU describes a group of disorders where the blood phenylalanine is raised to a variable degree.

A study by Walker, Clayton and Ersser (1981) of three-quarters of a million neonates tested for PKU between October 1969 and December 1978 showed that transient high levels of phenylalanine were falling appreciably and that this coincided with the introduction of low protein milk feeds. The use of low protein milks has not decreased the detection of classical PKU, but 'variant' cases may have phenylalanine levels only just above the normal range when receiving modified milk. As weaning foods or cow's milk are introduced, a considerable increase in the protein intake will occur; the blood phenylalanine will rise further. Therefore, all infants should be monitored by a paediatrician even if they do not initially need a special diet.

Screening laboratories in the UK take 240 micromoles per litre as the concentration of phenylalanine requiring further investigation. The Medical Research Council Working Party recommends that all babies with phenylalanine above this level should be notified to the MRC/DHSS Phenylketonuria Register even if dietary treatment is not considered necessary.

In October 1980 the Newsletter from the PKU Register indicated that over 1000 cases were being followed up. Female patients on the main register are transferred to the register of fertile women with PKU 'as they reach 14 years'. The aim is to achieve early notification of all pregnancies so that the management and outcome can be carefully documented. A study will then be possible which will enable better advice to be given to the rising generation of girls with normal intelligence when they wish to start families of their own. No consistent relationship has yet been worked out between diet, maternal serum phenylalanine levels before or during pregnancy and the outcome of the pregnancy.

Cystic Fibrosis

Dodge and Ryley (1982) make a strong case for the screening of all neonates for cystic fibrosis. They list the tests currently available and the advantages of early diagnosis, they mention the need for screening to be linked with a programme of treatment, regular assessment of the health of the child and research. Their argument for screening is followed by a commentary which suggests that the benefits of early diagnosis and treatment before symptoms occur need further assessment before such a programme of screening can be justified.

The article makes interesting reading for anyone wishing to understand more of the problems which involve doctors working with children, those concerned with research aimed at developing appropriate tests for screening for disorders and those who must advise on the justification of spending public money on population screening programmes. In future such programmes will probably show an increase in the number of examinations offered to selected groups, rather than to the total population.

Child Health Surveillance

Routine Surveillance

A baby should have two examinations by a doctor during the first ten days of life; the first within 24 hours and the second within ten days of birth. The purpose of these examinations will be to look for signs of illness, to note and record any defects which are present, to measure and record body weight, length and head circumference and to estimate the maturity of the baby. The mother should be present during the examination so that she can discuss any worries she may have about her baby's appearance or behaviour.

At regular intervals after this the baby will be seen either by a doctor or a health visitor. Certain important ages have been selected for developmental assessments and physical examinations: 6 weeks, 6 months, 1 year, 2 years, 3 years and 4 years, with a school entry medical examination shortly after the 5th birthday. In practice, it is often difficult to achieve this. In Sheffield, the children are called to see the doctor at the child health clinic at 6 weeks, 6 months and 3 years. The health visitor watches the child during the intervening periods using a short check list to detect poor developmental progress. In some practices the family doctor runs his own well-baby clinic; attachment of the health visitor to the practice, as part of the primary care team, enables her to combine her usual duties with this surveillance. Some authorities may rely entirely on health visitors with referral to senior clinical medical officers if they are worried. In the future more general practitioners will be taking on this preventative aspect of child health.

To look at the doctor's role in more detail, the 6 week visit is described. The health visitor will have made at least two home visits before the baby is 6 weeks and if she is concerned she will have alerted the doctor before the mother arrives at the clinic. Records should be checked to ensure that relevant details of the past and present health of both parents, the siblings and close relatives have been noted. Questions will be asked about the pregnancy, labour and the health, activity and well-being of the baby since the birth.

The examination of the baby will follow the pattern described for the newborn infant, but special attention is paid to developmental progress. The way the head is held, the posture in various positions, the reactions to stimuli such as noise, light and movement will be noted. A baby who has arrived after a full term pregnancy should be smiling in response to comforting sounds from the mother, fixing his or her eyes on her face and may be starting to coo when happy and turning to follow mother's face if she moves away. Certain primitive reflexes will still be present, but they will be in the process of disappearing. An example of these is the way in which a baby's fingers will close tightly around a finger when it is placed in the palm of the baby's hand.

A general physical examination is done and this will include a test for congenital dislocation of the hips. This should be carried out in the newborn period and repeated two or three times during the first year. The incidence of instability of the hip joint at this time lies between 3 and 6 per 1000 live births. However, not all cases can be detected at birth.

After the neonatal period, examinations of babies include a check on hip abduction, with the hips fully flexed. Limited movement should always be referred for a specialist's advice. Some infants with this condition become stable without treatment, but there is no reliable method for identifying these. The risks of not treating far outweigh those of splinting. Careful assessment of progress is needed as the time for which the hip remains dislocatable varies.

Some children present late with a limp as they begin to walk. This may be due to poor examination technique during infancy or failure to examine the hips of, for example, a very ill baby. In a retrospective study, David, Parris, Poynor, Hawnaur, Simm, Rigg and McCrae (1983) report a serious delay between the first symptoms of a dislocated hip and diagnosis. Parents and health care professionals failed to appreciate the significance of the symptoms.

This screening procedure depends on good examination technique in early infancy and an awareness of the importance of checking the abduction of the hips at regular intervals until the child can walk properly. Whether this should always be checked by a doctor is debatable. Professor Illingworth of Sheffield, for example, has personally recommended that health visitors should include it in their screening programme.

At subsequent medical examinations the doctor will continue to look for specific conditions and disorders – e.g. cerebral palsy. When mild it may be difficult to diagnose in the young baby but as the nervous system becomes more mature it is possible to check skills known to be present in children at certain ages. Tests of vision and hearing become more accurate as the child is able to participate actively in test procedures.

Measurements of height and weight continue to be important as early indicators of failure to thrive. Early referral of those with short stature is important so that appropriate treatment may be commenced.

The child's stature should be compared with that of the parents. The rate of growth must be estimated for a period of not less than three months. Burns (1982) recommends that patients with heights below the 3rd centile, taller children who are abnormally short for the family and patients with a poor growth velocity should be investigated.

At every examination during the first year of life the head circumference should be measured and related to the weight of the baby. Rapid growth may indicate hydrocephalus. Prompt medical treatment can prevent damage to the developing brain or the need for surgery with the insertion of a valve to drain away the cerebrospinal fluid which is collecting.

Babies who are of low birth weight need special observation. They need expert paediatric care, firstly in hospital and then when they go home. Regular reviews of progress will be carried out by paediatricians and early referrals made when other specialists need to be involved. If neonatal services are of high quality, we can expect these small babies to grow up without significant disability.

Developing Screening Procedures

The tests used depend upon the health authority: some favour Mary Sheridan's work and follow the guidelines laid down by her in 'Children's Developmental Progress from Birth to Five Years' (Sheridan, 1975). She recommends that we should look at four fields of development:

Posture and body movement.
Vision and fine movement.
Hearing and language: expression and comprehension.
Play and social behaviour.

Others prefer the Denver Developmental Chart which has been standardised by Dr. G. Bryant and her colleagues in Cardiff for British children, as the original work was done in America (Bryant, Davies and Newcombe, 1974, 1979). The chart indicates periods during which a particular skill can be expected to develop and when this period is over without this still having been developed the child may be considered to have delay in acquisition of that skill. Referral for expert advice should be sought from someone trained in development paediatrics (for a critique of this test see Chapter 3).

R.S. Illingworth has produced a particularly useful guide *Basic Developmental Screening 0-4 Years*. Guidelines for referral to a specialist are listed (Illingworth, 1982).

Medical Assessment at School Entry

Shortly after a child has started school arrangements should be made for an examination by the school medical officer. Clinic records of previous developmental assessments, details of events occurring around the time of the child's birth and a record of the immunisations given should be available. To supplement these every mother is asked to complete a questionnaire about her child's health and the opportunity is given for her to mention any worries that she may have about her child.

The Court Report (DHSS, 1976) leaves no doubt in our minds about the role of the school doctor.

Educational medicine is the study and practice of child health and paediatrics in relation to the processes of learning. It requires an understanding of child development, the educational environment, the child's response to schooling, the disorders which interfere with a child's capacity to learn, and the special needs of the handicapped. Its practitioners need to work co-operatively with the teachers, psychologists and others who may be involved with the child and to understand the influences of family and social environment.

Teachers have a valuable contribution to make. They can alert school doctors by reporting unusual behaviour, clumsiness or difficulties with classroom or outdoor activities – such as the following:

(1) Any fits, faints or episodes of seeming to be 'switched off'.
(2) Apparent difficulty with hearing.
(3) Poor speech to the extent that others have difficulty in understanding what the child is saying.

(4) Lack of comprehension appropriate for age.

(5) Apparent difficulty in seeing objects, difficulty with selection of play material by colours.

(6) Short stature compared with rest of the class.

(7) Breathlessness.

(8) Tiredness, or even actually falling asleep in school.

(9) Unusual pattern of walking or running, considering both arms and legs, on the flat and climbing stairs. Reluctance to join in playground activities.

(10) Unwanted movements, tremor, restlessness, fidgeting, tics or grimaces.

(11) Clumsy use of hands for table work − e.g. the grasp and use of pencil, scissors, building toys such as Lego. Lack of handedness being established.

(12) Incontinence, more than occasional accidents when first starting school. Similarly, repeated requests to use the toilet.

(13) Appetite or thirst much greater than peers.

(14) Behaviour problems.

At the time of the medical, screening procedures continue with the testing of vision and hearing; height and weight are also measured.

Hearing

The hearing is usually checked by asking the child to repeat a list of 12 words, 6 feet away from the examiner, taking care that the ear not being tested is covered and that the child does not have the opportunity to lip read. Catarrhal infections of the upper respiratory tract with intermittent loss of hearing are common between 3 and 7 years of age and any child not able to do the test easily, should be referred to an Audiology Department for an assessment (see Chapter 4).

If fluid is present − the so-called 'glue ear' − a small operation may be performed, removing the fluid and inserting a tiny tube through each ear drum so allowing air to enter the middle ear cavity. After 6 to 24 months the tubes or grommets usually come out by themselves.

It should be a regular practice for a team of school nurses trained in audiometric testing to screen all children of 6 years using the pure tone audiometry − the test often referred to as a sweep test (see Chapter 4).

Vision

This is checked at 6 metres using either letter matching or letter naming, testing each eye separately. The eyes are examined for a squint; this is particularly important if there is a family history of squint or vision in only one eye (see Chapter 3, page 54). Every effort should be made to assess the vision of those who are deaf or who cannot communicate well.

If a defect is found, the child should be referred to an orthoptist or ophthalmologist. Similarly, any child reported to squint when tired or poorly should be referred. The consequence of failure to treat may result in marked loss of vision as the child suppresses the image his brain receives from the squinting eye.

It is not thought necessary to continue to review short-sighted children in a hospital clinic; they can be seen by the local optician when they are about 8 years of age. However, routine vision testing on school children has been shown to be important. Tibbenham *et al* (1978), as part of the National Child Development Study based on all children born in England, Wales and Scotland from 3rd March to 9th March 1958, examined data on children at 7, 11 and 16 years. Their distant vision changed so that 18 per cent with normal vision at the age of 7 and 11 had developed a defect by the age of 16. Testing of vision is usually carried out by the school nurse.

Colour vision should be checked; school entry is the best time because colour recognition plays an important part in the modern teaching of both language and mathematics. The Ishihara Test Book is commonly used. Each test page shows a design in dots which makes up a number. The colour choice makes the number stand out from its background for the child with normal colour vision. The type of colour defect is worked out by checking with a score sheet; the commonest deficiency is red/green.

Children who are unable to give the numbers in this test can do the Guy's Test, if they understand the concept of matching. A set of plastic letters is placed in front of the child who should then point to the appropriate one on recognising the shape on the test page.

It is important for parents to be told if a child has defective colour vision as this will prevent them from taking up certain occupations — e.g. electrician, airline pilot, train driver. The figure usually quoted for males who have defective colour vision is about 8 per cent.

Neuro-developmental

Before undressing the child it is possible to do certain neuro-developmental tests even if the medical room is only the teachers' staff room or a classroom that is not being used for teaching purposes. Children of this age usually enjoy being checked, wanting to demonstrate to their mothers how well they can perform; it is considerably easier than working with three year olds.

To illustrate the various tests that may be done a check list is included, this is based on the recommendations of Bax and Whitmore (1973).

(1) Check for squint; check vision.

(2) Hearing of spoken word at 6 feet.

(3) Speech intelligibility.

(4) General appearance of child, noting symmetry.

(5) Tongue movement.

(6) Hand patting.

(7) Finger-nose pointing or object to object pointing; where the second object is moved about, child must lift elbow away from side of body during test.

(8) Rapid turing movements of wrists (diadochokinesia).

(9) Pencil grasp.

(10) Drawing a circle, square and triangle.

(11) Drawing of a man.

(12) Gait: noting arms and legs, freedom of movement and symmetry as the child moves freely round room. Fog's test is difficult to check at 5 years, i.e. ability to walk on outer sides of feet or on heels without waving arms about, but can usually be done by 7 years.

(13) Heel toe walk.

(14) Hopping.

(15) Reflexes and tone.

(16) Level of physical activity – note any unwanted movements.

(17) General behaviour during these tests. The doctor will be interested in how the child does the tests, considering willingness to co-operate and the ease with which he or she is distracted by other people in the room, e.g. sister or brother, or by sounds of other activities going on outside the medical room.

Time is often short when visiting a school but the search for children with minor disabilities is rewarding. The clumsy child may become the clown of the class, distracting other children and enjoying popularity for being silly, or may become withdrawn and miserable because never chosen for team games.

If a child is clumsy, careful consideration of other features that are present will assist in making the diagnosis and the appropriate method of offering help. These include neurological signs, immaturity and behaviour disorders.

The educational psychologist is usually involved with those children without neurological signs, but referral for a detailed team assessment is preferred where the reasons for the clumsiness may be found in the nervous system.

Physical

The neuro-developmental tests are followed by a physical examination. Routine medical examinations of school children, after the one at school entry, are no longer thought to be necessary. If the doctor is concerned about any aspect of the assessment or examination, the child can be called again for review, after an appropriate interval. Otherwise further consultation should depend on requests from the child's parents, the school nurse or the classteacher.

Some authorities have introduced screening for scoliosis — or curvature of the spine — in 12-14 year old children. This is done by asking the child to bend forward while observing the back for asymmetry of the rib cage. Twenty-five per cent of normal adolescents may appear to have scoliosis when checked.

There are three types of scoliosis: (a) caused by having legs of unequal length; (b) caused by asymmetry of the spine in the coronal plane; (c) progressive scoliosis. Group (c) is the important one. It is commoner in girls and the hollow of the curve is usually directed towards the right.

As a screening procedure this has still not yet received national recognition (Dickson, 1983): the number of positive cases is small; the age of onset is not precise, the prognosis is not always predictable. However, a greater awareness of the problem among those caring for children in their adolescent years with referral to a doctor of those having a curvature would allow careful selective monitoring. All those cases found to be progressive would be referred for an orthopaedic opinion.

Referral Procedures

In order to identify those children who need further assessment the health visitors in Sheffield, as in many other areas, have a checklist giving 7 or 8 items to run through either in the clinic or in the home (see Table 3.1, page 56). The health visitor is in a unique position, being able to build up a satisfying relationship with the mother and child from early infancy. Children who will not 'perform' in the clinic will often complete a task set at home in familiar surroundings, without any fuss.

As 3 years of age is so important when looking for those children who would benefit from early intervention by nursery or nursery school placement, considerable efforts should be made to ensure that someone will see the child. If he or she does not attend the health clinic the health visitor is asked to do a home visit. The child may, of course, be receiving part-time pre-school education but if not the health visitor should check gross motor skills, fine manipulation, expressive language, and comprehension. She should test the vision and hearing and note whether or not a squint is present. Socially, a child of this age should be alert and interested, asking lots of questions, playing with other children and should be toilet trained.

Community Assessment Clinics

If a health visitor or a clinical medical officer is not happy with the findings when the development is checked, a referral may be made to the family doctor or to a senior clinical medical officer for a more detailed assessment. The extent to which a problem is discussed before this referral is likely to depend on the nature of the problem, the certainty with which the referring person feels the problem exists and the understanding of the problem shown by the parents.

Detailed history taking is important and both doctor and health visitor will work together, carefully checking the various aspects of the child's development, particularly the vision and the hearing. A physical examination will always be done.

If there is significant delay in more than one field of development the doctor will discuss this with the parents and suggest the possibility of seeking expert advice. The family doctor should be consulted and if possible arrangements should be made for the child to be referred to an Assessment Centre or to the District Handicap Team. Of course, many children with recognised medical disorders can be given appropriate medical care and therapy without using such an assessment service. However, where the child is handicapped by the disabling nature of the medical disorder, or there is developmental delay for no apparent reason, the professional person most concerned with the management of the child may feel that it is necessary to arrange such a referral.

Children found to have delay in one particular aspect of development may benefit from referral for a specialised investigation or assessment, e.g. audiology or speech therapy and then review in several months. Others will benefit from a period of observation in a play group, nursery or nursery school. The parents should be fully involved at this stage as they will often have their own ideas regarding 'what needs to be done'. If referral to an Assessment Centre is advisable, the procedure that is likely to be followed there should be described, remembering to balance the need to give the parents and child the benefit of expert advice against the stress of being questioned and observed during the visit.

Multidisciplinary Assessment

The purpose of a full team assessment is to bring together an appropriate group of professional people with expertise in the diagnosis and management of handicapping disorders. A defect refers to any structural abnormality of the body, a disability indicates that function is impaired. In 1980 the following definition of handicap was established by the World Health Organisation: 'a disadvantage for a given individual resulting from an impairment or a disability that limits or prevents the fulfilment of a role that is normal for that individual'.

The process of team assessment can be divided into four stages:

(1) Forming the team from the appropriate professional staff available. This will depend on the nature of the problems presented by the child, but essentially consists of staff working in the educational, medical, nursing, phychological and social work fields as well as the various therapies.

(2) Gathering together the information which is already available: reports may be requested from the social worker, health visitor, teacher, educational   psychologist, nursery nurse, as well as from medical personnel.

In Sheffield the referring agent is likely to be a paediatric specialist, a community medical officer or the family practitioner. Elsewhere referrals are accepted from other disciplines directly.

(3) The collection of new information usually commences with a home visit by the medical social worker. It is helpful if a booklet is left with the parents describing the work at the Centre and the procedure that is usually followed. This is followed by the first visit to the Assessment Centre. Parental involvement should be encouraged at every stage. Careful observation will continue whether the child is

involved in specific test procedures or taking part in daily living activities, such as having a meal. It is important to note the child's attitude to learning, to achievement and failure and the way in which various situations are tackled. The positive aspects of character which will enable the child to deal with the disability are as important as the weaknesses. All observations are recorded. A detailed medical history is carefully taken and an examination carried out by a paediatric specialist.

(4) The case conference is held at the end of the assessment period. It is usually chaired by the paediatric specialist and all members of the assessment team are asked to attend. It is not always possible for everyone to be present, e.g. the audiology technician or orthoptist may have to be in a clinic outside the Assessment Centre. Other professional workers involved with the care of the child in the community should also be invited, e.g. the family practitioner, teacher or health visitor.

The purpose of the case conference will be:

(a) to hear the reports of the members of the assessment team, with the opportunity to discuss any difficulties that arise;
(b) to list the essential problems in order of priority;
(c) to identify the special needs arising from these problems and the ways in which they may be met;
(d) to suggest the outline for an individual programme of therapy and/or education remembering to involve the parents as well as the professionals;
(e) to arrange any further assessment or medical investigations, and the timing of review appointments.

If the parents are not sitting in at the case conference they will need to have the findings and recommendations discussed with them at the earliest opportunity.

It is important for a member of the nursing staff, a medical social worker or the health visitor concerned with the family to be present at this time, to provide emotional support. Genetic counselling may be offered, but the depth of the discussion will depend upon the outcome of the assessment and the parents' reaction to the findings. The programmes of care must be planned carefully and a 'key worker' chosen to ensure that the arrangements made are taken up. Other family responsibilities, the personalities of the parents, the distances to be travelled and details such as these must be considered if the planned intervention is to succeed. At the Ryegate Centre in Sheffield parents are interviewed after the case conference following an intensive two-day initial assessment.

Difficulties arise if the child is unwell, unwilling or just very difficult to assess when the initial assessment is over such a short period, but it does give a base line from which to work. Other assessment teams may choose to visit the child when the placement has been made in a nursery and then will meet to discuss future arrangements after a period of perhaps three months.

Surveillance 0–5 Years: Does it Work?

It has been shown that whereas mothers take their children to the local clinic regularly during the first year there is a gradual fall-off in the attendance rate as the child gets older. The need for advice and re-assurance declines as the immunisation is completed, children can be compared with others in the family or with those of friends and neighbours. If progress seems satisfactory the need for a check up at the local clinic may be considered to be of less importance during early infancy. However, the demand for this service still depends on the quality of the service offered (Hart, Bax and Jenkins, 1981).

One way of reminding parents to continue to make the best use of the services available is to provide them with a booklet before the mother leaves the maternity unit. In Sheffield, every mother receives one after her baby is born, enabling a comprehensive record to be kept from the very beginning. Details of the antenatal period, birth and first four weeks can be entered by the midwife. The doctor and mother can add details and then the health visitor will continue to add her comments as she takes over health care starting with her visit at 10 to 14 days. The parents can record the developmental progress as they would in any baby book. Immunisations can be entered with future appointments, visits to the family doctor or hospital can be noted together with details of illnesses, reactions to drugs and other important points which are so easily forgotten. If the family doctor uses a night-time deputising service, the doctor called for an emergency to the home may be considerably helped by a quick look through the child's personal health record. It should also be taken to the hospital whether a visit is for a consultation or for emergency treatment. It is now possible for all health authorities to adopt this excellent practice.*

The success of a surveillance programme will depend upon the

---

* *Child Health Record* published by B. Edsall and Co. Ltd, 36 Eccleston Square, London, SW1V 1PF.

training and experience of the staff available, the time allowed for this work and the local facilities. Doctors, health visitors, staff in day nurseries or nursery schools, if aware of the normal pattern of development, can bring to the attention of an experienced medical officer those children requiring detailed assessment. For example, a pre-school advisory teacher visiting a play group is able to ask the group leader about the children in her care. A chat with the health visitor concerned may be all that is needed to set the wheels in motion ensuring that any child has the benefit of expert advice at the earliest opportunity.

By building up a good relationship with voluntary workers running, for example, mother and toddler groups and play schemes, and by meeting others who run advice centres or organise toy libraries, our advisory teachers and health visitors can play a truly significant part in finding those children with special needs. At school age the school nurse becomes a key person, liaising with health visitors, clinical medical officers, teachers and parents.

In the past it has often been recommended that all children should be seen by medical officers for developmental testing. Realising that this can rarely be achieved, we must make it possible for other professional people who work with children to sort out those children in need of more detailed assessment. Ideally, we train everybody thoroughly so that they know exactly what they are looking for, offer the test material in exactly the same way making accurate observations about the way in which the child performs the task. Surely, this degree of accuracy must be left to the doctor trained in developmental paediatrics, the psychologist and the teachers who specialise in this work. But in the field we also need observant, interested individuals who have a good basic knowledge of child development, who can recognise when a child is falling behind and will be willing to refer him or her to the family doctor or clinical medical officer without undue delay. This is not to suggest however that we should not continue to aim for full child population developmental assessment at key ages. But it is no good imagining that we can persuade all parents to attend. Children with working mothers, children from gypsy families, children whose parents deliberately keep them away from nursery when they know a doctor will be visiting are a few examples of children in families who will not comply with our wishes. Zinkin and Cox (1976) stressed the need to reach these families with a service that is acceptable to them.

Registers in Childhood

'At Risk' Registers

In 1962 Mary Sheridan drew attention to the high incidence of handicap among certain groups of children. She found that 10 in every 1000 children who survive the neonatal period received special care and treatment for severe handicapping disorders. She suggested that registers of children at risk of developing these handicaps should be kept in the health departments of local authorities. She described a handicapped child as one who suffers from any continuing disability of the body, intellect or personality which is likely to interfere with his normal growth, development and capacity to learn.

The 'at risk' factors were divided into five groups:

(1) Adverse family history
(2) Prenatal hazards
(3) Perinatal hazards
(4) Post-natal mishaps
(5) Developmental warning signs.

A total of 36 factors was listed.

Two important assumptions were made in recommending the compiling of 'at risk' registers: (a) that the selected group of children would be small; (b) that this group would include most of the children who would subsequently develop handicapping conditions.

In practice results have been disappointing. There was clearly a wide variation in the interpretation of the criteria as listed by Mary Sheridan. It was also noted that the information received from maternity units was often incomplete. In some authorities as many as 60 per cent of children were entered on the register and in others 15 per cent. The register assumes a relationship between the selection criteria and the occurrence of handicap. Even careful follow-up of these children failed to identify more than about 50 per cent of children with handicapping conditions.

It was noticed that certain criteria seemed more important than others, that particular collections of risk factors were especially significant — e.g. low Apgar score with prematurity. The Apgar score denotes the condition of the baby at birth; the higher the score, the better the baby's condition. It may be repeated after 5 minutes. In an effort to make the risk register more acceptable, attempts were made to define more precisely the criteria which were thought to imply increased risk of handicap.

Oppé, Walkers and Rogers all suggested shortened alternatives to the Sheridan list. Forfar (1968) thought that a screening procedure for all infants could be combined with a particularly careful follow-up of infants in a 'high risk' group. This small group of 5–10 per cent of all infants would nearly all need special care during the neonatal period and their follow-up could be arranged at the hospital where they were born.

Despite the criticisms of at risk registers there is a strong indication for the clinical examination of all infants during the neonatal period, their screening for metabolic and hearing defects at the appropriate ages, and the careful observation of every child's developmental progress by doctors and health visitors.

The Non-Accidental Injury or Child Abuse Register

In 1974 the DHSS recommended that all Health Authorities should set up area review committees for the consideration of all aspects of the management of non-accidental injury to children. This included the keeping of a register which could act as a central point for professional workers needing to communicate with each other.

The register co-ordinates information about children up to the age of 16 years who have suffered non-accidental injury, where such injury is suspected, or where the child is thought to be at risk. Before a child's name is placed on the register, a case conference is called including all those workers professionally concerned with the child. If there is good reason to place the name on the register a key worker is appointed to watch over the child and report back to the register at regular intervals. If the worker is satisfied with the child's situation, the removal of the name from the register can be recommended, after a specified minimum period.

When there is immediate concern for the safety of the child, the provision of medical services and removal to a place of safety will necessarily be considered before calling a case conference. It is important that all those who care for children regularly continue to keep in mind the possibility of non-accidental injury.

By 1975 paediatricians were wondering how it might be possible to recognise the families in which children might be at risk of non-accidental injury, sudden infant death and physical or emotional neglect.

In Sheffield two systems developed: (a) all babies born in Sheffield were given a score at birth to work out the risks of sudden death in infancy (see page 40); (b) a 'green star' system was started at one of the hospitals (Gordon, 1979), where it was decided, by general agreement between medical, social and nursing staff, that all mothers in the perinatal period would be reviewed for adverse factors.

Six factors seemed to be particularly important:

(1) Mother single at time of conception, and under 21.
(2) Mother belonging to a known problem family.
(3) Baby in special care unit.
(4) Poor attendance at antenatal clinic.
(5) Mental dullness/illness.
(6) Other adverse social circumstances.

If two or more of these factors were present the health visitor was notified and she arranged to visit frequently during the early months of the child's life. This applied to about two fifths of births to Sheffield residents.

Spencer (personal communication) reviewing the success of this register now believes that the guidelines should be more specific enabling those working with mothers during the perinatal period to identify those needing special supervision more easily. The revised guidelines proposed are:

(1) Previous history of violence to children.
(2) Unsupported immature mother.
(3) Family disorganisation; poor social circumstances.
(4) Absence of normal 'nesting' behaviour.
(5) Signs of bonding failure.
(6) Prolonged separation in neonatal period.

A statistical method of predicting non-accidental injury has been evaluated in Sheffield, using the birth score. Future studies will enable a comparision to be made between statistical and intuitive methods of prediction. However, other studies (e.g. Lealman, Haigh, Phillips, Stone and Ord-Smith, 1983) have highlighted the problems in this area (see Chapter 10).

The Register of Congenital Malformations

The information comes from a variety of sources including birth notification forms from the midwives, still birth registration forms and copies of hospital discharge letters following the birth of the baby.

Health visitors and clinical doctors also send in relevant information to the person responsible for the register; this is usually a senior clinical medical officer. The information is also used to complete a form which is returned to the Registrar General at the Office of Population Censuses and Surveys. Naturally the validity of the information on these forms depends upon the accuracy with which the abnormality is described by the person sending in the details. The national scheme of notification of infants with congenital malformations only includes those identified within seven days of birth.

The Register of Handicapped Children

The specialist in Community Medicine with a responsibility for Child Health should be notified of all children whose disability is such that they may require special help from either the Social Services Department of the Local Authority or from the Department of Education. The register should be reviewed regularly, health visitors calling on the family and reporting back on the progress of the child. They should check that the hospital out-patient appointments have been kept and make sure that the family is receiving adequate help.

Handicap registers are still operated on a manual basis in some health authorities. Computers can offer improved facilities for locating records, flexibility in organising the data and a greatly improved potential for analysis. Registers operated in this way can contribute more fully to the planning and co-ordination of care of all children. To assist health authorities in developing computerised recording a Standard Child Health System has been made available. This is based on a register of the child population. Each health authority is expected to decide how to use the standard programmes.

Problems that still remain are:

defining the criteria for including the child on the Register;
deciding which data items should be included on each record; this must take account of potential users of information and procedures to ensure that children are not missed;
establishing communication procedures so that the register is kept up-to-date;
ensuring that the people who need the information will receive it in the most useful form;
establishing rights of access to data while ensuring confidentiality.

Some authorities will be concerned about the financial problems of changing to a mainframe computer and, for this reason and for the need for instant access to information, may prefer to use micro-computers.

The Warnock Committee (DES, 1978) recommended that a hand-book should be available for the parents of children with special needs, whether those needs are physical, educational or emotional. It can act as a guide to the services available both locally and nationally, being kept on one side and referred to as the need arises.

Sheffield has two handbooks: one for the parents of young children and one for school leavers. They were compiled with the assistance of those people who work with children with special needs, professionally or in a voluntary capacity. It must be recognised that there are periods of intense worry for the parents of handicapped children: the time of diagnosis, the time of school entry and then the period leading up to school leaving. Counselling is essential at those times and the hand-books can offer ideas for obtaining advice or help when professional help is needed.

A Register of those Children at Risk of Sudden Death in Infancy

In a classical cot death a child who is apparently healthy is put to bed by his parents and is subsequently found dead in his cot. More com-monly the baby, aged between 1 week and 2 years, has shown some symptoms of mild illness for the preceding 1–3 days and these have not caused concern. The baby then seems to be a little better, is given a feed and put to bed. Later the baby is found dead. The post mortem find-ings do not give a satisfactory explanation of the sudden deaths. The incidence is between 1 in 500 and 1 in 700 live births.

By careful analysis of all unexpected infant deaths it has been possible to identify certain predisposing factors. In 1973, the Sheffield Child Development Study began to collect information from obstetric units enabling a scoring system to be established. Since 1979 health visitors have provided additional information when the baby is one month old. At a home visit she completes a form giving such details as the following: the number of children in the family, the birth history, evidence of failure in bonding between mother and baby, breast or bottle feeding, with the care that is taken over making feeds if artificial feeding is taking place, whether or not the mother intends to visit the local child health centre. The details of enquiry are analysed together with information made available from birth records and those babies considered to be at risk of sudden death are identified. The health visitor and family doctor concerned are notified enabling them to give extra support and to be particularly sensitive to problems in infancy that might otherwise be considered to be of little importance.

Confidential enquiries following death in infancy continued in Sheffield as part of a national study from 1976 to 1979 and then as a local long-term exercise. The aim was to determine whether it might be possible to prevent the loss of babies with treatable conditions or those who died in the course of a minor illness. Taylor and Emery (1982) reported their results for a two-year period ending in March 1981.

The study emphasised the need for better preventative measures such as genetic counselling together with diagnostic tests to find genetic disorders early in pregnancy. It showed the need for further research into the causes of birth deformities. Detailed studies of the periods immediately before, during or after the babies' births are thought to be vital if the number of 'unexplained cot deaths' are to be reduced.

Research into this problem is one aspect, but we must not forget the parents' feelings. Their normal feelings of grief are compounded by feelings of guilt. Sympathetic counselling is needed and an explanation of the death should be given. Neglect at this time may endanger the well-being of subsequent children.

Future Trends in Child Surveillance

Future planning of effective health surveillance and screening procedures must be linked with research. First the Court Committee (DHSS, 1976a) and then the Warnock Committee on Special Educational Needs (DES, 1978) recognised the importance of a programme of developmental and health surveillance at regular intervals to support the parents in the important task of caring for their children.

'Research into Services for Children and Adolescents', published by the Department of Health and Social Services (1980), stresses the need to examine the effectiveness of health surveillance particularly in relation to cost, in the context of what are today's health and social problems.

This was followed by another publication by the DHSS in 1981 *Care in Action* outlining the groups within the population which should have priority. It states firmly that the local strategy of health promotion and preventative medicine should include:

improving the availability of genetic counselling and family planning,

encouraging early and regular attendance for antenatal care (including advocacy of breast feeding); screening for disabilities in young children; and providing dental care for children . . .
maintaining liaison with the education authority to ensure adequate arrangements for the health surveillance of children.

Illingworth (1979) has written of his experiences in child health clinics and stresses their value, whereas Hendrickse (1982) questions the need for this type of service. Others have evaluated the more specialised screening of vision and hearing at different ages and in children who have additional handicaps.

Rigby (1981) in his paper 'Child Health — a time for better understanding?' highlighted the need for the complementary roles of both general practice and the community child health service and asked for this to be recognised so that our children may enjoy the highest level of preventative services. It is hoped that the present reorganisation within the Health Service will provide the opportunity to introduce new programmes or modify existing ones to the advantage of our children and that we do not lose sight of our objectives while debating the best way of implementing them.

3 THE ROLE OF THE HEALTH VISITOR

Kathleen Jennings

A health visitor was defined by the National Health Service Act of 1946 as:

> a person employed by a local health authority to visit people in their homes or elsewhere for the purpose of giving advice as to the care of young children, persons suffering from illness and expectant or nursing mothers, and as to the measures necessary to prevent the spread of infection.

It is clear from this description that health visitors work not only with children but also with adult client groups. Although the focus of the present discussion is on children this fact should be remembered as this broader role of the health visitor has several implications. First there is the obvious issue of resources: health visitor time must be divided between all the client groups, not only very young children. Second, as with all professions, the present ways of working are to varying degrees a function of previous developments.

In order to put the work of the health visitor in perspective I will trace its historical development and examine present demands.

The Development of Health Visiting

Historical Perspective

According to many sources the origins of Health Visiting were to found in the voluntary organisations in Manchester and Salford around the 1850s. Early workers could be described as 'missionaries' and their work consisted of a service to the public based upon sanitary reform and charitable works. The approach was essentially one of didactic teaching and suffered many inadequacies, not the least being that the leaflets and pamphlets produced were distributed to many people who were illiterate.

Voluntary effort, as is often the case, led the way to official appointments and in 1861 the Ladies Sanitary Reform Association was established in Manchester. Between 1862 and 1890 some of these ladies were transferred to the staff of Manchester Public Health Department and names such as 'lady missionaries' and sanitary visitors gave way to the title 'health visitors'. After 1862 the employment of such visitors spread to other parts of the country and the developing emphasis of their service seems to have been upon health teaching and counselling.

If the original function of the health visitor was to teach the principles of health and the prevention of disease then the health reports from these early days suggest that there certainly was a need to be met. In 1871 the infant mortality rate in Manchester was 213 per thousand live births and 246 in Liverpool where 1 in every 4 children died before reaching the age of one year.

With passing years the recruitment of health visitors became biased towards those with a nursing background, while recognising however that there were distinct differences in skill areas between the two roles. In 1891 Florence Nightingale wrote: 'The needs of home health bringing require different but not lower qualifications and are more varied . . . She must create a new work and a new profession for women.'

With the advent of the notification of new births in Huddersfield in 1905, and by 1915 the compulsory notification in all other areas of the country, the health visitor was provided with information which created access to homes in possible need of her services. It should be noted however that from then until the present day health visitors have had no legal right of entry to households and effective work has always been based upon the establishment of good relationships between professional and client.

The number of health visitors has inevitably increased as has the scope of the work. The Jameson Report (DHSS, 1956) recommended approximately 1 health visitor per 4,300 population, although acknowledging that local conditions would require some variations. Hobbs (1973) quotes returns from 77 local health authorities where all but one fell below this recommended staffing level. Clark (1974) states that the ratio over the country as a whole was 1 to 7,000 population and even as poor as 1 to 15,000 in some areas.

The scope of the present-day health visitor's work is difficult to delineate given the very broad spread of professional training and expertise. The Council for the Education and Training of Health Visitors has identified five main aspects of the work as:

(1) The prevention of mental, physical and emotional ill-health or the alleviation of its consequences.
(2) Easy detection of ill-health and the surveillance of high risk

groups.

(3) Recognition and identification of need and mobilisation of resources where necessary.

(4) Health teaching.

(5) Provision of care: this will include support during periods of stress and advice and guidance in cases of illness as well as in the care and management of children. The health visitor is not, however, actively engaged in technical nursing procedures.

Training

The training of health visitors existed in some areas before the turn of the century. It was not until 1919 however that a generally recognised training was jointly promoted by the new Ministry of Health and the Board of Education. By 1925 it was requested that some obstetric knowledge was necessary on the part of the health visitor, because of the increasing emphasis on maternal and child welfare and the need for continuity of service between midwife and health visitor. In 1929 the Local Government Act provided for statutory rules and orders regarding the qualifications required for health visitors.

With the introduction and growth of the Welfare State the role of the health visitor continued to expand and the mental and social aspects of health began to be reflected in their training. In 1953 a working party was set up to advise on the work, recruitment and training of health visitors, the findings of which were published in the Jameson Report in 1956. The Report defined the function of the health visitor as primarily health education and social service, but with the emphasis firmly on health education.

While maintaining contact with families containing young children, the Report stated that health visitors should extend this role to become general family visitors. It was also suggested that health visitors had an important contribution to make in the fields of mental health, care of the elderly and hospital after-care. As far as prerequisite qualifications for training as a health visitor were concerned the Jameson Report recommended that registration as a nurse should continue plus a state midwifery qualification or a special three-month midwifery training relevant to health visiting.

Another main recommendation of the Report was that a new central training body should be set up, and accordingly the Council for the Training of Health Visitors, later to be named the Council for the Education and Training of Health Visitors, was instituted in 1962. To fit the health visitor for her expanded role which, it was envisaged, might be carried out in a particular geographical locality or as part of a general medical practice team, the syllabus of training was divided into 5 broad headings:

(1) Development of the Individual.
(2) The Individual in the Group.
(3) The Development of Social Policy.
(4) Social Aspects of Health and Disease.
(5) Principles and Practice of Health Visiting.

Since its inception in 1962 the CETHV has continued to assist the development of the profession by guiding practice and providing training principles in line with changing health and social conditions, new legislation, consumer expectations and new patterns of work. However, in 1983 the CETHV was formally discontinued, its functions being taken over by the new United Kingdom Central Council for Nursing, Midwifery and Health Visiting, and the four national boards for nursing, midwifery and health visiting for England, Scotland, Wales and Northern Ireland.

The Present Position

As stated earlier in the chapter the scope of the present health visitor's work is difficult to delineate. It has been noted that during the nineteenth century the chief concern was with control of infections, diseases and the role was basically that of sanitary inspector. Since that time the role has expanded to reflect the changes in health needs and social policy and the health visitor's role has moved more towards the emotional needs of children and the psycho-social aspects of disease. At the present time health visitors are concerned with visiting a wider range of families than any other comparable workers and because of this they find themselves discussing and advising on a wide range of subjects. This versatility of the health visitors is one of their greatest strengths but also can be a source of great frustration. Being a 'Jack of all trades' can lead to a dissipation of skills.

A major problem facing present day health visitors and health visiting services is that while training has equipped them for a wide role the size of the caseloads prevent this and inevitably priorities of work must be determined.

Looking more closely at some of the health visitor's work Clark (1973) presents a descriptive analysis of health visiting in Berkshire using information based on 2057 visits and 72 health visitors' reports.

It seems that most health visitors' visits were made to families where there were young children, but a substantial minority (29 per cent) of visits were to households where no young children were living; 18 per cent to the elderly and 11 per cent to households with neither elderly nor young children. The visit was usually made on the health visitor's own initiative but 14 per cent were initiated by the client and 7 per cent by the general practitioner. The purpose of the visit most commonly described was a routine visit to a child under five years, but these visits comprised only a quarter of the total. Visits usually lasted less than half an hour (in 79 per cent of the cases); 28 per cent lasted less than fifteen minutes, but a small number (3.4 per cent) lasted longer than an hour. 80 per cent of the visits were planned.

With regard to the content of the home visits, 51 topics were presented by the researcher and all 51 topics were mentioned in the findings. The topics most frequently recorded were infant feeding and the physical development of children in 36.8 per cent and 35.9 per cent of visits respectively. Of the ten topics most frequently recorded, five were specifically concerned with young children, but such topics comprised less than half of all topics recorded. Topics not specifically concerned with young children were recorded in more than 80 per cent of all visits.

It should be remembered of course that health visitors work in settings other than the home. Health education with groups can be carried out in many settings including schools, clinics and playgroups. Well-baby clinics may be conducted in local authority infant welfare clinics or general practitioners' surgeries. An important function of the health visitor is to act as a liaison agent and she can be making contact with a multitude of other professionals and agencies − e.g. social workers, teachers, educational psychologists, doctors, housing welfare officers, environmental health officers and voluntary agencies, to name but a few.

Screening of Pre-school Children

For the purposes of the following discussion the emphasis will be placed upon the health visitor's work with the pre-school child. This is largely an academic decision to make because, as I have discussed previously, the health visitor's role and the content of the home visits is likely to be multi-faceted. When making a visit to a home containing a six-week-old baby it would not be unusual for the health visitor to be discussing and/or advising on breast feeding, weaning, post-natal examinations, contraception, sibling rivalry, child development, adolescence, parental unemployment, housing, senility in ageing grandparents — to name but a few of the possible topics. Despite this generic role, it is possible to look particularly at the aspects of the pre-school child and to see how the health visitor's caseload is built up and how relationships with the public are established and maintained.

Notification of Births

All births, active or dead, must be notified to the Medical Officer of Health within a specific time. Following this notification the health-visiting service is informed and a birth record card is issued to the appropriate health visitor. Some health visitors work on a geographical basis and they accordingly would receive all the birth notifications for a particular group of roads and streets. Those who work as part of a general practice team would receive all the birth notifications for the particular doctor(s) to whom they were attached. Thus the health visitor will be notified, very shortly after the birth, of any new babies within her area of responsibility, whether they were born at home or in hospital.

There are also many other ways in which the health visitor learns about new births, some more formal than others. The health visitor may, for example, have visited the family during the antenatal period and/or have worked with the mother during antenatal classes. She may learn about the pregnancy and birth from her midwifery colleagues, or in some remote rural areas she may be employed as both midwife and health visitor. 'Picking up' information about the whereabouts of babies and young children becomes second nature to the health visitor. Because the health visitor is concerned about the development of all children from all walks of life, she can legitimately stop any new mother and baby in the street and enquire at any newly occupied home. Information concerning new clients to an area is also obtained when the family registers with a new doctor or registers an elder sibling for a school. The health visitor can obtain the original birth record from the appropriate authority if a pre-school child moves into her area.

Having all this information then concerning the babies and young children in her area of responsibility, what tasks might the health visitor undertake, bearing in mind that these tasks may vary from one health authority to another?

The First Visit

Mothers with new babies are usually visited in the home by the health visitor within 10–28 days of the baby's birth. The 'new-birth' visit is usually timed to follow on from the cessation of the midwife's role in the home in an attempt to provide some continuity and care for the mother and child. This visit may be the first contact that the health visitor has had with the mother and family and therefore is a very important one. It is on the basis of developing a warm relationship at this time that will set the scene for future work and co-operation. The main aims of the first visit for the health visitor will be to gain assurance about the physical, emotional and social well-being of the mother and baby, including the establishment of adequate feeding and sleeping patterns. The health visitor will usually undertake a full examination of the baby (even though this may have been done in hospital), ever alert to the early detection of abnormality but also to provide herself with a baseline upon which to compare the baby's future development. Both normative data and intra-individual data will be used to measure the child's progress through the pre-school years. If the baby is the first born then much of this first visit may be spent in reassuring an anxious, tired and possibly young mother. Great health-visiting skills are called into play during the visit in realising just how much information to give the mother all at once and what to leave for another time. The health visitor will certainly leave her office telephone number and the times and places of the infant welfare clinics. If the health visitor has a well worked out set of priorities for visiting her pre-school population she may also be able to give the mother a rough idea of when she will be paying her next visit.

It is worth noting again at this point that the health visitor has no statutory right of entry into any home and that the new-birth visit and subsequent visits are effected with the consent of the client and through the establishment of good relationships.

The Screening Process

Some of what the health visitor does in her work with pre-school children can be described as screening in that she applies one or more procedures to a defined population of children with the intention of identifying difficulties at an early stage. Within the scope of the health visitor's work such an identification of children at risk would result in the child's being referred to another medical (or para-medical) agency for futher investigation. Depending on the nature of the difficulty, however, this would not preclude the health visitor's offering the family advice and support for the child throughout the pre-school years. The health visitor would of course be receiving written communication from these other agencies about the specific diagnosis of the difficulties.

The types of screening procedures used and the age of application would again be subject to variation from one local health authority to another. However the following discussion will indicate some of the possibilities.

Hearing

Hearing defects can have major effects on the child's development both in the pre-school years and later learning in school. Health visitors are now administering a hearing test to all babies between the ages of 7 and 9 months.

Practice. The procedure for testing the hearing of babies at this age is usually conducted according to the Stycar hearing tests (Sheridan, 1968). The intention is to present the baby with familiar everyday sounds including speech as a preliminary screening device. The test is usually conducted with the help of an assistant who is trained to observe the child's reactions closely, and is therefore labour intensive.

The sounds required for the testing are produced by the human voice, a rattle, spoon against cup, tissue paper and handbell and are presented in that order. The tester will stand approximately 3 feet to the side of the child but outside his or her immediate range of vision. The distance varies from 1 to 3 feet according to the age of the child. It is important that unintended cues are not given, for example, visible shadows, perfume etc. as the observant child will readily make use of these. The assistant sits in front of the child trying to keep his or her attention.

The testing procedure involves presenting the sounds to both sides in the following manner. The speech sounds consist of a low-frequency vowel sound 'oo', repeated 2–4 times and high pitched consonant sounds 'tit-tit-tit', 'ps-ps-ps', 'pth-pth-pth' repeated rapidly 4–6 times. The speech sounds are produced at a quiet conversational level. The other sounds are delivered for 2–3 seconds: the rattle softly shaken, the spoon stroked against the brim of the cup, the tissue paper rustled quietly and the handbell tinkled gently. The child should turn in the direction of the sound. If no response to a sound is elicited two or three repetitions may be made with an interval of at least 2 seconds between.

Because of the risk of boring the child and losing further co-operation it is not worth proceeding with further repetitions.

If the child shows a clear-cut response to any 3 of the 5 sounds produced it is assumed that there is enough hearing to allow speech to develop. If the child fails to respond in an appropriate manner then the test should be repeated within a month. Any further doubt will result in the child's being referred to the audiology clinic for more expert testing (see Chapter 4).

It should be stressed that in addition to the information obtained from the above testing situation it is important to note the development of speech over the subsequent pre-school years. It is also necessary to keep a record of the mother's reporting of the child's hearing and speech behaviour at home, as parents have often been found to discover a hearing loss before professionals (e.g. Freeman *et al*, 1981).

Criticism. However the reliability of such a screening procedure as described must be questioned. First any test which requires a behavioural response on the part of the testee cannot be wholly reliable. Certainly if a baby does not respond appropriately then it does not necessarily mean that the baby has a hearing loss; the child may be unresponsive for a number of reasons unconnected with hearing loss – for instance sleepiness. A further complication to the procedure is that if the baby is suffering from a minor ailment such as a cough or a cold or even incubating one of the many childhood infectious illnesses he or she may fail to respond to the hearing test and a further one will be necessary.

From the health visitor's point of view the actual test, although short to administer, is labour intensive. For reasons of cost effectiveness the screening sessions are usually clinic-based and thus the risk of non-attendance is an important factor. The conscientious health visitor will of course follow up in the home any of the babies who are particularly at risk for any reason, including non-attendance.

On the question of the reliability of this form of hearing screening it must be said that all is not satisfactory. False positives (children who fail the test, but whose hearing is satisfactory) and false negatives (children who pass the test whose hearing is impaired) will occur, though hopefully fewer of the latter. In addition some children will be missed completely by moving home or failing to attend the clinic sessions. More criticisms of screening for hearing impairment are presented in Chapter 4.

More objective information about hearing screening has been made available through the Health Visitors' Association (HVA) (see Jones 1983). This association acts as a professional advisory body and a trade union for practising health visitors. In 1977 and again in 1981 the HVA conducted a survey of routine hearing screening conducted by health visitors, and information provided by district nursing officers reflected a good coverage of England, Wales and Northern Ireland. Some interesting facts and areas of concern are highlighted by the surveys. The HVA report a lack of standardisation both between regions and within regions in nearly all aspects of hearing screening, including the age at which children are screened and the training received by the health visitors.

The 1977 survey indicated that some districts were practising selective screening but an improvement on this was shown by the 1981 respondents where all infants aged six to ten months were screened in all areas. However in 75 per cent of the areas the hearing test was conducted only once as a matter of routine and anything up to four times in the remaining areas. The DHSS Sub-Committee (1981) recommended that all infants should be given a hearing test at eight months and three years, and that each authority should have a recognised policy towards hearing screening, a policy supported by the HVA. With regard to the training of health visitors for hearing screening, most did receive some form of training but the 1981 survey did reveal seven districts where no training courses were offered. Although this situation is a cause for concern, the HVA report that this is a great improvement on 1977 figures when over one third of districts did not offer training. It is an HVA recommendation that a standard outline of a district's training course should be specified and a certificate issued on completion of the course. This evidence of competence to undertake screening could be produced in the event of a health visitor's moving to work in another district.

It is apparent from the previous findings cited that there are areas of concern with regard to hearing screening, but the Health Visitors' Association appears fully aware of these and some improvements have been made as indicated by their surveys. Undoubtedly improvements will continue.

Vision

Screening and other tests of eyes and vision are clearly of importance during the pre-school years and the health visitor will need to be trained and familiar with these.

Vision. In the first few weeks of life note will be taken that the eyes are of normal size and appearance. The lens and the cornea should be clear, the pupils round, equal and responsive to light and the blink response should be present. By 2–3 months of age the eyes can be observed for fixation, horizontal following and conjugate movements of the eye. In addition to the above observations at 4–8 months following in both horizontal and vertical planes should be noted. Conjugate movements of the eyes and also convergence and visually directed reaching for objects may be observed.

At 7–9 months infants will be observed visually exploring the environment and will attend to and become preoccupied with objects around them. A test for visual acuity can be performed at this age if required by offering a smartie or similar sized object for near vision, and by using the Stycar graded balls test at 3 metres for distance vision (Sheridan, 1973).

For children of 3 and 4 years, health visitors in some areas (e.g. Sheffield) will use the 5- or 7-letter cards, respectively, from the Stycar Vision Tests as part of the systematic developmental screening of children.

The child is tested either with a parent or another familiar adult — e.g. a teacher in a nursery. The testing takes place in a well-lit room, and only after rapport with the child is achieved. First the health visitor determines that the child understands the task, which requires the matching of letters. The child is given a card with five letters (in the case of a 3-year-old) or seven letters (in the case of a 4-year-old) on it. This is repeated until the health visitor is sure the child understands the task, and is willing to 'play' the game. At this point the health visitor positions herself 3 metres away, while the child sits by, or on the lap of, the parent, and the left eye is carefully covered. The child is shown a series of letters, on a flip-over booklet, of diminishing size, and for each one must correctly point to the correct letter on the card. The test is repeated with the right eye covered. The letters are carefully graded to represent the levels of visual acuity.

Sheridan (1973) reports that the test can be used on 80 per cent of normal 3-year-olds at the first attempt. With careful preparation of matching experience, she argues, 'the percentage of testable 2's and 3's can be considerably improved'. Sheridan recommends referral to an ophthalmologist if the child fails size 4 letters at 10 metres (the equivalent of 6/9 vision), and retesting if the child fails the smallest letters, size 3 (the equivalent of 6/6 vision, vision at 3 metres).

Screening for squints is part of the Sheffield 9-month screening

— as indicated below, this is far from universal. It is repeated at 18 months and 3 years. The common forms of testing are the reflected light test and the cover test, and these may be conducted from 6-7 months onwards and repeated in the later pre-school years. With the reflected light test a small torch is held about 12 inches in front of the child's face in line with the bridge of the nose. As the child looks at the light the reflections in the cornea should be symmetrical and situated in the centre of the pupil.

With the cover eye test each eye in turn is covered and then un-covered whilst the child visually fixates on an appropriate smaller object. As the eye is covered note is made of any objection to the covering, movements of the uncovered eye in order to take up fixation, unsteady fixation by the uncovered eye or nystagmus. As the eye is uncovered note is made of any readjustment of fixation by that eye which might indicate a latent squint. As mentioned previously testing for squints may continue up to school age by the health visitor and/or the infant welfare clinic doctor. Visual acuity will usually be checked at 3 and 4 years of age using the Stycar Letter Charts. Colour vision will also be checked, particularly red/green in boys.

Some health authorities will encourage health visitors to refer direct to ophthalmic clinics those children who are causing concern. It is possible however that in some areas the referral may have to be made through a general practitioner. Authorities also differ with regard to the training of health visitors for vision and hearing screening. Some health visitors may not be required to test to the extent previously described and the children may be checked by the doctor at clinic attendance. This procedure will clearly not be servicing the needs of those children who are non-clinic attenders and the health visitor would be well ad-vised to have those testing skills at her disposal.

Criticisms. The population screening for visual impairment by health visitors appears to be much less well developed than hearing screening. Robertson (1981b) stresses the need for the early identification of certain visual disorders which are treatable, and where early treatment is necessary for optimal results. However, she suggests that this is far from wide-spread, and that there is no standard screening procedure for vision. She reports a survey of 20 general practitioners who offered developmental tests. Of the 91 children in the sample who were given developmental tests by the GPs and health visitors, 30 per cent were not screened for vision, and 70 per cent were not specifically screened for a squint.

Robertson suggests that the lack of universal screening is partly related to a lack of agreement among ophthalmic practitioners of what is a correct referral. A necessary requisite of a screening test is that there is a clear criterion of pass/fail leading, in this case, to referral to a specialist. Consequently some researchers suggest there is insufficient evidence to support universal screening for vision.

These problems are highlighted by a study by Robertson (1981c). Sixty children in one area formed the total sample, but only 45 were in fact screened at the age 3½ to 4 years. Of the rest, 2 had moved, 8 were not tested and 5 were already under surveillance by the eye department of the hospital. Using Stycar Vision Tests, and erring on the side of caution, Robertson referred 15 children to the orthoptist – i.e. 33 per cent of the sample tested failed the screening test. Of these 15, 5 were treated, 3 were considered suitable for observation, while 7 were considered satisfactory. In other words about a half of the children failing the test did not have a visual problem. With this low rate of accuracy, and the time taken on each child (15 minutes examination plus associated administration etc.) support is provided for those who question the evidence for universal screening for visual impairment. It must be said, however, that children are still entering school suffering serious visual problems which earlier identification would have prevented, by allowing earlier treatment (Ismail and Lall, 1981).

General Development

In addition to screening for sensory deficits the main area of screening with which health visitors are involved is that of general child development. Again it must be assumed that the screening procedures will vary from one district health authority to another and that the ages of the children screened will vary.

Practice. The changing attitudes towards child health and health visiting practices over the last decade which have been referred to earlier in the chapter are paralleled by a change in attitude toward infant screening. Previously the concentration was a narrow one looking mainly at physical defects or children 'at risk' but the approach has broadened to include the total assessment of the developing child. Health authorities would keep registers of children with obvious disorders – e.g. Downs Syndrome – and those deemed to be 'at risk' of developmental problems on the basis of their state after birth or in early infancy. It was hoped that such a register would enable the small number of high risk children to be monitored in detail during their early years. In this

Table 3.1: Example of Health Visitors' Screening Tests of Development

Name of Child ———————— Address ———————— Date of birth ————
General Practitioner ———————— Address ————————
Birth Weight ———————— Presumed Gestation ————————

			Demonstrated		Mother's Observation
Three Months	1.	Waves arms symmetrically	Yes	No	
	2.	Kicks vigorously with both legs	Yes	No	
	3.	Spontaneous social smile and cooing	Yes	No	
	4.	Eyes follow objects from side to side	Yes	No	
	5.	Turns eyes towards voice	Yes	No	
	6.	Ventral suspension — holds head up	Yes	No	
	7.	Comments			
		Signature of Health Visitor ———————— Date ————			
		Referred to ————————			
Nine Months	1.	Sits without support for 10–15 minutes	Yes	No	
	2.	Bears weight on both legs	Yes	No	
	3.	Picks up objects between index finger Right hand	Yes	No	
		and thumb and/or index pointing Left hand	Yes	No	
	4.	Babbles whilst playing	Yes	No	
	5.	Chews biscuits	Yes	No	
	6.	Squint present	Yes	No	
	7.	Hearing tests	Passed	Failed	
	8.	Comments			
		Signature of Health Visitor ———————— Date ————			
		Referred to ————————			
Eighteen Months	1.	Walks without falling	Yes	No	
	2.	Picks up toy from floor without falling	Yes	No	
	3.	Picks up small objects e.g. cotton	Yes	No	
	4.	Build towers of 3 cubes (after demonstration)	Yes	No	
	5.	Spontaneous scribble when given pencil	Yes	No	
	6.	Uses recogniseable words (if No — follow up at 2 years)	Yes	No	
	7.	Obeys simple commands	Yes	No	
	8.	Squint present	Yes	No	
	9.	Comments			
		Signature of Health Visitor ———————— Date ————			
		Referred to ————————			

Table 3.1 Contd.

		Demonstrated		Mother's Observation
Three Years	1. Jumps with both feet together	Yes	No	
	2. Builds tower of 9–10 cubes (after demonstration)	Yes	No	
	3. Imitates a bridge with cubes	Yes	No	
	4. Imitates a circle and line	Yes	No	
	5. Large intelligible vocabulary	Yes	No	
	6. Does he/she ask questions	Yes	No	
	7. Does he/she play with other children	Yes	No	
	8. Toilet trained during the day	Yes	No	
	9. Stycar Vision test result			
	10. Squint present	Yes	No	
	11. Teeth	Healthy Unhealthy		
	12. Comments			
	Signature of Health Visitor ————— Date —————			
	Referred to —————			

		Demonstrated		Mother's Observation
	1. Hops — Right foot	Yes	No	
	Left foot	Yes	No	
	2. Builds three steps with cubes (after demonstration)	Yes	No	
	3. Copies a cross	Yes	No	
	4. Draws a man with head and legs	Yes	No	
	5. Matches four primary colours	Yes	No	
	6. Normal conversational speech	Yes	No	
	7. Dresses and undresses himself/herself	Yes	No	
	8. Washes and dries face and hands	Yes	No	
	9. Toilet trained day/night	Yes	No	
	10. Stycar Vision Test — Right eye	Yes	No	
	Left eye			
	11. Comments			
	Signature of Health Visitor ————— Date —————			
	Referred to —————			

way resource allocation would have been effective. Unfortunately these hopes were not realised (see Chapter 10). The ideal is to screen all children with the implicit understanding that many factors impinge on development apart from physical defects. These factors are often ignored when some people ask the question, 'Why look at healthy children?' It is a sign of changing practice that baby clinics are now usually referred to as 'well-baby clinics' indicating that the modern emphasis is towards looking at the total development of all children.

Table 3.1 indicates how one district health authority tackles developmental screening, and at what ages. From the table it can be seen that the screening procedure takes the form of a developmental checklist where the child either meets or fails to meet a number of criterion behaviours. This example also includes reference to hearing and visual screening. The assessment can take place in the clinic or the home setting and in the case of non-clinic attenders the latter setting will be favoured. It is likely in many cases that the home setting will give a more realistic picture of the child's development, providing a familiar environment in which the child can play and be observed.

Clearly the results of any such screening test must be interpreted with caution. Experienced health visitors will use the information to augment all the other information they have concerning the child's development and the knowledge they have of the range of experience that the child has been exposed to. Failure to meet the criteria may or may not indicate developmental delay in the child, and the health visitor may wish to observe the child further using, if necessary, different criteria. In cases where the health visitor is concerned about a child, referral to a paediatric assessment unit is often possible either direct or through the general practitioner. In the event good communications should exist between all the professionals involved so that the parents can obtain maximum support and advice on how to meet the child's needs.

Leaving aside the small number of children who will present with obvious difficulties the screening tests can also provide an opportunity for the health visitor to discuss areas of child development with the parents. They can be encouraged to organise the child's environment and experiences so that the child can be maximally stimulated. In the case of inexperienced health visitors the screening tests can provide a supportive framework for observing children until a more extensive knowledge of child development can come into play.

Criticism. A screening test of general development which has been used extensively in the United States is the Denver Developmental Screening Test (Frankenberg *et al*, 1971). This is similar to that described here, but is more extensive at each age. In their 1971 paper, Frankenberg, Goldstein and Camp report that the DDST can be used by 'health screening aides' who have been specially trained. They report a validity study of 237 children whose scores on the DDST were compared with intelligence and developmental scales. The DDST results in a categorisation of each child as normal, questionable or abnormal. From their data it is clear that this, revised, version of the DDST produced a large number of false positives, using the individual assessments or developmental scales as a criterion. Of the children designated 'abnormal' on the DDST over half (17 out of 32) had a Stanford Binet or Bayley quotient over 70. Of those designated 'questionable' 91 per cent (48 out of 53) had such quotients, and 70 per cent had quotients of at least 80 (i.e. outside the bottom 10 per cent of the population). Most of the children failing the DDST, therefore, would be false positives — i.e. inappropriately designated 'at risk'.

In a later paper, Frankenberg *et al* (1981) report on an abbreviated and revised version of the DDST. They state that their earlier test was the most extensively taught to physicians in training, but that only 10 per cent used it in practice as it took too long. The shortened version takes only 5 to 7, as opposed to 15 to 20 minutes. Of the 197 children studied in their sample, 53 failed the short-form. Of these, 22 were designated 'questionable', and 7 'abnormal' on the full DDST. (Three children were untestable.) Thus only 13 per cent of those failing the short-form were considered 'abnormal' on the DDST — and remember that less than half those would be expected to have a quotient of less than 70, from the results of the earlier study.

Results such as these must lead us to treat such screening tests with caution. The DDST is used extensively in the United States and in parts of this country. It has the benefit of evaluative studies which raise questions about its accuracy. Most screening procedures used in this country, including that used in Sheffield and described above, have not been the subject of evaluation studies and their effectiveness is unknown.

Non-Accidental Injury

Another area in which health visitors are often greatly involved is the identification of children likely to suffer non-accidental injury. This is a very sensitive issue which has been the subject of many lurid accounts in the media following the death of Maria Colwell (see Howells, 1974).

Non-accidental injury is not rare; Kempe and Kempe (1978) report that it is reported 320 times per million population in the United States, and that their experience suggests that this is only a fraction of the total incidence.

The Kempes report a study which compared four sources of data to predict abuse or neglect, of which the most accurate was information noted in the labour wards and delivery rooms. This information, they state, gave a 75.6 per cent accuracy rate. Another measure based upon the parents' reactions to and caring for the child during the first six weeks had an accuracy rate of 54 per cent. The benefits of intervention and the accuracy of prediction were studied by comparing two groups of 50 mothers each, only one of which received intervention, and a control group of 50 low risk mothers. Of the 50 in the intervention group, 20 showed signs of 'abnormal parenting practices', whereas no low risk mothers did. In their first seventeen months of life, 22 children in the high-risk group and 4 in the low-risk group had at least one accident requiring medical attention, but whereas five in the non-intervention group required hospital treatment for serious injuries, none in the high risk intervention or low risk groups had such a need.

In this country, health visitors have also been involved in identifying children at risk of non-accidental injury. Generally this has been part of their task of general surveillance and has followed on from observations by obstetricians, paediatricians and midwives. Dean, MacQueen, Ross and Kempe (1978) report on a survey in Aberdeen of 7,700 children, of whom, 1,388 were presented to the Children's Hospital in their first two years with injuries or failure to thrive. They claimed that those children with health visitors' assessments coded moderate to great concern were more likely to present to the hospital with serious accidents, abuse or failure to thrive.

A later report by Woods (1981) describes an attempt in an area, Basingstoke in Hampshire, to develop a list of factors which are predictive of child abuse. In this project health visitors were given a detailed list of such factors, but then made their own decisions as to whether the child should be placed on an 'at risk' register. Four main areas were considered:

(1) Pregnancy – e.g. unwanted, late booking.
(2) Personality and social problems – e.g. low toleration of stress, poor family relationships.
(3) Parenting behaviour – e.g. poor bonding, husband's jealousy or rejection of the baby.
(4) Condition of baby – e.g. frequent illnesses, failure to thrive.

In addition all accidents or injuries were noted. A shorter checklist was completed in the maternity unit which was passed to the midwife. She passed it to the health visitor at 2 weeks. The health visitor completed her assessment by 6 weeks. Children considered at risk received more frequent visits by health visitors.

No evaluation of this study is reported, other than that fewer children were referred to the Social Services Department in the first year of operation.

Criticism. The identification of children at risk of non-accidental injury is far from simple. Although the Kempes report an accuracy of prediction of 76.5 per cent, most of these will be children correctly identified as not at risk. Of the children at risk, only 40 per cent were subject to 'abnormal parenting practices' and only 10 per cent in the non-intervention high risk group actually received serious injuries. Thus, the screening measures reported are, in fact, rather less efficient than is at first apparent. Widespread use of such measures, in their present form, would result in large numbers of children being wrongly designated at risk of non-accidental injury. Most are likely to be in the disadvantaged parts of the community.

This position poses a major dilemma. Such over-inclusive registers could be seen to pose a threat to civil liberties. They are often secret (i.e. the parents do not know they are on the register) and, as has been shown, inaccurate. Some of the criteria could be considered class- or culture-biased — e.g. just what are 'abnormal parenting practices'? On the other hand, it could be argued that the success of attempts like those of Kempes and of Woods are justified if just one child is saved from non-accidental injury.

Conclusion

The health visitor is a key person in the identification of children's special needs which may become apparent in the first four years of life, particularly in the time following discharge by the hospital and midwifery services and prior to school entry. Health visitors' practice, however, varies from district to district. Only recently have visitors in all districts started to screen all children for hearing loss. Some carry out structured general developmental screenings, many do not. The same applies to screening for vision. Screening for non-accidental injury is rarely carried out.

But in addition to conducting systematic screenings, health visitors do carry out general surveillance of these children. By their experience and presence they are able to identify many children who have special needs whether or not formal screening takes place. Observations by parents and the health visitor can be noted, and the child may be seen in home, clinic and the community at large. Unfortunately the effectiveness of this work is not known. Evaluation studies are limited to description of what the health visitor does, e.g. number of visits. Robertson (1981a) laments this and reports that some medical practitioners consider they are incapable of accurately detecting visual and hearing impairment. Certainly some children are missed.

Evaluating health visitor involvement in the pre-school years may allow the profession itself to use such information to work towards setting its own priorities within the service delivery as a whole. If this aspect of the health visitor's role were shown to be effective then such arguments could be used to obtain more staff to do a more efficient job of work.

It is evident from recent health visiting journals that health visitors as a profession are not shirking the issues of effectiveness and setting of priorities within their work. Whatever the outcomes of these many discussions and investigations it would seem likely that the systematic observation of young children and the support to parents of these young children will always form an important aspect of the health visitor's role. Evaluation research is necessary, however, to work out efficient methods of carrying out these observations and offering support to parents and children.

Finally, there is a need to extend examples of good practice in collaboration with other professionals, including teachers in nursery and infant schools, in order that the needs of children can be recognised and appreciated by those concerned.

4 AUDIOLOGICAL SCREENING AND ASSESSMENT

Anna MacCarthy and Judith Connell

Children with impaired hearing are now the subject of screening and surveillance by several professionals during their early lives. The first few years of life for these children are indeed crucial as impaired hearing is highly related to problems in the development of speech and language. The screening of hearing is therefore given a high priority in the early years as this is the time when speech and language are developing. Those children whose hearing loss is not discovered at this time are doubly disadvantaged as their language does not develop, often leading to educational retardation and behaviour problems.

Unfortunately, hearing impairment is a condition that many parents find very hard to accept in their children and it is not unknown for some to actively reject attempts by professionals to assess their child's hearing and prescribe suitable help (e.g. a hearing aid). For example, one mother, who was herself deaf, would not accept her daughter's disability until she was about three years old. Because of these reactions, professionals dealing with hearing-impaired children must show sensitivity and help the parents to accept their child's problem. Until that is achieved there may be little that can be done to help the child directly.

Hence, although the main focus of this chapter will be on the assessment of hearing itself, it must be remembered that there is a major need for work *with* parents. This is a necessity for all audiological professionals concerned, but in some cases the extra support of a social worker might be necessary.

The Professionals

Three stages in the identification of hearing difficulties can be described, with different professionals being particularly relevant at each stage. Those stages and the relevant people concerned are shown in Table 4.1. Apart from parents, these are professionals involved in the assessment of and for hearing difficulties. In addition, other professionals may be involved to provide further information on the child's

Table 4.1: Stages of Hearing Assessment and Intervention

Stage	People
Screening	Parents, Health Visitors, GPs, Clinical Medical Officers
Assessment	Audiologists, Audiological Technicians
Intervention	ENT Surgeon, Teacher of the Hearing-Impaired, Social Worker, Hearing Aid Technician

development. The educational psychologist, for example, may see a child to investigate the development of general cognitive ability and, later, educational attainment. Speech therapists, paediatricians and other staff may also see the child.

Parents

It is increasingly being recognised that parents are most important people in the process of identifying developmental difficulties in their children. Many professionals now argue strongly for 'parents as partners' and a number of books and pamphlets also now promulgate this view.

This development has come about in several ways. Some parents have been extremely upset and annoyed at the treatment they and their children have received. In some cases this has led to individual action, while others have formed groups of like-minded parents. Concern about the provision of health and education services for hearing impaired children has stung many parents into action, often with highly productive results.

The 1981 Education Act now requires parents to be intimately involved with the procedures for assessing and providing for their children (see Chapter 9). In addition, work through bodies such as the National Deaf Children's Society has heightened awareness of needs and strategies necessary to meet those needs.

We consider it of the utmost importance that parents are indeed treated as partners – not in a paternalistic, half-hearted fashion, but fully. There are several reasons for this. First, it is the parents' right to receive such treatment. Secondly, it is essential for the child that the parents trust the professionals with whom they are working. Thirdly, at the practical level, the presence and comfort of a parent during testing is often essential to facilitate accurate assessment. Our own practice, therefore, is to try to meet this objective of working with parents as partners.

The Audiology Service

The Audiology Service can be described as a network of professionals with a core team. The exact make-up of each and the location of the facility will vary from place to place. In some areas the team will be based in a hospital setting, the Department of Otology and Laryngology at Grays Inn Road, London is a good example. Many hospitals will have an Ear Nose and Throat Department. In other areas there might be a Regional Specialist Audiology Centre. The North-west is particularly forward in this respect having the Centre at Manchester University, and also a Diagnostic and Assessment Centre at the Royal School for the Deaf, Cheadle Hulme. A third variant is to have a Child Health Clinic, part of the DHA's provision for community paediatrics.

The location of each facility, and other local factors, will have a determining effect on the make-up of the core team and the consequent interrelationship between this team and the wider network of services. For example, hospital settings will have an ENT surgeon as part of the team but will not usually have psychologists. The Royal School for the Deaf at Cheadle Hume, however, includes in its team an educational psychologist and an educational audiologist. Audiologists working in Child Health Clinics would normally have a medical background and be clinical medical officers. This situation is potentially confusing to parents who will come across many professionals if they have a hearing impaired child. It is important for the sake of the parents, and especially of the child, that good working relationships are established both between professionals, and with the parents. As an example, the system in one city will be described.

In Sheffield there are presently two distinct services for children although they work in conjunction with each other. One is placed within the main Education Office in the centre of town and comprises a room for testing, which is sound-proofed, together with a waiting room and office. Its position in the Education Department can be traced back to the time of the School Health Service which once formed a separate functioning branch of medicine. This was abolished in 1974 when the Health Service was reorganised.

However, its position does have several advantages. First, being in the centre of town it is convenient for all children. Second, its *not* being in a hospital can be helpful to many parents and children. Some parents have an aversion to hospitals, particularly if they find acceptance of their child's handicap difficult, or if they have themselves had problems and hospitalisation. Many children, of course, find hospitals worrying places — a problem often aggravated by the overtly clinical ethos of some hospitals. Third, there is the practical advantage that children who attend the main School Health Clinic (as it is still called, despite the official changes mentioned above) can easily cross the road to the Audiology Clinic. Finally, the presence of the clinic within the Education Department facilitates interaction with education personnel. There are, of course, disadvantages which will be considered below.

The present Audiology Clinic was established in Sheffield, in response to an obvious need, about 30 years ago. It was started by an ordinary School Medical Officer who had to acquaint herself with the basics of audiology and how to run it with very little help or training from anybody. At that time little was known about either. She built up a limited but very efficient service seeing on average 900 school children for a Sweep Test (see below) and about 200 pre-school children each year. The Audiology Clinic passed into the hands of the present Principal Clinical Medical Officer in 1970.

Most Audiology Centres are run by a team of professionals with different qualifications and experience. Each concentrates on a particular expertise in testing, diagnosing and treating the children referred for further investigation because of some suspected hearing impairments suggested at the screening stage.

Clinical Medical Officer – Audiology. The person running this clinic is a Principal Clinical Medical Officer who has a full time responsibility to the post. Her experience has been with a wide range of work with children in schools, hospitals and clinics. Colleagues in a similar position elsewhere will have had comparable experiences, but as there is no standard training for the post there will be variations.

ENT/Consultant Medical Audiologist. A medical consultant who has specialised in disorders of the ear, nose and throat. He currently has 4 to 6 sessions per month in the clinic. He examines children and discusses their problems with other staff with a view to operating in suitable cases, and subsequently will review their progress. He is assisted by a Senior Registrar who also does about 4 sessions per month. The actual input by ENT specialists will vary in different parts of the country.

Peripatetic Teachers of the Deaf. There are 2 teachers who work with pre-school children and 6 for children of school age (including secondary). These are based at Sheffield's primary school for children with profound hearing impairment, but also visit the clinic. This is particularly true of the pre-school teachers. All are trained teachers who have taken extra qualifications to become Teachers of the Deaf and have much experience of children with all kinds of hearing impairment.

In some places, however, Teachers of the Deaf are expected to work with children of all ages. According to Nolan and Tucker (1981) this was the case in 11 of the 16 LEAs surveyed. We regard this as far from satisfactory. The geography of a large city does, of course, help here in allowing specialisation which is welcomed by parents and schools alike. These two Teachers of the Deaf also work with the Social Worker (see below).

Educational Psychologists. Two educational psychologists, spend part of their time working with the hearing impaired. This is, unfortunately, very limited at present owing to a lack of resources and averages about 2 sessions per month. Only some of this will be within the clinic itself.

There are very few educational psychologists who specialise in hearing impairment. Wedell and Lambourne (1980) report that only 18 per cent of field-worker educational psychologists work with the hearing impaired at least once a month. In most cases therefore, as in Sheffield, this work must be a small part of the overall workload. This is a far from satisfactory arrangement given the special skills required of such psychologists. Consequently use is also made of the few specialist psychologists available – e.g. at the Royal Schools for the Deaf at Margate and Cheadle Hulme, and at University and Hospital Departments which specialise in hearing impairment. One possible development for the future is the creation of regional specialist posts for a group of LEAs.

Social Worker. There is one social worker, employed by the Family and Community Services Department, who works with hearing-impaired adults, the parents of hearing-impaired children, and the youngsters themselves. In addition to basic social work training he has extra qualifications in work with the hearing impaired.

He runs a weekly group for the parents (in practice mainly mothers) of hearing-impaired pre-school children which is attended by the two teachers mentioned above. Other specialists visit occasionally either to give specific talks or to be available to the parents.

Speech Therapist. One speech therapist spends a limited amount of time with the clinic but, as with the educational psychologist, this is severely limited by current workloads.

Hospital Audiology Clinics

In addition to the clinic based within the Education Offices, there is a second clinic based within Sheffield's Children's Hospital. This is detached from the main hospital, and shares a building with the speech therapy department of the hospital.

There are several advantages to this arrangement. First, the hospital setting allows easy access to other hospital personnel and facilities. Secondly, there is a special benefit of being based together with a speech therapy department. This allows easy access to speech therapists for work with children, advice to parents and professional, informal discussions. Thirdly, although part of the hospital, it is physically separate and has adopted its own, non-clinical ethos. (However, it should be noted that Sheffield Children's Hospital has generally done much to make the stay of children, and their parents, as pleasant as possible.)

The clinic is run by a Chief Audiological Technician and there is one Senior Audiological Technician. The basic training is a two-year course leading to the Certificate in Sciences in Medical Physics and Physiological Measurement. This is followed by a year of study leading to examinations set by the British Society of Audiologists. At this point the person is eligible for a job as a Technician, but must have three years of experience before being able to become a Technician for pre-school children. There is a need for the development of links between the service for the hearing impaired and the speech therapy service in many areas. Speech therapists have important skills and knowledge to offer which are often not taken up. Most hospital Audiology Clinics will have a person with such training. This is, of course, different to the training route of clinical medical officers mentioned above.

Joint Service

Plans are currently in hand to combine the two audiological clinics. This is in line with a general movement across the country where a number of regional centres are being set up to provide diagnosis of and advice for hearing-impaired children. The rationale behind such a move is explained in Ives and Morris (1978). They report considerable concern arising from a survey completed by Ives in 1974 of over 2000 hearing-impaired children in the Midlands and North of England. This survey showed a significant lack of good diagnostic and advisory centres.

The plans in Sheffield do not go as far as Ives and Morris would like. The new Centre will bring together the audiological team, which will be in close contact with the speech therapy service. However, there are no plans to increase the input from educational psychologists.

Categories of Impairment

The term 'hearing-impaired' is now commonly used, but in itself is very general. To aid understanding of the child's abilities, various additional descriptions are used. The following are those recommended by the National Executive Committee, British Association of Teachers of the Deaf (1981):

Average hearing loss:
Slightly hearing-impaired: Up to 40 dB loss
Moderately hearing-impaired: 41 dB to 70 dB
Severely hearing-impaired: 71 dB to 95 dB (and post-lingual losses greater than 95 dB)
Profoundly hearing-impaired: Children born with, or who acquired before the age of 18 months, an average hearing loss of 96 dB or greater.

The Committee prefers these categories as the old labels deaf and partially-hearing, which have statutory definitions, have been found to be inadequate. The new definitions are based upon two factors: the degree of average hearing loss (across five tested frequencies, in the better ear) and the age of onset. These terms should help to describe hearing-impaired children more usefully, but there are still many variations within this population.

Types of Hearing Impairment

These are usually divided into conductive and sensori-neural impairments.

Conductive Loss

In this case there is a malfunction of the outer or middle ear such that the transmission of sound is impaired. It generally results in a slight or moderate hearing loss, although some severe losses are also found. Common causes are related to blockages in the outer or middle ear caused by fluid or objects (e.g. beads). A common, though nevertheless worrying problem, afflicts many children in their early years – 'glue ear'. Problems of catarrh and 'glue ear' can have a significant effect on children at a stage when they would normally be learning a great deal through talking and listening.

Usually, conductive hearing losses can be cured, or at least ameliorated, by medical treatment. For example, grommets (small tubes) can be placed in each ear drum to enable the middle ear to be ventilated. In many cases, however, no surgical intervention is required and the problem reduces as the child grows older. Here parents and teachers must appreciate how best to manage the child so that the reduced sensitivity to hearing is compensated for until the child outgrows the dysfunction of the ear. However, if the hearing loss is not recognised, such children can be seriously disadvantaged, especially at school. The development of reading, for example, is related to the development of an appreciation of the sound system of language, and the relationship between sounds and written symbols (letters and groups of letters). A child who cannot distinguish sounds or, worse still, hear certain sounds, will find reading more of a puzzle than the normally hearing. Some children, as a result of frustration because of such problems aggravated by missing instructions from teachers, develop behaviour problems which may quickly reduce following a screening of t' e hearing problem.

Sensori-neural Loss

Damage can also be caused to the nerve of hearing which extends to the brain centre from the inner ear. This type of hearing loss cannot be operated upon and so must be considered permanent. Often the cause will be unknown; in fact Nolan and Tucker (1981) claim that in up to 50 per cent of children with severe sensori-neural hearing impairment the cause remains unknown.

The causes can be divided into two main types. First, there are the children with *congenital* hearing loss. These are all born with impaired hearing, or rather impaired neural apparatus. Three types of cause can be identified:

(1) Hereditary. Some impairments are the result of genetic or chromosomal abnormalities.
(2) Prenatal. Some diseases, especially rubella (German measles), can have a severe effect on the baby in the womb if the mother is affected. With rubella the period of greatest risk is 12–16 weeks, and the effect of the virus is to effectively destroy part

of the cochlea (inner ear).

(3) Perinatal. Birth is a hazardous period for both mother and baby, and some hearing impairment is a result of problems at this time. Anoxia (lack of oxygen), Rhesus incompatibility, neonatal jaundice and severe prematurity have all been linked with sensori-neural hearing losses.

The second group comprises those children with an *acquired* hearing loss. Some virus infections and especially meningitis, inflammation of the membrane covering the brain,are the common causes.

A fuller description of the causes of hearing losses and of their treatment is to be found in excellent books by Nolan and Tucker (1981) and Freeman *et al* (1981). For our purposes there are several points to be made.

First, there is a great variation between children with a hearing loss, not only in its cause, and degree, but in the interaction between degree of loss and the child's other strengths and weaknesses. For example, a child with mental handicap in addition to a moderate hearing loss, might have more difficulty with auditorily presented information than a very bright child with a severe hearing loss. This interaction is important.

Secondly, sensori-neural losses are permanent. Future advances including cochlea implants might belie this statement but for the present it is a sad, but accurate statement. The likelihood of a cure for damage which is beyond the cochlea is very unlikely.

Thirdly, many causes of hearing loss have been recognised and steps taken to prevent damage (e.g. immunisation of adolescent girls against rubella). In about half the cases of sensori-neural loss, however, cause is not known.

Screening and Referral

Hearing loss is a serious and potentially damaging problem, especially with respect to language development. Fortunately there are some simple tests which can be used to screen young children to spot those who appear to have a hearing problem.

Some research is being carried out at present on screening children in the first few days of life using the Linco-Bennett Auditory Response Cradle. A new born baby is put into a cot with head supports and a small machine connected to the ear. Responses to sound are then examined. The work is still experimental and at an early stage (Evans, 1980) but promising. However, the question may be asked whether assessment or especially screening at this age is useful?

Screening

The first population screening of babies is usually carried out between the ages of 6 and 9 months by health visitors (see Chapter 3). Until recently some areas practised only screening of babies thought to be at risk of hearing impairment, owing to a rubella infection in the mother during early pregnancy, family history of hearing impairment or a difficult birth. However, the effectiveness of such a programme was poor. Nolan and Tucker (1981) report that in more than half the babies with sensori-neural loss diagnosed in their department at Manchester University the cause was either unknown or unpredictable. Given such a very low rate of effectiveness of the screening programme, there has been a move to screen all children. As Kath Jennings reports (Chapter 3), health visitors in all parts of the country will now practise total population screening.

If the health visitor is unable to test the hearing, or is dissatisfied with the result, a repeat hearing test will be arranged. If this is not passed the baby will be referred to the Audiology Clinic. A further screening will be conducted here. If this is failed, or results are unsatisfactory, a more detailed examination will be carried out (see below).

In Sheffield this second stage screening is conducted at the School Health Clinic, while the more detailed examination is made at the Hospital Audiology Department. In other areas both processes may be conducted in the same place.

Any child with a hearing loss should be identified before the age of one year. However, as in all systems, problems can occur. Appointments might be missed, the baby might be ill, or on holiday, the health visitor might be absent, or the service too stretched. In such cases a hearing impairment might not be confirmed until later than suggested here, a problem highlighted recently by the National Deaf Children's Society (1983).

All children are again screened in their early school life. In Sheffield, this is carried out when the child is 6–7 years and requires the screening of about 7,000 children per annum. This will be conducted by one of the School Nursing Sisters specially trained in audiometry. If the child is absent, a second visit is made. If excess wax is present in the outer ear this is softened (by introducing a few drops of warmed olive oil every night for a week) and the child is retested. If a child fails the screening test, a referral is made to the Audiology Clinic.

A study by Hodges (1983) in three Sheffield secondary schools discovered very few children with a hearing loss who were not known to the audiology service: only 8 from the 609 12-13 year old pupils investigated were kept under review by the Audiology Clinic or referred to the ENT specialist. Hodges concludes that a screening programme at this stage could not be justified.

This system therefore appears to work very satisfactorily, with very few children being missed, and those for only a short time. However, there are a number of issues to raise. First, especially with the babies, inaccurate results can be obtained because the child is in a distracting environment. Second, the long period between screenings can be problematic. It was mentioned above that many children develop problems of the middle ear in their early school days, say 3-7 years. It is quite possible, therefore, for a child to pass (correctly) the two screenings at 7-9 months and 6-7 years, but to suffer possibly serious hearing problems in the interim. Indeed many children are referred to us during this period, and for these problems.

Screening of children at the age of 3-4 therefore has much appeal, but is only likely to be very effective when a large proportion of children are in nursery schools or similar provision. Health visitors are not sufficiently numerous to visit homes for this population, and it is known that visits to clinics drop off sharply once the baby is more than one year old, particularly those considered 'high risk' (Zinkin and Cox, 1975).

Referral Process

As the different processes of screening and referral are so interdependent, it would be useful at this point to describe how they relate. The distinction to be made between these two processes is in terms of action. With screening, there has been a decision to carry out a simple assessment (the screening test) on a population of children. Referral, however, occurs when an individual child is identified as having – or probably having – impaired hearing. A request for referral might be made by a parent to one of a number of professionals.

A referral system might be 'open' or 'closed'. In the 'open' system anyone can refer the child. This would normally be the parent or health visitor, clinical medical officer, teacher or educational psychologist – i.e. professionals who have seen the child and become worried about a possible hearing problem. In a 'closed' system, however, referrals might be accepted only from a consultant ENT surgeon or a small number of other specialists. In Sheffield at present, both systems operate. The Education Department-based Audiology Clinic operates an open system, while the Hospital-based service has a closed system. The former clinic has a waiting list of one or two weeks, while for the latter it is normally up to nine months. Practice across the country will vary, as will the length of waiting lists. In our view, it is important that some action is taken as soon as possible, even if more intensive investigations must wait.

Screening and Assessment Techniques

The purpose of screening is to identify those children who have, or appear to have impaired hearing. These tests given, therefore, have a possible result of either pass or fail (although in practice health visitors will recognise borderline cases and must make a judgement to err on the side of caution or otherwise). These are the tests given by health visitors, and also in Audiology Clinics. Assessment, however, involves a more thorough appraisal of the nature of the hearing problem – levels of hearing loss across the speech frequencies and type. Tests used for this purpose are usually called diagnostic tests and will only be conducted at a specialist Audiology Clinic.

Screening

Distraction Test. This will be carried out by health visitors on babies of 6-9 months normally in a well-baby clinic, and is described in Chapter 3 (see pages 50-1). If a child fails this test it is recommended that a retest is given very soon afterwards (about two weeks). If the child fails once more, referral to a specialist clinic should occur. Here the test might be repeated before moving on, if necessary, to other procedures. Babies might fail the test owing to temporary hearing problems (e.g. related to illnesses), non-co-operation (either because of 'unwillingness' or having not reached the necessary developmental stage to complete the test) or faulty administration. Sensitivity to all possible reasons is required and specialists are normally happy to see children who fail the test and put parents at ease. Continuous re-examination of practice is required by health visitors, and audiologists, to avoid bad practice occurring.

At the Audiology Clinic the characteristics of the stimuli used will also be assessed. The sound pressure of each stimulus will be tested using a Sound Level Meter to ensure that the stimulus being applied is the same for all children, and complies with that intended. Without this check it is possible to over- or under-estimate a child's hearing by presenting a stimulus too loud or too soft.

Subjective Tests. Babies under 3 months give a reflex response to different sound stimuli giving positive evidence of some capacity to hear, but this does not prove that acuity is normal. The most important sound stimulus is the human voice — conversational and whispered. If a parent voices concern about her baby's hearing then one should examine that baby very closely indeed, because parents are very often right. The optimum age for testing a baby is between 7 and 9 months of age, allowing for prematurity of course, because by then a normal full-term baby is able to sit supported on its parent's knee and locate sounds by turning its head to right and to left in response to different sound stimuli.

An additional stimulus now being used is a 'warbler'. This is a small box which can be held in the hand unobtrusively near the baby's ear. It can let out warble tones, at the main frequencies, at three levels of intensity. This has the benefit of being a more sophisticated piece of equipment which can still be used in a play setting. There is currently a research programme in operation which is hoping to develop such a machine for health visitors to use.

Co-operative or Activity Testing. This is also known as Toy Discrimination and is normally given to children of 18-30 months. The first essential is to establish an easy rapport with the child. While the audiologist takes a detailed history of pregnancy etc., the child plays with toys familiar to a child of this age — doll, dog, car, cup, plate, knife, fork, spoon. We give simple instructions — 'Give mummy the cup . . . the fork . . .' etc. — first in a normal voice, getting gradually quieter (using a sound level meter for the measuring) — to find out if the child can hear a normal and a quiet whispered voice and can discriminate between similar sounding words like dog, doll; shoe, ship; car, cot; etc. During the testing the examiner must keep his/her mouth covered so that the child cannot lipread.

Not all children with normal hearing pass this test. Some fail to understand the instructions, while some decide to refuse to comply with them!

Performance Test. At a later age (about 2½-3½ years) a similar test can be used which is appropriate for children of this age. The child is trained to take part in a game — e.g. putting a ball into a box when 'go' is said. This tests response to low frequency sound. To test high frequency sound, we tell the child to put the ball in the box when a snake's 's' sound is heard. In both cases the game is started with the child being able to see the audiologist. Then the examiner moves out of vision, three feet away, and repeats stimulus sounds at minimal level. At least two successes at each frequency are required for the child to pass.

Pure Tone Audiometry or Sweep Test. With young children, of three years upwards, this test can be a modification of that just described. However in this test a whistle, of set frequency from an earphone, is the stimulus. With young children we only use one earphone, as two can be frightening. We also have the parent holding the earphone against the child's ear, for extra security. With older children, a double headphone is possible, when they can indicate they have heard a sound by knocking, lighting up teddy's eyes or performing some other suitable action.

The machine used, the audiometer, is carefully calibrated so that it can measure many different frequencies accurately. However, in normal practice six main frequencies are used, those important for speech discrimination: 250 Hz, 500 Hz, 1000 Hz, 2000 Hz, 4000 Hz and 8000 Hz.

The Sweep Test is used as a screening test in schools. In Sheffield all school children in their first or second year are screened (ages 6-7 years), currently about 7,000 children per year. For screening only the frequencies 500, 1000, 2000 and 4000 Hz are used. A child might fail the test in one or more frequencies. If this happens, the child is referred to the Audiology Clinic for further assessment. Children who are absent are revisited, and those with wax in their ears have it softened as described above and the child is retested after removal of wax.

When used for screening, the purpose is to test whether the child can hear a predetermined level at each frequency. This level is that which is normal among the hearing population, and this varies from one frequency to another with the ear showing similar sensitivity to sounds of 500 to 4000 Hz. For high and low frequencies the ear requires more energy for sound perception, and the audiometer is calibrated accordingly. If the child can hear all the sounds produced at this normal level he or she will have passed the test. Note that a reading of up to 15 decibels hearing loss is still within the normal range.

Screening – General Comments. In all the tests reported above the aim was to identify children who give evidence of a hearing problem, by failing the test in question. The type of test used varies with respect to the developmental stage of the child (which may not always match the child's chronological age). In all cases clinicians must be careful to apply the tests properly, but also with sensitivity. Young children can be put off by examiners with whom they do not feel comfortable and so fail a test which they should be able to pass. All clinicians should, of course, be sensitive to such eventualities, but even the most skilful can fail to make sufficiently good rapport with individual children. In all cases, however, it is important to err on the side of caution and give a full appraisal. On the other hand, parents and others who have care of children whom they suspect of a hearing loss, should not take a child's passing a screening test of hearing as the final word if they have reason to believe a problem exists. Faulty technique by the examiner can allow the child to pick up cues which allow an over optimistic result.

Assessment

Pure Tone Audiometry. The same instrument is used as was described in the section on screening. However the purpose now is to identify the exact levels of hearing across frequencies. Once more a young child can be asked to perform a task, as a game, such as putting an object in a box, or removing a ball from a stick whenever the tone is heard through the earphone. Each ear is tested across the frequencies mentioned above and an audiogram is plotted, as in Figure 4.1. The reading for each frequency is the hearing level by which the child's hearing is worse than the norm. In this example, the child has, for example, a hearing loss of 75 dB at 4000 Hz in the left ear. This is normally written as 75 dB HL.

An adaptation of this procedure is to use the audiometer not with a headphone, but with a small vibrator attached to the mastoid bone, situated behind the ear. With a headphone the signal is passed through the outer and middle ear to the inner ear, but with the vibrator the outer and middle ear systems are bypassed.

A normally hearing person will have results which are very similar for both methods. However, a child who shows normal hearing using bone conduction is presumed to have normal functioning of the inner ear but a problem with the outer or middle ear. This is indicative of a conductive loss. Where a loss is shown on both tests the implication is that there is inner ear damage, indicative of a sensori-neural loss. Finally, some children show a loss using both techniques, with a greater

Figure 4.1: Example of an Audiogram

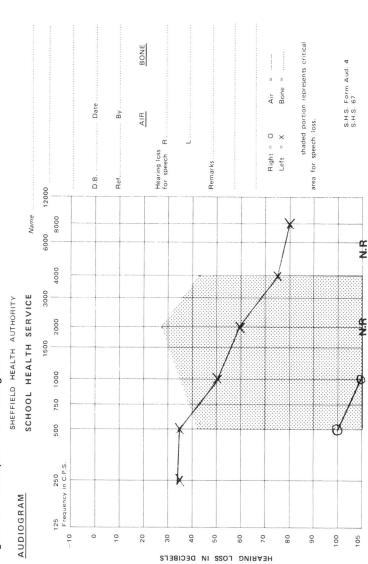

loss revealed by air conduction. In this case there is evidence of problems with inner ear, and outer and middle ear functioning.

With young children this test's usefulness is restricted by two factors. First, bone conductance cannot be tested on each ear separately as the whole skull is set vibrating (a method used with older children and adults, 'masking', is not suitable for children below the age of about 7 years). Second, the child must be old enough to take an audiometric test, i.e. usually 3 years and upwards.

Impedance Audiometry. This is a very simple test of middle ear function rather than a test of hearing *per se*. It comprises a small probe which is inserted into the child's ear. To this are attached three tubes. One is attached to a small pump which allows pressure to be exerted against the ear drum (tympanic membrane). The second is connected to a source of sound, while the third leads to a small microphone which picks up the sound reflected by the eardrum. A constant sound is played into the ear and the air pressure altered gradually. A graph is plotted to show the compliance of the ear drum.

A normal ear drum is flexible and so reflects little sound. Where there is a problem along the conductive pathway to make the eardrum stiffer, more sound will be reflected, i.e. not transmitted through the ear. As the air pressure applied to the ear drum is altered, the amount of reflected sound can be plotted as the ear drum's stiffness alters.

This is a very quick and simple test which can be done on very young babies. Young babies or nervous children can be cuddled, and the parents can hold the tube in the outer ear. Very few children are upset by it to the extent that they can't be tested. Yet despite its simplicity, it offers much information about the state of the middle ear. It can show eustachian tube malfunction, fluid in the middle ear, a scarred eardrum and other problems resulting in a conductive hearing loss.

Because of its simplicity, accuracy and usefulness it could be used to screen children in addition to assessing children referred to the Audiology Clinic. There is, however, a problem. Many children in their first five or six years suffer from middle ear problems leading to some form of conductive hearing loss. Most commonly this is some form of 'glue' or 'sticky' ear problem where excess fluid is present in the middle ear, so reducing the amount of sound transmitted. This is usually related to minor ear infections, colds, catarrh and similar problems. We estimate that in any one year hundreds, if not thousands, of children in Sheffield would be identified by the use of this test as having a conductive hearing loss caused by these problems. Thus any screening would identify a very large number of children in each area for many of whom a hearing loss would be transitory.

This problem received much publicity in the educational press in early 1983, with calls for screening to identify children suffering from otitis media, as this problem is called. Such demand arises from a legitimate concern that a child's learning ability, particularly for speech, and later for reading, will be impaired. For example, a letter from F. Mottram in the Guardian (1 February 1983) reported how his son had been a disruptive influence in school, was withdrawn and found it difficult to communicate. He was found to be 'deaf in one ear' at the age of six. Although the otitis media cleared up by the age of 6½, the parent reports that he took two years to catch up academically.

A review by Reichman and Healey (1983) supports the idea of a link between otitis media and learning difficulties. They report that approximately one in four elementary level children (equivalent to primary in the UK) identified by schools as learning disabled have experienced recurrent episodes of otitis media. However, support is also given for early identification followed by continued monitoring of treatment as the children receiving such intervention revealed minimal performance deficits.

But given the large numbers of children involved, what should be done if they are identified? In most cases the child will not need surgery (usually the insertion of grommets). Rather, what is required is that the parents and teachers are aware of the possible effects of this problem and compensate accordingly. Intervention is made more problematic by the fact that such hearing losses are usually fluctuating, although they may be more permanent, and probably therefore more serious among the more disadvantaged children whose general health is poorer. This issue is currently being debated within the profession but notwithstanding whether this screening is or is not introduced it is still necessary for teachers and parents to be aware of the possible presence of hearing loss for those reasons, and alter their behaviour accordingly. In the case reported above, the diagnosis helped parents and teachers to understand the boy's problems and alter their behaviour. The parent reports that the boy's social problems ceased at once: he became happier and more confident at school, and his relations with adults generally underwent a rapid change.

Speech Tests of Hearing

In addition to the tests of hearing discussed above, there are those which make use of speech. In each case the child is asked to respond to a spoken stimulus word, the exact nature of the test varying with age of the child.

Kendall Toy Test. This is suitable for children from about two and a half years. It requires the child to point to a toy (e.g. bus) from among a group of 15 spread out before him or her. The toys have been carefully chosen to allow specific speech sounds to be tested. The audiologist first ensures that the child can name each item and then asks for an item in a normal voice, while three feet away and outside the child's visual field. The audiologist then repeats the task for different items using a quieter voice, the level of which is measured on a sound level meter. Each ear is tested separately.

Manchester Picture Test. This is a similar test suitable for older children of about 4 years and upward, except that here a series of cards each with four pictures is used. Once more the child must point to one item. Each set of cards is designed to test the child's ability to discriminate particular consonants and vowels. Once more, the level of voice required, measured on the sound level meter, will be recorded for each stimulus.

Speech Audiometry. In this test a child is presented with a series of words, one at a time, through a headphone and is asked to repeat each word. The words are pre-recorded and presented at a predetermined level to one ear at a time. The child's response is scored in terms of how many sounds from the stimulus are repeated correctly. This test is usually not suitable for children below the age of about 7 years.

Specialised Techniques. The testing of children who are severely intellectually impaired or with an apparent severe or profound hearing loss may demand the use of more complex testing procedures. Several types of test can be conducted using equipment which is normally found only in regional centres and requires specially trained technicians. These tests are known as Evoked Response Audiometry and involve the use of electrodes which sense the slight electric signals which the nerve of hearing generates in response to sound stimulation. Some indication of hearing functioning can therefore be obtained for a child who may otherwise fail to respond to conventional testing. Another technique, electrocochleography, assesses the functioning of the cochlea directly but is carried out under anaesthetic by an ENT surgeon assisted by audiological technicians. These methods will not be described in detail as they are not generally available. Although giving some helpful information on different components of the hearing system, these expensive techniques are unable to give a full picture of a child's hearing ability and so need to be used in conjunction with traditional methods and careful observation of the child in normal settings.

Educational Implications of Hearing Loss

The tests described above have largely been those which assess hearing *per se*. But the educational implications of any hearing loss need to be considered in their own right. Two children with identical audiograms may in fact suffer very different degrees of educational disadvantage. Factors such as the child's general intellectual ability, willingness to persevere, resistance to distraction, parental support and help from teachers can all be very important in determining whether a hearing loss handicaps a child. Unfortunately, the recognition of this relationship between audiological and educational criteria is not always sufficiently well recognised. Many teachers of the deaf, for example, consider that children with hearing losses considered to be non-disabling, are being disadvantaged. There is disagreement about the levels of hearing loss which should be taken to indicate a child at risk.

These problems have been highlighted by Jacobs and Lynas (1982) in a survey of eight LEAs in one metropolitan region in the North of England. They obtained information in all the children in each area who had a hearing impairment and were receiving some special educational provision either within or outside the LEA area. They report that prevalence rates varied from 1.95 to 13.02 per 1000 school population. Although some slight difference in incidence may be expected, they suggest that the more likely explanations for such a range are variations in assessment facilities and, more especially, differences in ideas about the educational significance of any given hearing loss. They refer to studies which suggest that a hearing loss averaging 32 dB can have a depressing effect on educational attainments. A similar situation pertains with children who have a severe unilateral loss of 55 dB plus. However, it is not unusual for such children not to be considered as at risk. On the other hand, many teachers of the deaf, including the service in Sheffield, argue that children with any recorded hearing loss, even as low as 20 dB, should be recorded and monitored to ensure that their development is optimised.

Conclusions

Optimal hearing is essential for children to develop normally. Apart from those children with severe or profound hearing losses there are many thousands of others whose hearing is impaired, perhaps intermittently or to a lesser extent. The correct management of all these children is essential if they are to develop to the best of their abilities. Impaired hearing in early childhood can have the effect of impairing speech and language development, and can also lead to behavioural problems, related to frustration, or withdrawal.

Screening of children for hearing impairments is not as comprehensive as we would like. Bethan Davies, at a symposium on School Screening Audiometry in 1981, reported that the average age of suspicion of a hearing loss in this country is 2 years, and confirmation is 2 years 11 months. While this is the best in Europe, it leaves much to be desired. As Kath Jennings reports in Chapter 3, it is only very recently that all Authorities have instituted screening tests of hearing by health visitors.

The National Deaf Children's Society has recently expressed great concern about both the lateness and effectiveness of early screening. In their document 'Discovering Lateness', the NDCS report that the average age of diagnosis of hearing impairment has now dropped to about 18 months, and that the average age at which the first screening test was conducted was now 9 months. However the hearing loss of many children was not discovered at this first screening, according to a review of recent studies conducted by the Society (Mitchell, personal communication). In addition, many children miss screening procedures. A study by the Central Birmingham Community Health Council (1981), for example reports that only 32 per cent of the mothers of one-year-old babies in one electoral ward were aware of early developmental screening (including that of hearing impairment). Although some may have forgotten the tests, it is very worrying that so few mothers were aware of tests which should have occurred in the past few months. Furthermore, Nietupska and Harding (1982) report on a study of 8-year-olds in a social priority school where only 12 of the 30 children had normal hearing. Some children had losses which were damaging. Only 13 had had the stipulated pure tone audiometry sweep test, and even those who failed this were not referred on for an expert opinion.

The relationships between a hearing loss and its educational implication must also be recognised. Where a well-resourced service of teachers for the hearing impaired exists, children with quite small recorded losses can be monitored, or at least their teachers and parents can be alerted to monitor them and liaise with the teachers of the hearing impaired. This needn't prove unduly upsetting for parents if the nature and degree of the loss are explained. Similarly, teachers are usually happy to keep an eye on a child with a known or suspected problem. Monitoring systems used in schools often note hearing problems as one factor of which to be aware. For example, Clift, Weiner and Wilson (1981) report that health and physical factors (presumably including hearing, though this was not specified) were considered essential for inclusion on school record cards by 92.6% of the sample, and desirable by a further 5.2%.

This brings us to collaboration. The assessment of a child with a hearing impairment must be multi-faceted. The screening and assessment of hearing, the assessment of other factors and finally the optimal inervention require the skills of several different professionals. If the child is to benefit, these professionals must have a good working relationship, and communication must be efficient. Unfortunately the area of hearing impairment has been more divided by strife than many others. There is a history of conflict between medical and educational practitioners, and between educationalists who favour radically different teaching methods.

The Future

It is difficult to envisage the future in this field in respect of identification. It is likely that new and improved objective testing methods will be developed, but important as these are they can never replace the simple methods which have been tried and found useful over many years. There are more possibilities within the area of intervention with the improvement of hearing aids, including the greater availability of the less obtrusive ear level aids, and the advancement of surgical techniques — for instance, at present sensori-neural losses are considered permanent, but experimental cochlea implants in adults are underway. Also it is hoped that the incidence of severe and profound hearing loss can be reduced — e.g. by all girls being innoculated against German measles.

If children with severe and profound hearing losses are to be integrated into normal schools the need for improved technology is magnified. This is already happening, both with units attached to schools and with children integrated as individuals into normal settings (see Hegarty and Pocklington, 1982). Such a process has much to commend it in terms of normalisation and is usually welcomed by the parent. However, this is not always the case with the young deaf people themselves (Gill, 1982), who may feel they are being asked to lose their identity, language and the culture of the deaf community. If the incidence of deafness can be reduced and its amelioration improved, such fears will be less important and the hearing impaired will be best placed in ordinary schools (provided that sufficient resources are available).

This is a time of change and questioning for the severe and profound hearing impaired as old practices are questioned (e.g. the debate on oral versus manual or mixed methods of teaching) and school systems are altered, with segregated schools being replaced by units or other forms of integrated provision. But it must be remembered that the vast majority of children with hearing impairment are already attending normal schools. Their problems may be less severe, or transitory, but their needs still require identification and meeting.

Finally, we would emphasise that because of its central position in development, the early identification of hearing loss is essential. Although there is debate over some aspects of such a process, any child whose parents or teachers are concerned about hearing should be examined. We would reiterate the finding reported by others that parents who think their child has a problem are usually right. However, we would add that the need now is to help those parents (and teachers) who may not be so aware or sensitive. This requires an extension of regular screening, a development of the referral system with the necessary collaboration between professionals, and direct work with more disadvantaged parents.

5 THE SPEECH THERAPIST AND LANGUAGE DISORDERS

Kath Thompson

'Don't worry, he'll grow out of it', 'Speech therapists can't help a child who doesn't talk', 'He'll be alright once he starts school'.

These misguided and inaccurate remarks demonstrate the general ignorance which exists regarding the role and responsibility of the speech therapist. When such remarks are made by professionals who are untrained in the specialist area of communication, they are at best worrying and annoying, at worst positively destructive to the child's social, emotional and intellectual development. Martin Bax (1982) recently pointed out that an adult patient who presented a doctor with a note reading 'I haven't been able to talk for a year' would induce excitement and concern in the physician thus addressed. Yet, alas, the child of three who is not talking is still regarded by some physicians as having a problem which need not concern them greatly: 'He will grow out of it'.

What, one must ask, will he grow into?

Although some children with delayed speech do eventually acquire normal speech spontaneously, this may be at the expense of early social, emotional and intellectual development. There is convincing evidence that skilled intervention from a speech therapist can accelerate speech and language development in these children (Cooper, Moodley and Reynell, 1979). Further, the child's problems are not always over when he has acquired normal speech, because there is a strong association between early speech delay and later difficulties at school, particularly in reading, writing and spelling.

The reasons for such widespread ignorance are difficult to list, but perhaps should include the speech therapy profession itself for adopting a professional title which so poorly reflects its field of specialisation. It seems ironical that the very profession which deals with difficulties and disorders of communication should itself have such problems in deciding upon a suitable title. Crystal (1980) illustrates this by stating that the work carried out in clinics in the United Kingdom by speech therapists, is carried out in France by orthophonists, in Belgium and Germany by logopaedists, in the United States of America by speech pathologists and in Czechoslovakia by phoniatrists. Many speech therapists feel dissatisfaction with the present title, and the profession has been involved in votes and ballots on this issue. The reason for concern from many speech therapists is that the title focuses upon 'speech', which is far too restricting. The profession concerns itself with all abnormal manifestations of communication. When there is a breakdown, or lack of development of communication abilities, much more than speech can be affected. Even with the term 'speech' much more is involved than the simplistic notion of making sounds, or articulating. Many children are able to make a full range of sounds but cannot code these properly in their spontaneous speech, which may be completely unintelligible. Further, even when speech is fully intelligible, the child must acquire all the complexities of grammar and semantics if the final communicative act is to be regarded as normal. Many alternatives to 'speech' have been suggested. The word 'communication' has some favour – the official publication of the College of Speech Therapists is actually called *The British Journal of Disorders of Communication*.

The speech therapy department at the Sheffield Children's Hospital in which I work carries the title 'Department of Communication'. The word 'therapy' in the title 'speech therapy' has perhaps some shortcomings and can be very misleading. One particularly unfortunate implication is that speech therapists are involved only with 'therapy' – i.e. with treatment. This is not the case. Speech therapists are the only professionals who are ultimately responsible for the entire process of assessment, diagnosis and treatment of patients' communication difficulties. This is not limited to oral communication: non-oral communication is an area in which speech therapists have become increasingly involved. This is not appreciated by those who equate speech therapy with speech correction. There are children in whom the physical and/or mental resources are such that oral communication is not a realistic goal. As communication is a prime concern, alternative methods of communication may be introduced. It is becoming increasingly recognised that the speech therapist has a role in the assessment for and recommendation of non-verbal communication systems and communication aids as an alternative to or to augment inadequate verbal communication.

They do not work under the supervision or direction of a colleague from another discipline (e.g. a hospital consultant), nor are they bound to receive referrals only from a medical source. In this respect they are in a different category from other non-medical professionals who work in the National Health Service, such as radiographers, physiotherapists, etc.

It is hoped that the issue of professional title does not appear as trivial to the people outside the profession. It is not simply an issue of terminology, but reflects professional identity and status, academic standards and clinical autonomy. Speech therapists have a highly responsible role which is not reflected by their present professional title. This fact often proves misleading to doctors, administrators and particularly the public requiring speech therapy services.

Training

The purpose of speech therapy is to help children and adults overcome their problem of communication and in this it is closely allied to medicine and education. For employment in the National Health Service a certificate issued by the College of Speech Therapists is needed. This can be obtained by acquiring a specified degree qualification, from one of the recognised training institutions in the United Kingdom. The period of study is 3 or 4 years. No two courses are identical in their distribution of hours for various course components, nor in the themes singled out for special attention. But the courses will cover normal and abnormal development of language in children, and communication problems in adults, e.g. following a stroke.

After achieving the basic degree and licence to practise, speech therapists may go on to take a number of higher qualifications.

Staffing and Workloads

In 1972 the Quirk Report (DES, 1972) estimated that in England, Wales and Scotland well over 300,000 children and adults were in need of speech therapy services. Of this number over 270,000 were children, falling into the categories of pre-school (60,000); children in ordinary schools (180,000); educationally sub-normal–mild (12,000); educationally sub-normal–severe (17,500); and physically handicapped (3,000). Other categories, such as partially hearing children and autistic children, would increase this total still further. The Quirk Report also estimated that the average caseload of a speech therapist at that time (1972) in the United Kingdom was approximately 100 patients. If only a proportion of these children are seen each week, bearing in mind the need for time for analyses, preparation, reports, discussion, research, teaching, liaison and other administrative duties, it is obvious that any

Table 5.1: Summary of the Results of a National Survey of Speech Therapy Provision

District	Population	w.t.e.	% of Quirk
Omagh N. Ireland	42,700	4	175
Central Birmingham	185,000	12	110
Sheffield	544,000	28	85.9
Salford	252,600	12.2	80
Harrogate	125,000	6.2	75
North West Surrey	203,500	8.6	66
East Dorset	404,000	11	49
Leeds Area	750,000	24	55
Portsmouth/S.E. Hants	519,000	15.3	50
Liverpool	450,000	17.2	27
South Tyneside	150,000	2.8	17

Source: McGuin (unpublished).

speech therapist has insufficient time to do all the work which needs to be done. Some increase in staffing levels has taken place since 1972, when Quirk recommended staffing levels of 6 whole time equivalent (w.t.e.) speech therapists per 100,000 population.

A national survey of population and staffing levels was undertaken by Janet McGuin, District Speech Therapist in Portsmouth and South East Hampshire Health Authority, and the results produced in April 1982 (McGuin, personal communication). This shows the population figures for the various Health Districts and the number of whole time equivalent speech therapists employed. This figure is then shown as a percentage of the Quirk Report's recommendations for staffing. A summary of these results is shown in Table 5.1 with Districts chosen to reveal the range of variation. At the extremes are Omagh and South Tyneside. Omagh has an establishment 75 per cent greater than Quirk recommended, while South Tyneside's establishment is less than a fifth of the suggested level. Overall, only 12 per cent of Districts were at the Quirk recommended levels, while 20 per cent were staffed at a level of 50 per cent or less of these levels.

Only 17 of the 131 Districts surveyed had ratios at or better than the level recommended by Quirk, while 27 had ratios of 50 per cent of Quirk or worse. South Tyneside had the worst ratio at 17 per cent of the Quirk level. It is clear, therefore, that speech therapy services nationally are understaffed.

The Need for Early Identification

A study by Fundudis *et al* (1980), part of the Newcastle Child Development Study (Neligan, Prudham and Steiner, 1974), provides evidence for the need to identify some children with speech and language problems early in life. They followed up those in the sample of 3,300 children, all those born in 1962 in Newcastle, who were considered to be speech retarded at 3 years. This definition was based upon health visitors' reports using the criterion: 'failure to use three or more words strung together to make some sort of sense by the age of 36 months.' This sample comprised 133 children, or 4 per cent, and 102 were traced for retesting at 7 years.

Fundudis, Kolvin and Garside report that at 7 years two general groups of children with speech and language problems could be identified. First there were those whose intellectual, psychological or physical functioning was significantly abnormal, in addition to their language difficulties. This group included children with marked intellectual impairment (IQ below 65), specific clinical syndromes (e.g. elective mutism, infantile autism) and demonstrable neurological disorders (e.g. cerebral palsy). These were called the *pathological deviant* group. The second group comprised those who at 7 years showed no signs of other such impairments, and were labelled the *residual speech retarded* group.

At follow-up, 18 children fell into the pathological deviant category. Prevalence rates for sub-categories, e.g. infantile autism, were similar to those from other studies — i.e. such disorders were very rare. However, the number of children in the residual speech retarded group represented 2 to 3 per cent of children of school age. This group was found to score significantly worse than a control group on tests of reading, verbal intelligence (Wechsler Intelligence Scale for Children) and language (the Illinois Test of Psycholinguistic Abilities) as well.

Not all the children identified at 3 years continued, at 7 years, to have major speech and language difficulties. However, for many of the children in the speech retarded group it was commonly assumed that they would soon overcome their speech disability. For many this was not the case and, as reported above, they tended to suffer educational problems later. Fundudis *et al* argue, therefore, for a screening programme to identify such children, followed by a thorough assessment by speech therapists, but, because some identified at 3 years will mature naturally to have no difficulties at 4 or 5, they also suggest that such a programme should include periodic re-examination over the first 5 to 7 years of life.

Similar conclusions arise from a study by Silva (1980) of 937 children in New Zealand. He concludes that children identified at 3 years as delayed in both expressive and receptive language 'are at very high risk for later developmental delay, especially in intelligence and language'. He suggests a simple first stage screening test of three-year-olds. To pass, the child must speak in sentences of four or more syllables.

Programmes of Screening

Pre-school. Screening programmes are not common, despite the arguments of researchers such as Fundudis *et al* and Silva. In some areas, screening of general development is conducted and in such cases the appraisal of language will be part of such a process. The Denver Developmental Screening Test discussed in Chapter 3, for example, has items on language development. The screening test used by health visitors in Sheffield is another example, see Table 3.1. The items from that which are relevant to language are as follows:

9 months	Babbles whilst playing.
18 months	(1) Uses recognisable words (If No — follow-up at 2 years)
	(2) Obeys simple commands.
3 years	(1) Large intelligible vocabulary.
	(2) Does he/she ask questions?
4 years	Normal conversational speech.

The problems inherent in screening for language are readily apparent from this example. First, some items are very subjective. What does 'intelligible' mean? What kind of questions? How frequently? What is normal conversational speech? Note also that those items scored at 3 years differ from those used in the Newcastle study. In practice, trained and experienced health visitors must use their judgement, but this will be a potential source of variation in identification — one health visitor may err on the side of caution, while a colleague may do the opposite.

A further complication arises as appraisal of language must take place in the context of the child's behaviour. Some children refuse to talk or respond to strangers during these early years. In such cases no direct appreciation of the child's language ability can be achieved. In such cases the comments of the parent(s) are the sole criterion. Parents will vary in their understanding of normal language development and may fail to appreciate that a problem exists. It is not possible to judge from the Newcastle study how many children were missed at 3 years and subsequently would be found to have speech and language problems.

Thus, while there is a good case to be made for early identification of speech and language problems, and while screening by health visitors has been shown to be viable by the Newcastle study, its overall effectiveness has not been fully evaluated. Where a district does have comprehensive screening by health visitors and easy referral to speech therapists who have reasonable workloads, a useful system can be developed. But it is necessary to be aware that there are significant dangers of missing children at the pre-school stage. In cases of doubt, referral should be made to a speech therapist.

Screening in Schools. When a child enters nursery or infant school, one of the methods of screening used by educationalists may be used (e.g. the Keele Pre-School Assessment Guide described in Chapter 6, or the Infant Rating Scale, described in Chapter 7). In both cases, teachers will be considering the child's language progress, both expressive and receptive, and trying to identify difficulties.

The number of children identified by such scales is usually unknown, but information is available on the Infant Rating Scale (see Lindsay, 1981a). The results of teachers' ratings of 1,342 children of 5–5½ years on the expressive language items of the IRS are presented in Table 5.2. It is apparent that a large number of children (2.8 per cent) were considered to have major problems of articulation, but in addition about 2 per cent also had problems with language usage.

A follow-up of the children rated on the IRS shows that there is a clear relationship between language ability at 5–5½ years and school attainment at 7 and 9 years. For example, correlation between the Language Subscale of the IRS and the Young Group Reading Test at 7 years, and the Primary Reading Test at 9 years was 0.51 ($p < 0.001$) in both cases (for further details see Lindsay, 1981a).

These results are in line with those derived from the Newcastle study by Fundudis *et al* (1980), and indicate the usefulness of and necessity for teachers of young children to be aware of the need to identify children with speech and language problems at an early age.

Table 5.2: Percentage of Children rated at the lowest point on the Infant Rating Scale Level 1, Expressive Language Items (N = 1342)

	Item	Percentage
Expressive	Very poor articulation; difficult to understand, or does not talk.	2.8
	Immature vocabulary; mainly limited to single words or does not talk.	2.0
	Always uses incomplete sentences with many grammatical errors; does not talk.	1.9
	Unable to tell a comprehensible story.	2.4

Source: Lindsay (1981a).

The Role of the Speech Therapist

Screening procedures for speech and language problems are not common and when they do take place they are normally conducted by other professionals: health visitors for pre-school, and teachers for school-aged children. These professionals then refer children to speech therapists if they appear from the screening to have speech and language problems. The main role of speech therapists, therefore, is in the detailed assessment of children referred to them by these and other professionals, although they will also have an important role in the development and evaluation of screening procedures for speech and language if these develop.

Speech therapists do not expect other professionals involved in screening programmes to make any decisions regarding the necessity for speech therapy or diagnosis of a communication problem. Rather, the speech therapy service expects that any child whose communication is causing concern, to the parents or another professional, should be referred for a full assessment. Where a screening programme operates, failure of the test should result in referral, but referral should not be limited to those children if a child passing the test is still causing concern.

There are dangers in giving cursory screening tests which concentrate entirely on small samples of utterances and do not explore the speech in function nor the skills which underlie or accompany it.

Referral

Referral for speech therapy is 'open' throughout the country. An open referral system means that anyone can refer the child for speech therapy assessment, including the parents. It is not necessary to go via a family doctor, a consultant, or any other person, to request a referral to speech therapy. It is possible for any member of the public to approach the service directly. Where children are concerned, referral is recommended as soon as any communication problem is thought to exist. There is often nothing to be gained by 'waiting to see if he grows out of it'. All too often it is the case that, a year later and finally in the speech therapy clinic, not only has the child not 'grown out of it', but he or she has developed any of a number of secondary symptoms (withdrawal, temper tantrums, enuresis) often related to a language problem.

The vitally important years for language development are between 1½–4½ years, during which time there is normally very rapid language development. Therefore it is advisable for any child suspected of having a language difficulty to be referred during these years. If a problem is present, it is far easier for the speech therapist to remediate language during these three years of development, when skills are being helped at the normal developmental stage, than to try to 'make up ground' after the age of 5 years.

Additionally, communication difficulties in the pre-school years are not conducive to healthy social and emotional development, and this can have far reaching effects which may disturb the family as a whole. It is essential that these early language difficulties are identified and managed appropriately. One thing communication-disordered children are unable to do is to tell you about their difficulties.

Assessment – General Issues

Once the child has been referred for speech therapy, an appointment time and date will be arranged for the parents to bring their child to the speech therapist's place of work, which may be a hospital, a community clinic or some other establishment. It is rarely the case that speech therapy assessments are performed in the child's home, mainly due to pressures of time. However, it may be necessary for the speech therapist to arrange a domiciliary visit at some point, if the child requires treatment. If treatment is necessary, this usually takes place at the speech therapist's place of work – the hospital or the clinic – though sometimes this can take place at school or nursery.

In assessment, the speech therapist will consider all aspects of the child's communication to determine if any disorder is present. The main aspects of the child's communication which the speech therapist will consider include:

speech and intelligibility
understanding of language (i.e. verbal comprehension)
expressive language (i.e. use of words, vocabulary, content, grammar
    and style)
voice quality
fluency

In addition, when assessing an infant or handicapped child, the feeding skills of mastication, sucking, deglutition (swallowing) will be closely studied. This is because those organs that are used at a later stage in speech production, have earlier functions in chewing, sucking and swallowing.

If a disorder is diagnosed, the speech therapist will carry out further investigations to determine the cause, or aetiology. All children admitted for speech therapy at the Sheffield Children's Hospital receive a routine hearing test. Occasionally, referral for an X-ray is necessary, to gain fuller information on tongue and palatal movements. If necessary, the child may need assessment by another professional, such as a psychologist, neurologist, paediatrician, E.N.T. consultant, depending upon the nature of the child's communication difficulties. Factors which may cause a communication problem are wide-ranging, and the speech therapist must give due regard to all of them. These include:

environmental factors
emotional factors
intellectual factors
developmental factors
audiological factors
neurological factors
structural factors
physiological factors

The speech therapist uses a combination of informal and formal methods of assessment. The first type includes observation of the child's general conversation with the parents in the waiting room, and of the child's free play. The latter includes structured approaches either in a play setting or using standardised tests. A fuller description of these instruments, and an appraisal of their usefulness can be found in Muller, Munro and Code (1981).

Multi-disciplinary Approach

The nature of many communication disorders (the cleft palate syndrome, for example) is such that many professionals, with different backgrounds and approaches, may be involved with any one child. Communication amongst these various agencies is, of course, essential to ensure a unified, balanced approach to the child. This state of affairs can often be somewhat confusing, and time-consuming, for the parents. Attendance at different clinics, receiving different advice (which can sometimes be perceived as contradictory) is confusing and worrying for the parents and not always in the child's best interests, especially as clinic attendances mean absences from school. Professionals must work together on the complex difficulties of communication. For this reason, joint clinics between speech therapy and other disciplines have been started. For example, at the Sheffield Children's Hospital, joint speech and hearing assessments may be arranged or patients may attend the speech ENT clinic to receive comprehensive care. Children attending this clinic frequently present with syndromes involving a combination of symptoms which cut across professional boundaries, such as the cleft palate syndrome. A plastic surgeon is involved in performing the relevant surgery and the speech therapist is involved throughout to supervise feeding patterns and later speech and language management. Orthodontic treatment is often necessary. The ENT consultant may be involved due to an increased incidence of upper respiratory tract infections in these patients. If the infection moves via the eustachian tube to the middle ear, resulting in otitis media, this causes an additional complication. The middle ear may be poorly aerated because of poor muscular control of the tube's opening by the tensor palatini muscle. As a result, hearing problems are common in this group of patients. The service to those patients is improved if speech therapy, ENT and audiology appointments are co-ordinated. Not only is this more convenient to the patient (and less disruptive to schooling), but the quality of service is improved. With joint clinics it is easier for professionals to co-ordinate their intervention so that, for example, the ENT consultant may operate to improve hearing at the time the speech therapist feels is most essential with regard to the development of language skills.

Joint professional endeavours are also imperative when dealing with parental unreliability and often very poor attendance at the hospital or clinic. Very often transport difficulties or parental apathy may be present. The latter is a very real handicap for any child. If a child is not being brought for therapy other agencies — health visitors, social workers, volunteers — can be contacted to encourage attendance. Occasionally, however, the speech therapist sees hours of assessment and treatment planning time wasted, when a child is not brought for appointments.

Conclusion

The ability to communicate meaningfully is an essential part of life and the need to identify those children who are having difficulties in developing communication is self-evident. There is some evidence that screening programmes of children of about three years could be helpful in this, and some health visitors are now carrying out such procedures. However, it must be remembered that the causes of communication difficulties are many and varied and a full assessment is usually required to identify the exact nature of the child's problem. This assessment will enable the speech therapist to predict whether the child's difficulties can be expected to resolve spontaneously, or arrangements should be made for a course of therapy.

What is required, therefore, is a combination of an effective screening procedure and easy referral for a surveillance of all children in their pre- and early school years.

As Robert West stated: 'Life without speech is empty; and life devoid of communication is scarcely better than death.'

6 LOOKING FOR TROUBLE: A TEACHER'S POINT OF VIEW

Mary Jane Drummond

Introduction

A teacher's point of view is substantially different from that of most of the other professionals who have contributed to this book in one important way. All children go to a school of one kind or another, but only a very small number of children ever visit a speech therapist or an audiologist. The proportion of children in special schools is also very small – less than two per cent in 1980 (Hegarty and Pocklington, 1981) – and very few of these children will be less than seven years old, so that mainstream primary teachers meet and work with the greatest possible variety of individuals. Other professionals may wish to commit themselves to working with the whole of the population in the age group – health visitors, for example, or psychologists, who would rather not limit their work to children who have problems. But the pressure of numbers often means that these intentions remain intentions, and it is only teachers who meet children, every working day, from across the whole range of personality, ability and developmental level. Inevitably, this affects the way in which we teachers approach the task of identifying children with difficulties; and furthermore we have to take into account the fact that children between the ages of three and seven are changing all the time, but sometimes in undesirable ways. We have to be aware of the self-fulfilling prophecy by which we may identify 'low ability' children and form inappropriately low expectations of them: these children are very likely to meet our expectations and progress at a slower rate than the children treated as 'high ability'. Although early research on the self-fulfilling prophecy (Rosenthal and Jacobson, 1968) has been discredited (Thorndike, 1968), there is now ample evidence for the effects of this labelling process (e.g. Burstall, 1978; Rist, 1975), so that teachers not only have a responsibility to identify real problems that need intervention, but they must also, at the same time, avoid creating unreal problems for normal children by forming inappropriate expectations of them. Most of the so-called 'Warnock 20 per cent' are children who do not have intrinsic disabilities, but for whom there is a mismatch between their own abilities, attitudes, hopes and wishes, and the diet provided for them by the school.

In this chapter I will consider the ways in which teachers set about monitoring the progress of all the children in their care – not just the minority of children with special needs. I will concentrate on those aspects of development that are most relevant to teachers – children's cognitive, emotional, social and physical developments.

Children and Schools: the Setting

In many local education authorities, including Sheffield, children are offered a place in school in the term in which they reach the statutory school age of five.

But this simple rubric covers a bewildering variety of practices. To begin with, children's pre-school experience may affect their entitlement to a place in school. Children who have not been to a nursery school, but who have stayed at home with their parents, or who have been looked after by childminders are, in some schools, offered a part-time place in the term before the term in which they are five (not an easy concept to explain to anyone). Some schools go further and admit children only once a year, in September, so that some children (those with summer birthdays) start school two terms early, when they are only just four. But in some LEAs children who attend a nursery school or class, part-time or full-time, are not eligible for these early places and so may start school up to two terms later than children of exactly the same age. However, this regulation applies only to children attending nursery schools or classes provided by the education authority; it does not apply to children in Day Nurseries, which are provided by the Social Service Department, or to other types of part-time pre-school provision such as playgroups, or work-place nurseries.

The variety of pre-school provision and experience means that there is no such thing as a 'typical' five-year-old starting school. Five-year-olds' experiences of life so far have been, even in a fairly homogeneous catchment area, so enormously different. Teachers must expect that children will respond to their first experience of school in as many different ways as there are children. Another consequence of the confusion of the pre-school scene is that some of the people who have looked after the pre-school child will send detailed written records to the school, and others will not. Some of the places where pre-school children are cared for are easy for teachers to visit, and some are not.

There may be excellent liaison between a school and a pre-school establishment, or there may be none at all. These issues have been investigated in a recent study by Cleave, Jowett and Bate (1982) who offer practical guidelines for fostering continuity between home or pre-school and the school.

Even after children have been admitted to school, there is a tremendous variety in what may happen to them there, simply in organisational terms. For example, in Sheffield, children may go to an Infant school, where they will stay until the September after their seventh birthday. So some children will leave after three full years in the Infant school, some after two years and a term; some children will be 7 years 11 months when they leave, and some will only just be seven (and these are the children who have had least time in school). Or, children may go to a First school, which they will not leave until the September after their eighth birthday; they may go to a Junior and Infant school, where they spend seven years, transferring to a secondary school in the September after their eleventh birthday; or finally, they may go to a Nursery, First and Middle school, where they may spend the years from 3 to 12 in the same institution though in three different departments. The confusing variety of pre-school experiences is only matched by the variety of school experiences available within a single education authority.

When considering a child who may have special educational needs at the age of six, five or earlier, it is important to remember this highly variable background.

Classroom Organisation

But the variation does not end here. Even within a single type of school, there are a number of different practices that have important consequences for children starting school. They may enter single-age classes for all the children who are five during the academic year (often called reception classes in Infant schools or F1 classes in First schools). Then in the following September they may move on to a new teacher as a class of 6-year-olds – and so on. But some children are taught in mixed-age classes (sometimes called vertically grouped or family grouped classes). There may be two or three, or even, in First schools, four age groups in one class. In fact, there is commonly a combination of single-age and mixed-age classes within one school.

There is variation too in the staffing of the classes. When vertical grouping was first introduced the idea was that children should stay with the same teacher throughout their three (or four) years in the school. But few schools now adopt this system completely and it is much more usual for a child to spend a year with each of three (or four) different teachers. This practice means that there must be some established and efficient way for teachers to pass on to each other what they know about the children they teach.

Other variations in classroom organisation stem from the design and layout of the school buildings. Since the late 1960s many schools have been built with an open-plan, or semi-open-plan design, where there are sometimes as many as 60 children in one 'base' shared between a number of teachers working more or less co-operatively. There are a number of advantages (as well as a number of disadvantages) in this system and some schools with traditional classrooms have converted pairs of classrooms to create shared teaching areas. All these practices have an effect on the number of adults that children are expected to form relationships with during their first years in school, and so may in themselves make life very much harder for those children who have difficulty in responding to adults.

Starting School

When I started teaching in 1966, forty reception children arrived at my classroom door at 9 o'clock one morning in September, and at least thirty of them were weeping bitterly. Since then all teachers have learned a good deal about making children's entry into school a much less harrowing experience for them and a less overwhelming one for the teacher (see Cleave *et al*, 1982). We try to make it easier for children by introducing them gradually to the school, the buildings and the teachers; we try to make it easier for the teachers by gradually introducing the children. So that, for example, in the small infant school where I now work, we organise a series of visits to the school for the children with their parents, and we try to visit the children in their nursery schools and classes too. We have just started a system of visiting children in their own homes (a practice that many schools have used for some time). We are lucky in having a playgroup that meets twice a week in an empty classroom in the school, so many children already feel quite at home in the place, long before they start school. But these visits are not organised solely for the benefit of the children. The teachers benefit too: we can begin to know the children as unique inividuals; we can begin the long slow process of continuous observation that goes on throughout the children's time in our school.

To add to our own first impressions of the children we collect a sheet of notes from their parents. We ask them not just for factual details (telephone numbers, special diets) but for information about their child's friends, hobbies and interests; we say in effect 'tell us about your child . . .' It is the first step, we hope, in an extended conversation between home and school about our shared interests and concerns.

Recognising Problems in School

One thing is certain: all children have problems at some time or another during their school life. There are a million possible causes, and a million possible manifestations: the list of possible permutations and combinations is impossibly long. So teachers have to try to classify the kinds of problems that they encounter in their work: and at this point certainty ends, because what teachers say and do about recognising and categorising children's problems varies enormously from teacher to teacher, and from school to school. And this is not a trivial variation; to a considerable extent, the way in which we as teachers define children's problems is a reflection of the way in which we define the purposes and nature of early childhood education.

Checklists

Some schools and teachers use a checklist approach, and once a term, or more often, the teacher completes a checksheet for each child. On these sheets possible areas of difficulty or concern are grouped together into broad categories familiar to all teachers from the psychology lectures of their initial training. A typical set of categories would be: physical, emotional, social and cognitive development. Within each broad category there will be subsections and smaller boxes to tick, maybe even sub-subsections.

Many teachers have produced their own checklists, a result of discussions either within a staffroom or at a teachers' centre. Many are intended only for use in one school, while others have been devised by research teams for wider application.

An example of the latter is the Keele Pre-School Assessment Guide (Tyler, 1980). It is intended to measure 'changes in those aspects of behaviour which directly reflect the aspirations and values of the adults responsible for the children's care' (Hutt, Foreword to the Guide). It is designed for use with nursery children by the teachers themselves. It is divided into two parts. Section 1 comprises six dimensions on which the child is to be assessed on a 7-point scale, e.g.

X   X   X   X   X   X   X

_____

Tends to   Mixes well
play alone   usually plays
                                                    in group

In Section II there are 15 aspects of development (e.g. Sorting and Classification Skills) which are grouped into four general categories: Language, Cognition, Socialisation and Physical Skills. For each item the teacher must choose the most appropriate of five descriptions of the child's present level. The scores are then plotted on a 'wheel'. Teachers are advised to complete the chart every 4-6 months to mark the child's progress. No evidence of the reliability or validity of the KPAG is provided, and some of the scoring criteria of items may be ambiguous.

The chief attraction of this approach in all its guises is its broadness: the physical problems listed may range from speech difficulties to dietary or toilet problems; the cognitive category may extend over the whole of the primary school curriculum. But the model of learning and the view of education that underlie this approach seem to me to be unsatisfactorily vague and diffuse. Furthermore the natural development of young children does not take place, as the use of this system implies, in a number of discrete strands of being, where cognitive and affective processes are independent of each other.

Objectives

The previous example is based upon a developmental approach: normal milestones are listed and ticked off when passed. Another approach is to set objectives for each individual child. These may also be related to normal milestones — e.g. 'By the age of 4½ years he/she should . . .' Again, there may be some merit in the potentially broad scope, where key questions may range from the concrete: 'Can he/she tie shoelaces/ eat with a knife and fork/write name, address and phone number?' to more complex and abstract requirements: 'Can he/she speak in complete sentences/create an original story/give a correctly sequenced account of a recent event?' But the danger of this approach is the implication that children who do not achieve pre-specified goals at a predetermined time are problem children or children who need special help. Defining aims and objectives for particular ages and stages seems not to take account of what we know about the enormous differences (often purely developmental) between individuals that are so characteristic of young children.

This aims/objective approach is possibly more common in certain types of junior schools, where children who do not succeed in learning their tables, or perform well on spelling tests are classed as 'remedial' and given extra tutoring in these areas. But it is not unheard of in infant and nursery classes, where a four-year-old who doesn't know the names of the colours, for example, may be the subject of quite unwarranted concern. A further consequence of this way of looking at the education of young children is that it leans toward the most easily quantifiable aspects of learning. The pace at which children acquire nuggets of knowledge is seen as more important than the less easily answered question of what they can do with their knowledge.

A refinement of this approach is to set objectives for an individual child as part of a learning programme (see Ainscow and Tweddle, 1979). In this system, the children are not being rated against a normal peer group, but against themselves. This approach has been the subject of much debate (e.g. Hogben, 1972) and is not popular in nursery and infant schools, as it fits uneasily with the more common, 'child-centred' approach. However, there is evidence that it is a useful and indeed necessary method of teaching and assessing the development of some children with special educational needs (for example see Becker, Engelmann, Carnine and Rhine, 1981). Teachers of children with more extreme problems will find this useful in determining the exact nature of the difficulties, and the rate of the child's development.

Assessing Learning Processes

A more recent, and for me, much more promising approach is based on a recognition that children's learning and development can be classified in a way that cuts across the physical/social/intellectual model we noted earlier. The materials published by the Progress in Learning Science 'Match-Mismatch' Project (Harlen, 1977) investigate the extent to which children learning science are acquiring certain skills, attitudes and concepts. The authors deliberately set out to move teachers away from a knowledge-based view of the curriculum (and all that it entails in terms of teaching and assessment). Instead they try to demonstrate how the skills (e.g. problem solving), attitudes (e.g. curiosity, inventiveness) and concepts (e.g. classification, causality) that we value, or should value, in education can be described as a developmental sequence of behaviours. And they go on to discuss activities and teaching methods that will help children pass through this developmental sequence. Children's problems are here defined within a much more complex and much more revealing view of learning than in other systems we have looked at.

Conclusions

Within any of these systems for describing children's learning in school, the onus is on individual teachers to observe, record, evaluate and act on any problems they may discern. Inevitably, the areas of education they value most highly will be the ones where they are most likely to see cause for concern. The teacher with a fervent belief in the import-ance of the 'basic skills' will be more aware of the reading performance of each child in the class than a teacher whose primary concern is the children's growing ability to socialise, to share, and to act co-operatively. The occurrence, the distribution and the gravity of problems perceived by teachers vary greatly from class to class, from school to school, even from one area of a city to another; and what is important about this variation is that there may be no simple correspondence between the perceived problems of children and any more objective set of criteria.

Sensitive teachers, and good schools, will be able to detect their own prejudices and concealed values so that they can build up a truer picture of each child's progress. Some teachers achieve this by adopting a view of the curriculum that has been characterised by Stenhouse (1975) as the process model. In this view, teachers concern themselves less with the products of the education they offer — the completed seven- or eight-year-old child — and more with the whole process of being in school for each unique individual in their care. Education, in this view, is more than the transfer of knowledge and skills from an experienced adult to a naïve young learner. It encompasses not only growth in knowledge, in skills and in concepts, but also in the critical attitudes and affective concerns that drive and motivate the individual's learning. Teachers come to see the children they work with as whole people, using in their learning all their human characteristics.

It seems to me that unless teachers take up this view of the curri-culum as the sum of everything that happens to children in school and begin to see their learning, and their development, in a holistic rather than fragmented way, they will not be as accurate or as effective as they could be in recognising and assessing children's problems.

Recording Problems in School

I have argued that the way in which teachers formulate the purposes of their schools, and the education they offer, can affect the ways in which they recognise and define children's problems. Similarly, the way that teachers see these problems has a considerable effect on the way they choose to record them and the action they take to solve them.

The evidence on the effectiveness of educational screening of children in the age range up to six years is not impressive (see Chapter 7). Even though such screening is an increasingly popular activity, its lack of proven accuracy and effectiveness should make us very wary. While many LEAs have developed screening procedures for young children (see Cornwall and Spicer, 1982 for a review) Sheffield LEA has since the mid-70s adopted a policy of encouraging schools to develop their own systems for monitoring and recording children's learning (Lindsay, 1980). In this section, therefore, I will concentrate on these developments.

All schools keep written records of some kind, and there is, inevitably, a tremendous variation between schools and between individual teachers in the fullness, accuracy and relevance of these records (Clift *et al*, 1981). In the school where I work, we have spent a good deal of time over the last four years working on our record system, and this system, imperfect and under constant revision as it is, may serve to illustrate some of the important issues in record keeping.

Stages in Record Keeping

There are three main stages at which it is important for teachers to gather information about each child in their care.

(1) At Entry — e.g. information from parents, and nursery or other pre-school (if applicable).
(2) On-going — e.g. information about the child's day to day or weekly progress; important extra information from home as events happen; termly overviews.
(3) On Leaving — information to pass to the next teacher or school.

These three stages demand different types of information; they serve different purposes; and they call for different methods of acquiring and recording the relevant information. For example, records made at stage 2 are mainly concerned with day to day planning, and problems that arise in the here and now of the classroom. Stage 3 records, however, must comprise a summary of the information that will help the next teacher, without harming the child.

Profile Sheet

We think that the most important item in the set of records that we keep for each child is the Profile Sheet — a blank page with the child's name, date of birth and date of starting school. Here we attempt to put down, at least once a term, sometimes more often, a thumbnail sketch of each individual as he or she strikes us at that moment. It is a deliberately anecdotal account and relies for its effectiveness on the spontaneity of each set of comments. The entries don't attempt to cover every possible aspect of development and learning, but pick out a handful of key features of that child, in that week, on that day, in that class. After only a few entries the Profile Sheet gives a fascinating picture of the whole child as a developing human being.

But we don't keep these records simply to be read as literature: they are very valuable in helping us decide on a course of action.

Joel. In February this year Joel (5.11) was very unhappy coming into school in the mornings. Not every morning, but on 2 or 3 occasions I saw him weeping in the cloakroom, clutching his mother and insisting that he was sick and wanted to go home. With help from the non-teaching assistant we were able to settle him in his classroom but we all felt we needed to talk the problem over together. Joel's mother felt quite strongly that Joel should be moved to another class, and that his unhappiness was caused by the teaching methods and the atmosphere of the class he was in. She contrasted his present attitude with his happiness the previous year in another class. We felt uncertain about her interpretation because, after the first half hour in school, Joel seemed quite at ease and relaxed in the classroom, applying himself with interest to a range of activities (though he did often ask how long till he could go home!) .When we turned back to Joel's Profile Sheet for the previous year we saw that his class-teacher had been worried for some time about Joel's distress at leaving his mother. Indeed it wasn't until towards the end of the year that she noted for the first time that Joel has come into school on his own, quite confidently. After re-reading this record it seemed to us that Joel had a long-standing difficulty in leaving his mother, rather than a recently acquired problem in his present classroom. We decided to try to give Joel special help first thing in the morning and not to move him to another class, which might make him even more anxious. Within a very few weeks Joel was once again happy and eager to come to school.

Records of this kind, where teachers note incidents that may seem trivial, can take account of very individual quirks and personalities that just don't appear on checklists, however comprehensive. For example, I saw recently in a nursery school a 'Personality Record Sheet' with a very large number of headings, including one for 'Attitude to Adults (Authority)'. In this section the teachers had to tick the appropriate description from a set of four alternatives:

Consistently helpful and obliging
Mostly satisfactory – sometimes rude
Unreliable and unpredictable
Defiant, challenging, pleases self

There may be something to be learned from a record of this kind, but it can't give a really individual picture.

Linzi. When Linzi started school her mother told us (and noted on the parents' record sheet) that Linzi had a great fear of illness, accidents, blood, doctors and nurses. We expected difficulties when routine medical examinations became due, and we were right. The day the dentist came to school for the annual inspection is a day we will never forget. But over the last two years, we have tried to help Linzi to conquer her fears and it was with a tremendous sense of achievement that her teacher wrote recently 'Linzi had her hearing tested today! and then visited every class in the school to tell the children not to be frightened of the doctor, it didn't hurt!'

One objection that teachers sometimes make to open-ended records of this kind is that a full and truthful account of a child as he or she is now might prejudice a teacher whom the child meets later. Behaviour problems in particular are often soft-pedalled by teachers in their new written records, if not in their casual conversation, in the supposed interests of the child: one of the most disruptive and aggressive children I have ever taught had been characterised by his previous teacher on the record sheet as 'a lively little boy'. However our own personal experience of writing franker records than many teachers would approve of has convinced us that more difficulties can be caused by concealing information or playing down a problem than by being outspoken.

Parent Record

A useful supplement to the profile of each child is the record sheet that parents complete for us before the child starts school. Knowing how the parents see the child can be a good corrective to one's own bias or prejudice and so we also keep a record of the discussions we have with parents through the year and at the termly Open Evenings. Here we record in a few brief phrases the information and assessment passed from teachers to parents and from parents to teachers: the sheet gives us a good picture of the parents' changing concerns and interests.

Records for the Basic Skills

Some schools prefer to reproduce their maths syllabus, in a shortened form, on each child's mathematics record, and to mark off with a series of ticks, crosses and circles when a child is introduced to and when he or she masters each of the concepts within the syllabus. Some reading records consist of a list of all the 'reading books' in the school, which are to be ticked off as the child reads them. We have chosen instead to give relatively less importance to the particular level (or book or sum card) that a child has reached, and to leave more space for the teacher to comment on the child's confidence, application and sense of achievement, as well as current difficulties of understanding or expression.

One of the characteristics of children between five and seven is the enormously wide span of achievement across a particular age group: a 'normal' six-year-old may be reading at the five-year-old, or at the eight-year-old level; a 'normal' seven-year-old may just be starting formal operations with numbers, or calculating areas and working with decimals — the range is dramatic. Record sheets that are based on levels of achievement will highlight those children who do not move steadily up the ladder, from level to level. But it is unrealistic to expect all children to make progress in this way. Many children, for example, who have not achieved independent reading at 6½ years, are not necessarily children with real learning difficulties; they are just children who haven't learned to read yet.

David. David came to us from another school in December, aged 5 years 4 months. His nursery records showed that he hadn't started to talk to anyone until he'd been in the nursery for over a year, and that he had then needed speech therapy for poor articulation. His drawings were very primitive, just a few unconnected lines, and during the rest of that year with us he remained very quiet and seemed to make little progress. In the following September, just after his sixth birthday, things seemed to be changing. His drawings became more lively and full of detail, and more important he began to talk a great deal more − to adults and to children. But in spite of these major improvements he still hadn't started to read. After consultation with David's parents we called in the educational psychologist. His verdict was crudely put: there is nothing preventing David from learning to read − he just hasn't done it yet! He reminded us how our records showed that David was making progress in all areas, at a certain pace, except in this one skill of reading, and he underlined the importance of David's now very good use of spoken language for a wide range of purposes. Luckily David's seventh birthday is in August so it has been easy to arrange for him to stay another year with us rather than leave for the Junior school with the rest of his (strictly) chronological age group. We are confident that he will learn to read during the next year.

For each child we also keep a record sheet for practical maths and for phonic skills. The practical maths sheet, like the one for computation and written mathematics, asks for comments, rather than levels of attainment. On the phonics sheet we have tried to focus on the extent to which children apply specific phonic skills in reading and in writing, not just whether they have been 'taught' them; but I'm still not certain whether the information we record on this sheet might not be better handled in some other way.

Children's Work

One last ingredient in each child's folder, and a very important one, is a collection of drawings and pieces of writing. Here again, the spread of achievement within a single age range is very wide. The accumulating set of examples enables us to look at each child's progress relative to him- or herself, rather than to some notional standard, valid for all children.

At other schools, at various times, I have used other record systems: in one school we kept detailed language records; some schools complete records of each child's play activities; other schools pay more attention than we do to physical aspects of learning and development. But in all schools there is one more important reservoir of written information about each child: the voluminous records that children make of themselves, in the form of their stories, mathematics, project books, paintings, drawings, and models. Written work in exercise books particularly is likely to take up quite a large proportion of children's time once they can write independently. When these activities are dated and annotated, preferably with quotations from the discussion between teacher and child that follows the activity, they can act as a valuable source of information about a child's learning, and possible problems.

Unwritten Records

In all schools, written records are supplemented by unwritten records. Informal discussion with staff, non-teaching staff and parents is an important way of monitoring children's progress. Anyone who knows the child can be a valuable source of information, and those who work with children outside the classroom are sometimes in the best position to observe crucial aspects of learning. For example, the dinner-time supervisors are likely to give a very accurate picture of a child's changing friendships: a child who is worrying his or her classroom teacher because of apparent loneliness or isolation may be found to have formed a close relationship with a child from another class, which can only be expressed at dinner time.

The school atmosphere in which this informal discussion takes place is vitally important: there is little to be admired in staffroom discussions of certain famous malefactors that degenerate into a rigmarole of complaints against the child. But there's a lot to be said for an atmosphere in which all the adults working in a school, including cooks and caretakers, do spend a lot of time talking about the children, simply because they are so interested in them and intrigued by their complexities and personalities. In the right atmosphere adults come to talk about the children they work with almost as if they were part of a huge extended family. Certainly in the school where I work we all talk about the children a great deal. We mark their birthdays, accidents, family illnesses or sporting achievements in our casual staffroom conversations. When we work together to put up exhibitions of work, we look for pictures or writing by children we taught last year, or whose brothers and sisters we know, and we talk about the way they are developing. I believe that this kind of dicussion, far from being idle gossip, is an important part of becoming more aware of the children we teach. In effect we supplement our written records by this continuous stream of unwritten comment and anecdote to such an extent that the idea of formal testing across the school, or a screening procedure for a particular age group, seems fairly ludicrous. What could it tell us that we don't already know? Screening is what you do to strangers.

Interpreting Records – the Next Step

Many teachers object to keeping detailed records for an admirably pragmatic reason. 'After all,' they say 'who reads them?' I do have every sympathy with infant school teachers who cannot persuade junior school staff to read their lovingly compiled biographies of closely observed children, but within the infant or first school, the problem is rather different. I believe that all records should be read, first of all, by the person who writes them (as well as by the Headteacher, deputy or Head of Department). It's as you read back over the accumulating picture you are putting together that you can decide whether, for the moment, a child does not give cause for special anxiety, or whether you need to take extra action.

When record writing and record reading reveal a child with serious problems the teacher has to decide what type of action to take. There are I think three possible courses of action available to the school, or the teacher. Two of them are only appropriate for certain specific problems or kinds of problems, while the third course of action seems to me to be a most powerful strategy, valid for all children at any time. These three courses of action are:

    to use published tests
    to refer to an external agency
    to collect, by observation, more information about the child

Using Published Tests

The usefulness of educational screening tests is discussed more fully elsewhere (see Chapter 7). Other tests available to teachers are so-called diagnostic tests including the Daniels and Diack *Standard Reading Tests* (1958) and the *Swansea Test of Phonic Skills* (Williams, 1971). These can be useful, but experienced teachers should be able to derive as much useful information from their own assessment procedures. For example, for a child with reading difficulties one very useful technique is that of miscue analysis; the teacher listens to the child read, in the normal way, but makes a record of the child's errors. These errors are then analysed to give detailed insights into the child's difficulties. For a highly practical account of how to use this important technique see Helen Arnold's *Listening to Children Reading* (1982).

There are occasions when standardised tests are useful, especially when a teacher is inexperienced. And teachers occasionally make sweeping assumptions about a child; here the use of a standardised test can show the child's abilities to be very different. In these rare cases the next step is normally the involvement of an outside professional such as an educational psychologist.

Referral to an External Agency

The decision to refer a child is only taken for a relatively small number of children. Occasionally we refer children in order to eliminate possible sources of anxiety — for example, the school nurse and doctor will do hearing and vision tests for children who may have physical problems of this kind. But more often we refer children because we know we need help: we feel we cannot tackle this particular problem on our own. Other chapters in this book deal with the way in which the support agencies receive and process referrals from schools, so that all that needs to be said here is that even after the decision to refer has been taken, the child remains in school, and is still the responsibility of the teachers. Referring a problem does not make it go away, any more than testing does; the teacher still has to act to solve the problem, but now in co-operation with others.

Observing Children in the Classroom

This third strategy is the most valuable one that a teacher can turn to for a number of reasons. It is appropriate for all types of children and all types of problems; it does not involve extra time in the classroom or withdrawal from the class; and best of all, structured observation can begin to generate ideas about how to tackle a child's problems. Methods of observation are described in Irwin and Bushnell (1980) and Sylva, Roy and Painter (1980).

But observing children, or one individual child in the classroom, is not an easy assignment. It is fascinating to see how curriculum projects of recent years have focused on this one vital strategy, and have tried to help teachers to become more systematic and less intuitive observers of the classroom scene. Whereas in the 1960s the main drive of the big curriculum projects was towards producing new materials for teachers to put in front of children, by the beginning of the 1970s the idea was gaining ground that there could be no curriculum development without teacher development. And it's a measure of the importance of this one part of the classroom teacher's work that over the last ten to fifteen years so much time and money should have been spent on the business of building up a teacher's skills of observation and informal assessment.

Some of the projects I have in mind are concerned, at one level, with a specific area of the curriculum. The Schools Council Project

'Communication Skills in Early Childhood', for example, is an attempt to help teachers understand more about children's use of language in the classroom. Teachers who use the pack of workshop materials (first published in 1976 and revised in 1983) learn to use quite specific terms to describe the purposes for which young children use language. Assessing children's language skills can now be done in a much more accurate and effective way, though still informally, than it could in the past (Tough, 1976, 1977). Furthermore, as teachers listen to, and record children talking, they become painfully aware of the extent to which the child's language skills, or lack of them, are the product of the teacher's language. They learn how their own talk may well be an important factor in the quality of the child's talk. In other words the process of observation sows the seeds for the action the teacher needs to take; first you get better at listening to children talking, then you get better at talking to them yourself.

In a very similar way the Schools Council Project 'Structuring of Play in the Infant/First School' (see Manning and Sharp, 1977) uses a workshop approach to show teachers ways of observing children's play that will help them see the learning – or lack of it – that is involved. The detailed observation schedules that teachers use in their classroom alert them to opportunities for learning that may have been missed in a particular play activity; teachers can use their own observations to discover weaknesses in their provision, or their participation in children's play.

But for all their ostensibly curricular focus these two projects are, at another level, concerned with a much more general skill. They both set out to give teachers the confidence and the ability to assess and evaluate for themselves the learning of the children they teach and the effectiveness of their teaching.

This generalised skill is itself the focus of a more recent pack of materials from the Continuing Education Department of the Open University: *Curriculum in Action* (Merritt, 1981). Teachers using these materials challenge themselves with six deceptively simple questions, which are to be answered by classroom observation:

(1) What did the children actually do?
(2) What were they learning?
(3) How worthwhile was it?
(4) What did you (the teacher) actually do?
(5) What did you learn?
(6) What will you do next?

Simple as they sound, these questions can have a dramatic effect, not just on the way teachers think and talk about their teaching but on what they actually do. The materials offer a range of activities, observation techniques and discussion formats that help teachers to make the continuous observation that is necessary all day, in every classroom, into a much more systematic and refined method of evaluation. Teachers learn to evaluate, as part of their day to day existence, the child's learning, the teacher's part in that learning, the whole context of the classroom and, inevitably, in due course, the whole school environment.

Conclusion

In this chapter I have described one small part of the teacher's work: how we learn to recognise children with problems and how we try to define and describe those problems in the most constructive way. But this is only a first step. Next we need to learn how to tackle the problem and, if possible, surmount it. When we look carefully, we may find that the school itself, or the classroom or the teacher may unwittingly be the cause of, or contribute to, the child's difficulties; but even if the origins of the problem lie elsewhere, unless something in the complex pattern changes, the problem will be perpetuated. Our task as teachers is to find ways of adapting our practices to help children overcome their problems. We need to learn how, if we want to change the child, we must change ourselves.

7 THE ROLE OF THE EDUCATIONAL PSYCHOLOGIST

Geoff Lindsay

'I'm not letting my child see a psychologist – he's not mad.'
'My child doesn't need a special school.'
'Anyone who sees a psychologist needs his head examining.'

Introduction

Psychologists have been and probably still are a group of people whose work is surrounded in mythology and even fear. The most common type of remark about psychologists, in my experience, is one which shows a confusion with psychiatrists – and a particular view of psychiatrists at that. 'Are you going to psychoanalyse me?' is a favourite opening gambit used by many people when they meet psychologists socially. Visions of a couch and an elderly, preferably bearded Viennese man mumbling in the background seem immediately to come to mind when the word 'psychologist' is mentioned! Although the profession has grown, and consequently more people have encountered psychologists, there is still a good deal of confusion and lack of understanding about their role.

Types of Psychologist

There are many different types of psychologist and they can be classified in several ways. Common to all is a degree in psychology, or one with a major psychology component. However, most graduates in psychology do not become employed as psychologists as such. In common with other graduates they obtain jobs where the type of degree may not be relevant. What is of interest for our purposes are the two remaining types of psychology graduate who actually work as psychologists. The first group comprises academic psychologists. These teach psychology in institutions of higher education (e.g. Universities, Colleges of Education) or work as researchers in psychology. They may enter employment with a first degree, or often having also taken a Masters or doctorate which will be research-orientated.

The second main group of psychologists comprises those graduates who have gone on to undertake professional training in addition to their first degree. Of these professional psychologists, the groups which are most relevant to young children with special needs are the educational and the clinical psychologists, and particularly the former.

Number of Educational Psychologists

Educational psychologists are mainly employed by Local Education Authorities (LEAs), although there are some professionally qualified educational psychologists who work in higher education (e.g. tutors to training courses in educational psychology) and some who are in private practice. There are currently about 1,350 educational psychologists working in the United Kingdom. As a profession it has grown rapidly since the 1960s. At that time there was a national shortage of educational psychologists and it was not uncommon for large Local Education Authorities to have only one post. A government Committee was set up to investigate the numbers of, and need for, educational psychologists and its report, published in 1968, advocated an expansion of training courses to produce trained educational psychologists to meet the needs identified (Summerfield Report: DES, 1968).

In the late 1970s, the Division of Educational and Child Psychology (DECP) of the British Psychological Society conducted a survey of the work of educational and clinical psychologists working with children (Wedell and Lambourne, 1980). One of the recommendations arising from this survey was accepted by the Warnock Committee, which was considering provision for children with special educational needs, and was incorporated into its recommendations, namely that there should be 'at least one educational psychologist to every 5,000 children and young people up to the age of 19' (The Warnock Report: DES, 1978, p. 267). This was a significant increase on the level advocated in the Summerfield Report ten years earlier which had been one educational psychologist to 10,000 children of school age (i.e. 5-16 years). At the present time Psychological Services are, on average, staffed at a level commensurate with that advocated by Summerfield, but, although the figure advocated by the Warnock Committee is not ungenerous, the workload has increased greatly during the past 15 years — so much so that it would require nationally between two and three times as many educational psychologists as at present. Furthermore, as the Warnock Report states (p. 266), the figure of 1:5,000 children and young people of 0-19 years is derived from the evidence of the DECP survey and does not, therefore, take account of the additional demands imposed by the recommendations of the Warnock Committee, many of which are now law, having been incorporated into the 1981 Education Act, which came into operation on 1st April 1983.

The actual number of educational psychologists per area varies with respect to both the size of a Local Education Authority and its generosity of provision. Sheffield, for example, has an establishment of 13.6 full-time equivalent educational psychologists for a school population of about 94,000 and a population of 0-19-year-olds of about 145,000. To meet the minimum requirements of the Warnock Report, the present staffing level would need to be increased to about 30. In Scotland the system is rather different and the ratio of educational psychologists to children and young people is significantly better. In 1981 it was reported that there were 311 educational psychologists in Scotland, and 1,037 in the rest of the United Kingdom (Professional Affairs Board, 1981). It can be seen from these figures, that educational psychologists are a scarce resource. In Sheffield, the average educational psychologist might have four or five medium-sized secondary schools (each of about 800-1,000 pupils), 20 to 25 primary schools, and a number of special schools and units. In some of the less well-endowed LEAs, and in some county areas with many small schools, these figures could rise to a level of 50-80 schools per psychologist.

Number of Clinical Psychologists

Clinical psychologists are mainly employed by the National Health Service (NHS), although some are in private practice, or in higher education (e.g. tutors to courses in clinical psychology). There are about 1,100 clinical psychologists working in the NHS (Professional Affairs Board, 1981), but only a minority of these work with children. It is estimated that about 300 clinical psychologists work with children, but for most of these this is a part-time commitment and children form part of a wider age range of clients. For example, a neuropsychologist may see mainly adults but the occasional adolescent. However, some clinical psychologists work exclusively with children (and their families) normally in hospital settings. Of particular relevance here is the fact that many of the psychologists who work in Paediatric Assessment Centres will be clinical psychologists, and so many parents of more severly handicapped children will come in contact with clinical psychologists.

Training

Educational psychologists have a training in both psychology and education. Probably the most common pattern of training at this time consists of the following four stages: first degree in psychology; post-graduate certificate of education (a qualification to teach); at least two years teaching experience; and finally a post-graduate qualification in educational psychology. There is also a sizeable group of people who qualify as teachers first, then teach (often for 5 to 10 years or more) and while teaching undertake a psychology degree, before undertaking the post-graduate course. In both cases the pre-qualification experience comprises academic psychology and practical teaching experience.

The post-graduate training period is usually one year, which is generally agreed within the profession to be too short. Improvements to the system of training have been under consideration for several years, and in Scotland it is planned to do away with the teaching experience element *per se*, but to build into the post-graduate training an educational component. This is unlikely to happen in the rest of the United Kingdom, but discussions on extending and improving the integration of training are being held between the profession and the LEAs and Department of Education and Science.

Clinical psychologists, in comparison, usually undertake a post-graduate qualification after their first degree. There is no requirement that they undertake other experience, although many do research degrees, or work in other areas of the NHS before taking their post-graduate qualification. This is normally of two years' duration, but some courses are three years, a length favoured by the profession.

Many of the elements of the training of educational and clinical psychologists are common. A broad range of academic psychology is learned by both. The main differences are that educational psychologists are experienced in the educational system, from their practice as teachers, their academic knowledge of that system and their work with children. Clinical psychologists, on the other hand, are experienced in the NHS, and have a wider range of client groups, including the elderly and psychiatrically disturbed adults. Their experience of children is often limited, although some will choose options on their courses which allow greater experience with this client group.

Problems seen by Educational Psychologists

The focus here is on the work of the educational psychologist with young children in their pre- and early school days. It is important to bear in mind, however, the children that a typical educational psychologist sees will also include primary and secondary age pupils, and some who are post-16. The DECP survey (Wedell and Lambourne, 1980) found that nearly half (46.8%) of educational psychologists frequently saw children of two years and upwards, but only 13.2% frequently saw children in their first two years of life. A similar proportion (47.7%) of the clinical psychologists who work with children saw those of two years or more but 27.2% frequently saw children in their first two years.

The types of problems experienced by children in these early years which bring them to the attention of an educational psychologist are varied but can be loosely grouped under several headings. It is important to point out, however, that many children do not fit neatly into categories (indeed many parents would say that their children don't fit neatly into any categories!). For example, a child may have both learning and behavioural difficulties, or a problem with mobility caused by a physical handicap, and a hearing loss. It was partly for this reason that the Warnock Committee advocated abolishing the old system of categories (e.g. educationally subnormal, blind, deaf) and replacing them with a statement of the child's special educational needs. However, the following categories relate to the types of problems which are presented to an educational psychologist, rather than what needs may be discovered after investigation.

The clusters of problems can be described as follows:

(1) Learning Difficulties – severe, moderate, mild, specific.
(2) Sensory Impairment – visual, auditory.
(3) Physical Impairment – e.g. cerebral palsy.
(4) Behaviour difficulties – e.g. aggression, stealing.
(5) Emotional problems – e.g. unhappiness, withdrawal.

In some cases the educational psychologist will work with other professionals in order to better understand and subsequently help the child. For example, a child with cerebral palsy will have a physical impairment which will demand the help of a physiotherapist but may also have certain learning difficulties related to the brain damage, requiring the intervention of a teacher and a psychologist. A fuller description of the work of educational psychologists is available in Wedell and Lambourne (1980).

Screening

The purpose of screening, as has been discussed in Chapter 1, is to identify children who either have or might later develop problems. It is immediately obvious that for educational psychologists this aim presents various practical difficulties, in terms both of the large range of children with whom they are asked to be involved and the practicalities of finding those children. However, educational psychologists have been greatly involved in screening, particularly in the past ten years.

When to Screen

It has been common in many authorities to screen children in the top infant or bottom junior years (i.e. at about 7-9 years) and it is often the educational psychologist who has supervised these initiatives. The Bullock Report (DES, 1975) found that these years were the most popular for screening and that the usual focus was on reading. In addition, some authorities would screen maths or general intellectual ability.

However, an increasing dissatisfaction was expressed about this method of screening for children with difficulties. The main problem with this process, it was argued, was the timing. If we screen children of this age we are *confirming* that they have difficulties. The corollary is that they will have been having problems in school for three or four years, and by the time they reach this stage may have an acute sense of failure. Consequently their motivation is often reduced, so compounding the original learning problems; in addition to these difficulties many children begin to be disruptive or apathetic. Would it not be better, it was argued, to identify these children before they failed?

This possibility was advocated in the Bullock Report and mirrors similar activities, based on the same rationale, undertaken by, for example, the medical services. It involves a move away from the identification of problems which already exist, to those which will exist unless something is done to prevent their occurrence. It is therefore one example of the general class of 'at risk' screenings.

As far as educational psychologists are concerned there are some practical problems concerning when a screening procedure may take place. Before the age of five years, many children are more or less inaccessible. Until this time, not all children either attend nurseries or other pre-school provision, or the various clinics where access to them could be obtained. Educational psychologists do work with very young children, either those referred as individuals, or as a result of the psychologist's work in various clinic settings, but they are not able to screen all children until they have reached the age of compulsory school attendance, i.e. five years.

In addition, little children who enter a new setting such as school require, and deserve, a time to settle down and become used to their new lifestyle. Consequently the earliest time that a full screening could be undertaken by an educational psychologist is after at least half to one term in the infant or first school. The focus of the subsequent discussion, therefore, will be on 5- to 7-year-old children.

What to Screen

A survey by Cornwall and Spicer (1982) of the LEAs in England and Wales found that 41 per cent conducted screening in the third infant year (i.e. when the children were seven). Sixteen per cent screened 6-year-olds and 23 per cent screened 5-year-olds. (It isn't possible to tell from the data whether these were different LEAs.) Educational psychologists were the most usual organisers of LEA's screening (in 48 per cent of cases).

The two questions of what and when to screen interact. The Bullock Report (DES, 1975) found that the most popular measure on which children were screened was reading (albeit on a large number of tests which differed from one LEA to another). The case was still the same when Cornwall and Spicer (1982) surveyed LEAs again. Once more, the most popular ages for screening were top infant, lower junior, and the main focus was reading.

If screening is to be conducted on younger children, its content must be different. While a sizeable minority of children enter school having already developed a useful initial reading ability, the assessment of reading at this age would not be appropriate − most children would 'fail'. Consequently research has been conducted to discover what abilities should be assessed at this age. What are required are measures which will identify children who are not necessarily having difficulties now, but will have them later.

The theoretical aspect of this is essentially a distinction between the assessment of target skills (e.g. reading) and supposed prerequisite skills. In fact, all that is necessary is to identify abilities and disabilities which correlate with later success or failure, but the common model has been to focus on those abilities at 5 years (or earlier) which are thought necessary to develop reading.

Screening procedures at this age, therefore, have included measures of abilities which are thought to be necessary for success at school. They have also been limited to those abilities and characteristics of children which are relevant to this age. Pre-school procedures (e.g. the Keele Pre-School Assessment Guide, described in Chapter 6) and developmental screening of even younger children (described in Chapter 3) include tests which are even more removed from the target skills, such as reading for example.

There has been much research which has investigated the types of tasks which are related to later performance in children. For example, many researchers have studied groups of children at about 5 to 6 years on a wide variety of tests, and then correlated the results from their assessments with test results in, say, reading at 7 or 8 years. One famous study was conducted by De Hirsch, Jansky and Langford (1966) in the United States, who examined 53 children (30 boys and 23 girls) whose ages ranged from 5 years and 2 months to 6 years. They were given a total of 37 tests while at Kindergarten, and the results on these tests were correlated with performance in typical educational skill areas such as writing, spelling and reading at the end of first Grade. The tests used at Kindergarten included investigation of the child's laterality, gross and fine motor skills and visual perception.

Many other studies in the United Kingdom and other countries, have taken a similar format — i.e. trying to identify the tests of children's ability in the early school stages which correlate with performance in school subjects at about 7 or 8 years. From such research it was hoped that the best correlates could be discovered and that these would be the best predictors of later performance. If these best predictors were then combined in one test, all children could be easily screened at the start of their school careers.

Examples of the types of tests used include:

(a) Visual orientation:

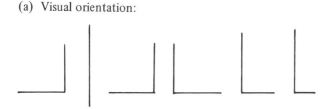

In this test the child must indicate the shape which is the same as that presented on the left. Young children are not able to do this task successfully as they do not consider orientations to be relevant — after all in the normal lives of pre-literate children things stay the same in essence no matter what way round they are — a sweet is still a sweet however it is moved!

(b) Auditory discrimination:

(1) At a simple level a child might be asked to distinguish between two everyday sounds (e.g. a train and a car). At a more difficult level the child might be asked to show which of three pictures begins with a certain letter sound (for example S).

(2) The child might be asked to show which letter is represented by a sound.

As a result of these studies a number of scales for screening young school children have been produced. An early one in this country was the Croydon Checklist, devised by Sheila Wolfendale and Trevor Bryans in the early 1970s when they were both working as educational psychologists in the London Borough of Croydon (Wolfendale, 1976). Subsequently, *The Somerset Developmental Checklist* (Lawrence and Blagg, 1977) and the Humberside *Infant Screening* (1981) have also been produced and published nationally. In addition many Local Education Authorities have produced their own screening tests which have been compiled by local educational psychologists, teachers and advisors. In Birmingham, for example, the *Screening Instrument* has been used throughout the city. This is a combined screening test and rating scale completed by teachers devised originally by Rawsthorne, 1967 (see Tansley, 1976).

Most of these instruments are tests and require the skill to perform some standard activities in a defined way. However, some are either exclusively or in part rating scales completed by the teacher. In this case the psychologist has been involved at the level of producing the scale and helping the teachers interpret the results, but the actual administration is done by the teachers themselves.

Examples of Screening Instruments

Two examples of screening instruments will be described to highlight the common characteristics and problems of these procedures. The first, the Aston Index (Newton and Thomson, 1976) is a series of tests completed by the child while the second, The Infant Rating Scale (Lindsay, 1981a), is a rating scale completed by the teacher on the children concerned. Both instruments are suitable for children of about

5 to 5½ years and both also have a Level II suitable for children of 7 plus. In addition each test has been subjected to a number of evaluation studies and each is intended to be of direct help to teachers by offering a profile of strengths and weaknesses.

Aston Index

Description. The Aston Index was designed to identify children with learning difficulties with written language. Level I is designed as a 'first screening' measure for children who have been in school for about 6 months, and comprises the following items:

(a) General Underlying Ability
   (1) Picture Vocabulary.
   (2) Vocabulary.
   (3) Goodenough Draw-a-man.
   (4) Copying Geometrical Designs.
(b) Performance Items
   (1) Write or copy name three times.
   (2) Phoneme/Grapheme correspondence.
   (3) Visual Sequential Memory (symbolic).
   (4) Visual Sequential Memory (pictorial).
   (5) Auditory Sequential Memory.
   (6) Sound Blending.
   (7) Sound discrimination.
   (8) Laterality (including knowledge of left and right and common sequences).

The authors claim that: 'All the test items are easily available to teachers ("open tests") and require no lengthy specialist training for their administration. They can all be administered quickly and on several occasions (e.g. on consecutive days) and some may be given to a whole class at a time' (Newton, Thomson and Richards, 1979, p. 56).

However, some of the items require interpretation and problems of agreement may occur with untrained teachers. Also the Index is found to be quite lengthy by teachers and needs to be given individually to children of this age, so increasing the amount of time necessary for a screening procedure.

The items in this Index comprise new tests and previously existing tests (e.g. Schonell Graded Word Reading Test, at Level II). Some were chosen to assess 'underlying ability' and are similar to items in standard intelligence tests, while the Performance Items were chosen as 'those which have been found to correlate with this kind of reading difficulty' (Newton *et al*, 1979, p. 59) – i.e. dyslexia.

Evaluation. Several studies are reported by Newton *et al* (1979) concerning the usefulness of the Index.

(1) *Reliability.* Test-retest reliabilities are given for some of the items. The results for a sample of 15 children of 5½ to 6½ years show item test-retest correlations ranging from 0.67 to 0.89 (median 0.75) over a period of one to two months. These results are reasonable, but the sample size is very small. More worrying is the fact that no reliabilities are presented for tests scored subjectively (e.g. Copying Geometric Designs and Name Writing).

(2) *Concurrent Validity.* No results are represented for concurrent validity of Level 1.

(3) *Predictive Validity.* Two studies are reported on predictive validity, using 120 children drawn from six schools from different socio-economic areas within one LEA. The children were given the Aston Index Level I between the ages of 5 years 6 months and 5 years 9 months. They were retested with Level II including the Schonell Reading and Spelling Tests, two years later. Correlations of items with reading ranged from 0.05 for Picture Recognition to 0.63 for Sound Blending. Correlations between reading at 7 years and Overall Score (0.60) and Performance total (0.63) were reasonable, but that for General Underlying Ability was low (0.31).

When the sample was divided into those children who could at 7½ years read at or above their chronological age, and those who read below their chronological age, differences seemed to exist on each item of the Index. The 'at risk' group was found to have progressed on some items only to the level of the 'not at risk' group when they were 5½ years.

These results provide some support for the Index as a predictor of problems with written language at 7½ years. However, a further study, using Bayesian statistics, reveals that for the cut-off score chosen, about as many children deemed 'at risk' at 5½ years were reading satisfactorily at 7½ years, as were reading below their age level – 19.1 and 21.4 per cent respectively (see Table 7.1).

In all, 40.5 per cent of the sample were considered at risk according to the Index, but only 21.4 per cent scored below their age level on reading. The test had an overall 'hit' rate of 75.3 per cent, mainly made up from the 53.9 per cent of children rated not at risk at 5½, progressing satisfactorily at 7½ years.

Table 7.1: Frequencies of Children in Categories, expressed as percentages

		At Risk	Not At Risk	
Criterion	At Risk	21.4	5.6	27
allocation	Not At Risk	19.1	53.9	73
(Reading				
Ages)	Total	40.5	59.5	100

Source: M.J. Newton *et al* (1979), *Readings in Dyslexia*, p. 86, Table 14.

Conclusion. The Aston Index is a test widely used by teachers, although its claim to be a screening test must be tempered by the time of administration. It has a number of evaluative studies which allow us to judge its value. Although it shows reasonable predictive power, it will misclassify a large percentage of children as 'at risk' when they are not. As a screening test it must, therefore, be used with some care.

Infant Rating Scale

Description. This is a 25 item scale which is completed by the child's teacher after about 1 to 1½ terms in school (Level I). For each item there is a five point scale, each point of which is defined. Teachers must score each child on each of the 25 items according to their everyday behaviour — i.e. there is no test situation. Tables of norms are provided to show how common or rare each type of behaviour is.

There are five subscales: Language, Early Learning, Behaviour, Social Integration and General Development. Each subscale comprises between three and eight items. An example of a Language subscale item is Sentence Construction.

5	4	3	2	1
Always or nearly always uses grammatically correct sentences; uses conjunctions such as 'if', 'because'.	Few grammatical errors; uses long sentences with conjunctions; only occasional errors with past tense (e.g. 'catched').	Satisfactory.	Frequently uses incomplete sentences; short utterances only — about five words or less.	Always uses incomplete sentences with many grammatical errors; does not talk.

In this case, only 1.9 per cent of the children on whom the IRS was standardised scored at point 1, and only 11.0 per cent scored at point 2.

The IRS differs from the Aston Index in being a rating scale rather than a series of tests, and therefore by being based upon the teacher observing the child, rather than the child performing set tasks. In addition, the IRS aims to provide information over a much broader range of areas.

Evaluation. The IRS has been evaluated in several ways, and reports are contained in a number of publications; the key references are Lindsay (1979a, 1981a, b).

(1) *Reliability*. A study of test-retest reliability was carried out on 49 children by their teachers, with a two-week gap between ratings. Test-retest correlation ranged from 0.65 to 0.93 for the items (median 0.85) while the Total scores produced a reliability coefficient of 0.96.

A subsequent study by Povey, Latham and Cliff (1983) reported on inter-rater reliability. This also was satisfactory with reliability coefficients of 0.82 and 0.97 (total scores) for two classes of children assessed by their classteacher and headteacher.

These results suggest that the IRS is a reliable instrument both over short periods of time and when used by different teachers who know the child.

(2) *Concurrent Validity*. Lindsay (1979b) reports a comparison of 105 children assessed at the age of about 5-5½ years (mean age 5 years 4 months). Those designated 'at risk' on the basis of IRS total scores recorded significantly different scores from a not 'at risk' group on a variety of measures of general ability and visual auditory discrimination. In all cases the differences were significant at the 0.001 level.

(3) *Predictive Validity*. Several studies are reported on predictive validity (Lindsay 1979b, 1981a, 1981b).

Correlations between the Language and Early Learning Subscales of the IRS at 5 years, and the Young Group Reading Test at 7 years were 0.51 and 0.56 respectively ($p < 0.001$ in each case), for a sample of 480 children. When the results of Level I IRS were compared with the Primary Reading Test results at 9 years, for 297 children, a similar result was obtained: correlation coefficients of 0.51 for Language, 0.49 for Early Learning. When a step-wise multiple regression analysis was carried out on a selected sample, the IRS contributed most to the correlation at 0.73 (Lindsay, 1979b).

Table 7.2 shows the results obtained when the predictive efficiency of the IRS was measured using classificatory statistics.

Table 7.2: Percentage Efficiency of IRS Level I scores in predicting Reading Failure at 7 years

IRS	Overall Efficiency	True Positives	True Negatives
Language subscale	75.2	47.7	81.4
Early Learning subscale	76.1	45.5	80.6
Total Score	80.0	31.6	89.5

Source: Lindsay, 1981a.

Thus, while overall the IRS had a 'hit' rate of 80 per cent, slightly over half those children designated 'at risk' on the Language or Early Learning Subscales were found to have satisfactory reading at 7 years. (n.b. The cut-off chosen here was lower than that chosen for the Aston Index, so reducing the apparent accuracy of the IRS compared with the Aston Index.)

Conclusion. The Infant Rating Scale is an easily administered screening instrument which is quite simple to use, but does require a teacher to observe children and then reflect on their behaviour. It is very reliable, shows reasonable predictive power, but will misclassify about half the children, who appear to be 'at risk' when they are in fact not. The manual, however, makes it clear that it is to be used as part of an on-going system of monitoring children by the teacher.

Evaluation

Lack of Studies

According to the survey by Cornwall and Spicer (1982), 53 per cent of LEAs made use of 'home grown' products when screening children. That is, rather than use published tests or scales, they make use of instruments developed locally. Unfortunately examination of these initiatives reveals that these instruments are usually poorly evaluated and, indeed, often not evaluated at all. Tests published by reputable companies, on the other hand, can be expected to have been the subject of evaluation studies.

One instrument (Tansley, 1976) which had been used in a major English city since 1971 but had 'not had a large scale statistical enquiry . . . carried out to measure the progress of the children concerned' (Gray and Reeve, 1978).

The lack of evaluative studies is understandable. Often a working party of psychologists, advisers and teachers have produced an instrument which appears satisfactory but have had insufficient resources to evaluate its accuracy and usefulness. However, such a practice is clearly not defensible. Screening tests can result in important decisions being made on a child and the accuracy of the measuring instrument must be known if such a practice is to be defended.

Evaluation studies of screening instruments for 5- to 7-year-old children are available, but particularly on American screening tests. Some school readiness tests date back to the 1930s and are sometimes used as screening tests, although they normally require individual administration lasting 30 minutes or more (as does the Aston Index). But a major landmark was the publication in 1966 of *Predicting Reading Failure* by De Hirsch, Jansky and Langford.

This work was followed in the late 1960s and 1970s by a plethora of other instruments, usually the result of similar though often less extensive studies. Some instruments were extensively studied, but often single reports would appear in the literature of only one aspect of the instrument, so making evaluation difficult. Work in the United Kingdom really got underway in the 1970s with reports by Wolfendale and Bryans (1971) of the Croydon Checklist (Wolfendale, 1976) and Bailey and Rogers (1979), Cornwall (1979) and Marshall and Gilliland (1976) of screening instruments developed in their own LEAs. All of these reported only limited information to allow evaluation — they can best be described as interim reports.

More recently some instruments have been produced which have been evaluated. The Aston Index and Infant Rating Scale have been considered in some detail. The Swansea Evaluation Profiles for School Entrants (Evans *et al*, 1979) are the result of a major research study and allow their use to be evaluated. But the current position is that there is a dearth of good evaluative studies of many British screening tests, most of which are locally produced.

Results of Evaluation Studies

A review of screening instruments by Lindsay and Wedell (1982) was highly critical of early identification procedures. In addition to the problems discussed above, those scales which did report evidence for their usefulness were often found wanting. Most of these are American.

A survey of some of the literature reveals the following conclusions about some of these instruments:

    coefficients tend to be too small to be used justifiably to make individual decisions, particularly with minority group children.

(Oakland, 1978)

these data question the concurrent and construct validity of the Slingerland Screening Tests as a screening test for learning disabilities.

(Meade, Nelson and Clark, 1981)

In most instances the majority of children whose Pupil Rating Scale suggested a learning disability did not evidence severe or generalised academic difficulties.

(Margolis, Doherty and Sheridan, 1981)

most inadequate [the Kindergarten Auditory Screening Test].

(Margolis, 1976)

the West Riding Screening was inefficient in selecting children identified on the three chosen criteria six years later.

(Rennie, 1980)

In some cases the problem appears to be simply one of poor test construction. For example, McCandless (1972) says of the Boehm Test of Basic Concepts that 'none of the criteria of formal test construction is satisfied'. Certainly one wonders how well some of the 'home grown' products would stand up to evaluation. Rennie's study of the screening used in the West Riding before 1974 found that 'of the 300 children in the relevant schools functioning in the bottom 10 per cent for reading ability at 13 plus, only 65 were identified by an educational screening at top infant level' (Rennie, 1980, p. 48).

But even the best produced instruments, at this age, appear to be of limited use as the consideration of the Aston Index and Infant Rating Scale has shown. In general they are efficient at identifying the children who will *not* later have educational difficulties, but less efficient at identifying those that will. A further example is given by Potton (1983) who evaluated the relationship between the Croydon Checklist, given at 5 years, and the Young Reading Test, given at 8 years, on a sample of 395 children. While 84 per cent of the children deemed not vulnerable by the Croydon Checklist were satisfactory on a reading measure, 60 per cent of those who had reading problems at 8 years had *not* been picked up by the Checklist.

This finding replicates those of Satz and Fletcher (1979) and Lichtenstein (1981) on different instruments and is similar to the results reported above for the Aston Index and Infant Rating Scale.

Some of the results are statistical artifacts, depending on where one chooses to draw a cut-off line to decide when a child is 'at risk' or not.

However, a consistent finding has appeared. Screening of children 'at risk' of educational difficulties is far from simple and certainly not as accurate as early proponents of its use had hoped.

Monitoring Children's Learning

In the light of these disappointing results, what is to be done? Clearly the simple, and simplistic, use of screening tests and scales is not justified. Questions have been asked of the simple model of educational 'at risk' screening. In this an appraisal of children is made in their early school careers and a yes/no decision is made: they are either 'at risk' or not 'at risk'. The evidence which has been accumulating compels psychologists to consider a different system. In this, the child is seen as a changing person, for whom prediction is uncertain. Therefore, appraisal must be a continuous affair. This is not to discount the use of well-proven screening instruments, but rather to say that their usefulness must not be overestimated. They must be incorporated into a continuous monitoring system. In many cases they may add little to what a good teacher can derive from everyday activities, but on occasion they can add an important new perspective. The need to structure one's observations and thinking using such a scale can, in itself, be of great help.

Educational psychologists have therefore developed ways of working with teachers such that the best instruments available and the teachers' and psychologists' own skills can be used more effectively. This occurs both at class and school level and at the level of the LEA. Many educational psychologists mount in-service courses for teachers. In Sheffield, for example, over the past eight years, psychologists and advisers have been collaborating with school staffs, to develop ways of monitoring children's learning (Lindsay, 1981c). A project in Barking with similar aims has also shown success (Trickey and Kosky, 1983).

Conclusion

Educational psychologists become involved with identifying children's special needs in a variety of ways. Often, especially with pre-school children, this will follow a referral by another professional who has seen the child, or a request from a parent. When this occurs the psychologist will assess the child in a number of different ways, depending on the problem. But educational psychologists have also been keen to act not simply as the recipients of referrals, but also to go out and identify those children with special needs. In practice this occurs once the child is in school, although some educational and clinical psychologists working in hospital settings might identify special needs in very young, usually severely disabled children.

Screening has increased in popularity during the past decade, and educational psychologists have been heavily involved in this development. They have administered this system and also developed screening instruments. However, the evidence on the effectiveness of early identification measures is not totally encouraging. As I have shown here, there has been a lack of evaluation of the instruments produced and those which have been well researched show limitations.

The evidence points to the need for the development of a more integrated form of monitoring, with psychologists helping teachers and parents, who have daily face-to-face contact with the children, to teach, observe and record their children carefully. This requires good instruments and availability of educational psychologists. It also requires that good, positive partnerships are built up. These developments are already happening and, if staffing ratios are brought closer to the minimum levels recommended by the Warnock Committee they may be extended. At such a time more parents (and teachers) will have a ready access to a psychologist who will cease to exist as a stereotyped, sex-mad Viennese.

8 THE SOCIAL WORKER: FRONT LINE AND LAST DITCH

Bryan Craig

It is quite unusual to read about social work in connection with schemes of early intervention in the Health and Social Services. This is because social work is primarily, though not exclusively, a service of last resort — the ambulance at the foot of the cliff. It has not reached the stage of development attained by the Health and Education Services, where considerable resources have been allocated to preventative practices.

The two areas in which social workers have been at all involved in systematic early identification procedures are those of child abuse and social/emotional problems of young school-aged children. In the former case their involvement has usually been in collaboration with medical services. Discussion of such initiatives is presented in Chapters 3 and 9. School-based identification programmes, at this time, rarely involve social workers, but if and when school-based social work develops, the scope for such initiatives will increase. An example of one such initiative is presented later in the chapter.

The Social Worker

Teachers and Health Workers — particularly those who do not have much or any contact with the social workers — frequently hold derogatory stereotypes of social workers as being in their early 20s, long haired, untidy, clad in jeans and sandals, bearded — if male — condoning the worst excesses of disturbed and delinquent behaviour and preaching revolution to their disaffected clients. This stereotype has replaced the 1950s version: the middle aged woman do-gooder with brogues and two-piece costume and somewhat mannish air, meeting her own needs by over-controlling and over-nurturing her lame dogs and strays.

Stereotypes, particularly amongst professional groups, are half-truths and distortions which are magnified as the whole truth, to provide an Aunt Sally at whom anger, arising from professional rivalry, can be directed. Social workers, just like other professionals, have a range of stereotypes which they employ. But the reality is different.

The Central Council for Education and Training in Social Work (National Institute of Social Work, 1982) estimated that in 1980, in Local Authority Social Services Departments there were about 15,700 front-line Field Social Workers, 5,000 Team Leaders or Area Managers, and 4,000 in central management or advisory posts. In Sheffield with a total population of about half a million, the Family and Community Services Department in early 1983 contained 7 Divisional Officers, 28 Social Work Team Leaders, 175 Generic Social Workers and 65 Specialist Social Workers. In addition there are 5 Principal Community Workers and 39 Community Workers of various types.

Nationally over 70 per cent of front-line Social Workers are qualified, and other surveys by Age Concern, 1981, and the Association of Directors of Social Services, 1981 (in NISW, 1982) suggest that 65 per cent of these are aged between 25 and 45; only 3 per cent are below 25, 20 per cent are between 25 and 30, 45 per cent between 36 and 45. Seventy-three per cent have been in post for at least 2 years and 40 per cent for more than 5 years. So the popular image of the Social Worker being young and inexperienced is a false one.

Eighty per cent of Field Social Workers work in area offices, 15 per cent in hospitals, 1 per cent in general practice or child guidance clinics and a further 2 per cent in other settings.

Training

The appropriate qualification for social work practice, the Certificate of Qualification in Social Work, awarded by the Central Council for Education and Training in Social Work, is held by 73 per cent of Local Authority Fieldworkers and over 90 per cent of Social Services Managers. The qualifying courses, which are available at Universities and Polytechnics, are of 12 months duration for relevant graduates and of 2 years duration for non-relevant graduates and applicants with 'O' and 'A' levels. Exceptionally, applicants with no formal education qualifications will be accepted if they can satisfy the college – by its own examination and tests or by other means – of their ability. In addition, 4-year courses in social sciences recognised by the Council for National Academic Awards offer a 4th-year social work option which leads to the CQSW.

Personal characteristics and relevant experience are highly rated in selection procedures, along with intellectual capacity, and courses are balanced between academic study and supervised fieldwork practice, which a student must complete successfully in order to pass the course.

Typically the subjects studied are: Social Work Theory and Method, Social Policy and Services, Sociology, Psychology, Human Growth and Development, the Legal System and Relevant Legislation. These subjects are often integrated within specific themes such as the family, young offenders etc.

Courses usually offer options for students wishing to enter specialist settings, e.g. Probation, Psychiatric Social Work, Residential Care. Within the last 5 years a number of colleges have advertised options for social workers in Education settings, e.g. school-based Social Work, Child Guidance and Educational Welfare. As there are no formal criteria established for the content of these options, and as some colleges are not able to send out a description of the content or duration of the option, it is difficult to establish whether this form of training offers the best method of developing the skills necessary in the school-based Social Worker.

It is also questionable whether Social Workers should go straight from a CQSW course to work in a school. In order to develop sufficient professional and personal confidence necessary for work in a school and with workers from different professions a school-based Social Worker should have generic experience after qualifying in order to gain a grounding in the mainstream of work and particularly to be able to know and tap into the resources of the Social Services Department.

School-based Social Work

Amongst the 2 per cent of Social Workers to be found in other settings will also be found the 50 or so school-based Social Workers employed by Local Authority Social Services Departments. Within Great Britain there are only a few pockets of School Social Workers employed in various authorities. There is at yet no national drive to appoint School Social Workers because there is as yet no general awareness of their potential contribution. Those that do exist tend to be located in Haringey, where there is a big programme of school social work, and in Wakefield, Durham, Lothian and Strathclyde.

It is important here to draw the distinction between the school-based Social Workers and Education Social Workers. School-based Social Workers are employed by Social Services Departments, to whom they are accountable, and whose resources they use; they are usually attached to one or two schools only. Education Social Worker is the title claimed by some Education Welfare Officers. These are all employed by the Education Department having the prime responsibility to secure the presence in school of non-attending pupils; they may service as many as 8 to 13 schools.

School-based Social Workers because of their setting have working arrangements which are considerably different to those of their main-stream Generic Social work colleagues who are based in area teams.

A Generic Social Worker will expect to deal with a whole range of individual and social problems 'from the cradle to the grave'. A school-based Social Worker will work primarily with children and families. The Generic Social Worker will probably spend one day per week taking new referrals 'on duty', the school-based Social Worker will not do official duty, but whenever he or she is in school will be open to receive referrals. The school-based Social Worker will become a member of two organisations, the Social Services area organisation and the school, and will have to find ways of reconciling the demands of each as well as those of children and families. The Generic Social Worker is more or less free to plan his or her work during the day, whereas the school-based Social Worker is constrained by the open hours of the school and the timetable, which restricts the availability of staff and children. But they will be in much closer working relationships with teacher and health staff than their area-based colleagues.

'Problems' to which the School Social Worker Responds

There is a problem about using the word 'problem'. Within the spheres of health, education and social work, the word is often used to des-cribe in general a specific condition or behaviour of an individual – e.g. depression, anxiety, lack of control.

The ideas and practice of screening and early intervention belong to the liberal philosophy of public service provision, which locates prob-lems and pathology in the individual. The appropriate professional response is made to the 'problem-bearing' individual; something is done to him or her to make an improvement – compensatory education, counselling, medical treatment. The desired result of the activity is that the individual condition or behaviour will change for the better so that he or she corresponds more closely to a norm as defined by the profes-sional concerned.

The effects of this approach are that individuals may be controlled and patronised, allegedly for their own good – although they may have little real chance to have any say in the matter; and more particularly the public service agency, the school or the society is shielded, by the location of the problem in the child, from examining its own contribution to the generation, maintenance or aggravation of the whole problem condition or behaviour.

The Social Work Approach

The contemporary social work approach to individuals and their problems is based on a different analysis. The school, the public service agency or the society is not seen as an immutable 'given' requiring others to adjust to it. Rather the school or the organisation or the society is seen as an organic living entity whose members interact with its consumers, customers, clients. They in turn have an impact on the organisation or institution, just as the organisation and institution influences them. Thus, as Rutter, Maughan, Mortimore and Ouston (1979) have shown, schools, depending on their ethos, can positively or negatively influence children's behaviour in terms of attainment, subsequent employment, attendance, court appearances, etc.

The assumption that the school or welfare agency is acting in the best interests of its consumers, clients or customers and that therefore there is no need to examine critically the effect it has on its public in contact enables the political power of the institution in relation to its public to remain unchallenged. In reality the relationship of a client to a social services department, a patient to a doctor or a pupil to a school is a political relationship which defines and limits the extent to which the individual is able to exercise autonomy in respect of the sphere of his or her life in question.

Social workers deal primarily with society's deviants: offenders, mentally ill people, those with physical and mental handicaps, 'problem' families, one-parent families, battered children etc. As a result they develop a particular sensitivity towards the way in which 'normal' people and institutions reinforce whatever is the form of deviance by the process of labelling and of passing the individual through the official system, designed to cure, manage or contain the deviant behaviour. For example it has been fairly well established by research studies (Merriman, 1981; Millham, Bullock and Hosie, 1978) that the passage for young offenders through the juvenile justice system reinforces the development of delinquent careers, particularly through their entry into community homes, detention centres and borstals. However, diversion from that system and towards community-based alternatives reduces offending behaviour. Consequently social workers would tend to view the concepts of earlier identification and screening as problematic within the school setting if it leads to labelling the individual child or family, for example, as 'inadequate', 'disruptive', 'feckless', etc., or to the location of the problem in the individual without examining the relationships between the individual child with this school system, with the family and with the community and the wider society, in which resources for living are inequitably distributed in accordance with its power structure.

Typically social workers use, amongst others, an interactionist perspective to understand the relationship between these elements, and school social workers in particular do so, since they have to be aware of the expectations which the school has of them. They tend to focus not only on the elements in the system but on the relationships between them. The elements are the school, the child, the Social Services Department, the family, the community. So the Social Worker focuses on key relationships within this network:

The child and the school.
The family and the school.
The child and the family.
The child, family and community.
The child/family and Social Services Department.
The school and the community.
The school and the Social Services Department.
The community and the Social Services Department.

There are two main symptoms of problem conditional behaviour which school staff experience and which they may refer to a school social worker: the failure to learn, to attain, as well as might be expected of a child of particular age and the failure to relate appropriately to peers, school staff. In some ways the failure in relationships with a teacher for example, may be partly responsible for the failure of a child to attain, especially at the infant and primary level.

Such groups of symptoms may result from one or much more likely a combination of the following elements:

(a) *The condition or behaviour of the child.*
Physical Disability — deafness, poor sight, obesity, speech defect.
Illness — e.g. anaemia.
Psychosomatic — enuresis, asthma.
Emotional — anxiety about self, relationships, performance.
Withdrawal — depression, avoidance, inattention, attention-seeking.
Aggression — disruptive behaviour, bullying other children,

angry reactions to school staff.

Cognitive — retardation, specific learning difficulties.

Deviance — stealing, lying, disobedience.

(b) *The condition or behaviour of the family*. Low income, marital conflict, lack of parental care or control, ill-treatment, isolation, alienation, neglect, emotional or physical ill health of parents.

(c) *The condition or behaviour of the community*. Child's poor relationship with peer groups in schools and community, racial tensions, class or religious intolerance, delinquent sub-culture.

(d) *The condition or behaviour of the school*. Failure to motivate children, lack of appropriate resources or curriculum for disadvantaged children. Over-controlling attitude to children, insensitive handling, discriminating and stigmatising practices, non-acceptance of working-class culture. (A more detailed taxonomy will be found in Rutter (1975) and Algie (1975).)

An example of the problematic relationship between a pair of the elements can be seen in the following:

(e) *Home/school relationship problems.*

Conflict of aims and expectations, norms and values.

Physical separation of home and school.

Social alienation of parents.

Ineffective communication.

It is worth noting at this point that the school social worker is based in the school and aims to develop co-operative relationships with school staff. The fact that in some instances the practice and organisation of the school contributes to or generates some of the problems which children experience means that on occasions the school social worker has to seek to change attitudes, practices and the organisation of the school or at least has to point out to school staff what is happening. For example, a child in a primary school class was frequently misbehaving, causing difficulties and disrupting the lessons of a particular teacher. The child was from a single parent family. The classteacher persuaded the Head to refer the child to Social Services with the recommendation that the child be received into the care of the Social Services Department. A social worker investigated the referral and arranged for the child to be assessed at a day assessment centre for young children, which made it unnecessary for the child to leave home. The conclusion was that he showed no signs of abnormal behaviour, and discussions with the mother indicated that the child and mother had a good loving relationship. The social worker discussed these conclusions with the headteacher, and persuaded her to transfer the child to another class, for a trial period of two weeks. The child settled successfully in the class and showed no signs of the difficult behaviour which he had exhibited previously in his first class.

The teacher's analysis was that the problem lay within the child whereas in reality the problem lay within the relationship between the child and the teacher. The fact that the social worker was able to create the opportunities for a thorough assessment of the child, enabled a more realistic and less damaging solution to be found to the problem.

This case highlights the importance of having the skills of a social worker available along with the resources to which he or she has access. It also demonstrates the importance of a social worker's accountability being to the Social Services Department and not to a school. If a social worker were on the staff of a school and accountable to a Head there would be both subtle and overt pressure on the social worker to accept the definition of problems in line with the educational perspective.

Screening

The concepts of screening and early identification are not current with Social Services thinking, as they are within the educational and medical fields. This is primarily because Social Services are basically crisis-orientated, dealing with the worst first, operating as an ambulance at the bottom of the cliff rather than as a fence at the top of the cliff. Basically social workers do not go looking for problems; one of their key activities is to establish that the level of severity of a potential client's problem is great enough to justify their intervention. School social workers are one of the few groups of social workers who may be involved in the process of screening as a result of their association with educational practices.

Conversely it can be argued that no comprehensive process of screening can take place without the involvement of social workers. Both headteachers of the first and middle school involved in the Sheffield project have stated quite firmly that the involvement of a social worker within the school completes the 'trinity' of major caring agencies whose resources and objectives are geared in various ways to meeting the needs of individuals and of society. All Sheffield schools have access to the whole range of educational advice, support and provision. Each Sheffield school is serviced by a school nurse and a school medical officer who act as access points to the whole range of specialist medical services.

However, there is no direct or systematic relationship between schools and Social Services Departments and the whole range of resources which they deploy. Education Welfare Officers although attempting to develop a social work approach to their role are unable to bridge the gap between the educational and social services. This problem is general throughout the country.

The value of the involvement of the social worker in the welfare network and screening process means that the important issues of professional boundaries can be dealt with. For example, without a school social worker, teaching or medical staff may decide that a child or family problem is primarily one within their own professional province and that there is no contribution for social workers to make. Alternatively, they may decide that the problem is wholly a social and emotional problem for a social worker to deal with and that they have no contribution to make. The presence of a social worker in discussions of problems of individuals and families will serve to challenge some of these boundary assumptions and through a process of discussion and negotiation professionals will be able to learn more about each other's roles and resources, skills and approaches as well as the limitations and the boundaries of their work as a firm foundation for co-operative working relationships.

One of the basic problems about the processes of screening and early identification is the assumption, based on scientific determinism, that − given the necessary knowledge and information − it is possible to predict which children are going to be problematic in the future. Research into human behaviour in fact demonstrates that human beings are not predictable to the extent that one can identify those who are going to show some sort of deviant behaviour. It is possible to look back and pick out possible causes of a child's problem behaviour in the present but it is just not possible to say with any confidence that out of a broad population of children specific individuals will either become depressed, be non-attenders or become criminals.

Research into cases of child abuse has shown, for example, that while we may be able to predict that parents who batter their children are likely to come from a certain socio-economic group and from certain age groups, it is not possible to identify individual parents, who are likely to cause harm (Frude, 1980).

There is a danger, indeed, that by making this deterministic assumption one can bring the self-fulfilling prophecy to come into play. This is particularly noticeable when younger siblings of children who have been disruptive in school are admitted. There is an automatic expectation that 'they are all tarred with the same brush'. Expectations are very powerful and if the whole staff of an infant school is expecting a newly admitted child to show disruptive tendencies then it is quite likely that he or she will respond to their expectations or that behaviour may be misinterpreted, in line with those expectations.

The Sheffield School Social Work Project

Social workers share the problem of other professionals, e.g. educational psychologists, of not having ready access to pre-school children. Consequently the first time they can conduct a systematic programme of early identification is when the child enters a school or pre-five establishment such as a nursery. However, the involvement of social workers in schools is a new phenomenon, and as yet little written evidence is available on the role of school social workers either in respect of work with schools in general or in procedures for early identification in particular.

Consequently one particular project will be discussed with particular reference to the procedures for early identification, and the lessons learned from this will be considered.

Origin

In December 1978 the Chairman of Social Services requested that plans be drawn up for an experimental project basing social workers in school which should be set up under the Urban Programme. Four schools were chosen: a comprehensive, a paired first and middle school, a school for ESN/maladjusted children and a school for deaf children. Senior staff of both Education and Social Services Departments met to shape the project and later individual discussions took place between the Heads of the schools and the divisional Social Services officers.

The objectives of the project were:

(a) to explore and assess the use of intensive case-workers as part of multidisciplinary teams in schools;
(b) to assess where social work support can be most effectively used within the education service.

The paired first and middle schools, which have a combined roll of about 600 children, are based in the centre of one of the city's cheapest housing areas, which attracts residents who have most difficulty in coping with their life tasks and responsibilities. An indication of the educational levels in the surrounding community is that in September of 1982 43 children were admitted to the middle school, only 7 of whom had an IQ of over 100.

The middle school's policy is to look after as many of the children as possible in the area. This means very few referrals for special education. In 1981 only one child was referred for special education and only 2 were referred for special education on transfer to a comprehensive school. The school's aims are to be a resource to the community, to be responsive to the community and to provide services from the school that the community needs. The Head has, therefore, built up strong contacts with social and health services in the area. All professional views are taken into account.

The first school's aim is to meet the educational needs of children and families. However, in such a disadvantaged community many educational problems are experienced by the children. When these educational problems are explored often social and emotional problems are revealed, so in order for the children to make any educational progress the social and emotional problems have to be tackled. Therefore, the school has social objectives, which are to bring into the school professionals from other disciplines with powers to compensate for and ameliorate the root problems which are about basic social deprivation.

Therefore, the attachment of a social worker to this pair of schools was very much in line with the school's acknowledged social objectives which provided a firm foundation for co-operation.

The Welfare Network and Referrals

There is a well developed and flexible system of pastoral care within the two schools, the hub of which is the social adjustment unit. This is staffed by a member of staff from each of the first and middle schools. Together with the school social worker and the education welfare officer they form the core of the school's welfare network. Referrals from either school are made to the appropriate member of staff, or parents or children refer themselves direct. Referrals, problems and action are discussed and resulting plans implemented.

In attempting to meet the needs of all children, the school has set up a unit for children with learning difficulties, behavioural problems, etc. The social worker and the education welfare officer work very closely with this unit.

In the summer term 1980 school staff were asked to complete a simple form stating the child's name, address and the problem. This referral would then be discussed at a weekly allocation meeting consisting of the core team of education welfare officer, school social worker and two teachers previously mentioned. This group generally has the most knowledge of the child, and between them they decide the most appropriate person to offer help. These meetings are intended to be a frank discussion about a case and the discussions are treated as confidential. This referral system has been successful and has resulted in referrals from both schools.

The social worker receives on average one referral approximately every 6 weeks which involves substantial work. Two-thirds of these come from the first school and the other third from the middle school. However, there is a large number of brief contacts and short term work cases which do not figure on the case-load returns. There are very few referrals from the nursery.

Although the social worker has direct access to both the headteachers the main contact is with the unit leader. Within both schools there is a network of all the teachers who have direct access to their unit teacher in order to refer cases. However, teachers can have direct access to the social worker also. The headteacher sometimes refers cases direct to the social worker after discussion with the unit teacher. It is important that the school social worker focuses primarily on the unit as it is difficult for her to contact one out of 15 teachers. Both headteachers let this social worker operate and do not hope to know everything she does.

Often parents go direct to the unit for support and help and thereby bypass the Heads who see this as quite acceptable. Confidentiality is recognised to be important within the school. Sometimes parents don't want the classteacher to know that they are receiving help from a social worker. Both formal and informal systems of referral and communication operate freely.

Because of the high needs in the community which the schools serve there is a high concentration in the welfare network on achieving the task of meeting needs and dealing with problems of people in the community. There is little emphasis on maintaining discreet professional roles. The general aims and objectives of the schools have been parallel to those of the school social worker. The 4 people in the welfare network have a similar value system in that they see children and parents as individuals and not units in an institution. They wish to work co-operatively as people and to understand each other as people and not purely as professionals.

Types of Screening Process

There are a number of screening approaches which a social worker can adopt in conjunction with medical and teaching staff. Basically, they relate to the entry of the child into the institution of the school, the transition within the schools and finally the transfer to secondary education.

The Pre-entry Screening. When the list of rising 5s and early admissions has been clarified the school social worker, reception classteacher, education welfare officer and if relevant the nursery class teacher or head of nursery school can pool the information they have available. The social worker can check the divisional social work records and the school nurse can have available what is likely to be the most crucial information from the health visitor's records. In some areas there is very poor communication between health visitors and infant or first school staff, so that much useful information is not made available which could greatly facilitate teachers' attempts to help children and families. Where the school has an established practice of visiting all parents of new entrants prior to their first term, 'live' assessments can be introduced to a joint screening process. Where this is not the practice visits may need to be made or further contact with health visitors or other professionals known to be involved in order to build up a picture. In either case subsequent visits by the school nurse or social worker or education welfare officer may be necessary.

At this stage the value of the screening process should not be exaggerated. Information will be available which may give a clue to future problems which may be encountered but a child's reaction to attending school for the first time and the process of settling down cannot be predicted effectively in advance, so a second stage review of newly admitted children is necessary at the end of a first term.

School-based Screening. The first school which shares the attachment of the social worker in Sheffield uses the Croydon Screening System (Wolfendale, 1976). The main purposes is to plan the class grouping of new entrants to the school. Additionally, the scheme is used as a staff development approach so that they become more aware of behaviour or clusters of behaviour which might indicate that there are specific problems which should be dealt with. It is also used as a basis for providing an information record for the children in school. For example, the scheme can be used on a termly basis and changes in a child's behaviour and functioning noted and decisions made either to increase, change or reduce the resource made available to deal with a particular problem.

The importance of continuous use once the scheme has been started is that firstly a once-and-for-all or sporadic use of the scheme produces only a static or unrelated picture of a child at a point in time. To be of full value the scheme has to be used on a regular basis in order to gain the beneficial effects of comparison over, say, two terms, which enables discriminating judgements to be made about appropriate responses to make to the child's needs. Also, a once-and-for-all snapshot of a child means that there is a danger of him or her being labelled as being such and such a problem child, whereas he or she might only be going through a phase of a certain sort of behaviour, which might later be discarded with or without intervention.

Conclusions

The involvement of a social worker in such a programme is clearly more complex than a simple one-off screening procedure. Here the teacher is primarily screening problems, but in close collaboration with the social worker. Decisions on whether the child is identified as having a problem are the result not only of the screening test itself, but also of the interpretation of the result in combination with the teacher's general awareness and knowledge of the child and family. This in turn is reinterpreted following discussions with the social worker. Such a process can still be regarded as screening, as it is based on relatively limited samples of information and is directed at identifying children for further, fuller investigation. However, it is a more complex process than, say, a blood-test, or the use of the Croydon Checklist alone. It fits into a model similar to that suggested for health visitors, for example, (see Chapter 3) whereby screening test results are considered in the context of a general monitoring or surveillance. However, the system here is more involved because of the nature of social and emotional problems, as discussed above.

Assessment

Following a screening process, or in most cases a referral from another professional or requests from clients themselves, the social worker will conduct an assessment of the problem.

A social work assessment is traditionally called a diagnosis, following the medical model of a patient–doctor relationship, in which the patient has some pathological symptom and the doctor has the means of under-standing and remedying the condition.

However, there are important distinctions between the medical and social work concepts of diagnosis. First, in social work one cannot separate in time, diagnosis and treatment. If a mother on her first inter-view with a social worker explains the difficulties she is having with her 8-year-old son and during the process expresses a lot of feeling – 'gets it off her chest' – 'treatment' has already started, and so has a relation-ship. Similarly the mother probably wants help straight away and won't wait for an unspecified length of time for a 'diagnosis' to take place. The diagnosis is not a once-and-for-all process; as more and more facts and feelings emerge through discussion, a social worker gradually builds up a view which he or she reassesses continually in the light of new information.

Second, in diagnosis social workers recognise that clients have made an appraisal and found a way of explaining the cause of their problems, which may or may not be accurate, but which nevertheless influences their approach to dealing with the problem.

However, social work thinking and practice is moving away from the medical model of diagnosis and treatment and of the authoritarian doctor–patient relationship. Social work is moving towards a more interactionist, dynamic approach to the assessment of problem situa-tions; the linear processes of diagnosis, treatment, evaluation by the expert is being replaced by a joint explanation by worker and client of the nature and effects of the particular problem being experienced, working together on solutions and jointly evaluating progress made. The local impracticability of attempting to separate 'treatment' and 'diagnosis' is illustrated in the following situation.

Teachers expressed their concern to a school social worker about the behaviour of two siblings. They were withdrawn and non-communicat-ing. When the social worker saw the mother, marital problems were revealed. The mother talked about the angry way in which she relates to her husband. After exploring this area and the woman's childhood relationships the social worker has a hunch that the woman is relating angrily to her husband because she has some unresolved feelings towards her father, whom her husband resembles physically. A social worker gently suggested that there might be a connection between the way she related to her father in the past and the way she relates to her husband now, and the woman gradually let this realisation sink in.

The interpretation made by the social worker serves the purpose of both diagnosis and treatment.

The social worker has checked out a diagnostic hypothesis about one of the roots of the marital problem and at the same time, by giving insight, has enabled the client to understand her behaviour and establish a point of departure for one area of change in the marital relationship.

Sainsbury (1970) describes diagnosis as

> . . . a process of discovering problems of significance in the information directly obtained or inferred. It is tentatively constructed and refined throughout the whole period of contact with the client. It is a way of thinking about situations so that help is made available now and in the future. Its value can be assessed only by its relevance to:
> (a) the solution to the social problems presented.
> (b) the clients' material and emotional needs (both in the present and, where unfulfilled, in the past)
> (c) the capacities of the agency and the worker to help.

It is not a static conclusion, for it reflects changes in situations brought about by new events and by the effect of the help already given. To the extent that it is a shared activity with the client, it is dynamic in that it is directly instrumental in changing the situations by enhancing the client's perception of them.

The actual process of a social work assessment involves the worker in:

> receiving direct information from the client and impressions about the client, in the way he or she relates, and levels of feeling expressed, including body language;
> building up a picture of the problem in terms of facts and feelings in play, including significant issues for the client or the family, the extent of the problem;
> eliciting further information about other areas of a client's life – e.g. family interaction, and response to the problem;
> structuring the information in a coherent pattern and checking the accuracy with the client;
> forming hypotheses about key behaviours of the client/family and possible means of intervention to allow change to take place;
> revising hypotheses and structure as new information emerges.

In this way is achieved a working understanding – preferably shared and agreed with the client – of the causes of the problem situation, the nature of the relationships between the client, the problem and the environment, and areas of behaviour or functioning which need to be addressed in order to achieve the desired change.

So a school social worker is interested in the interaction between the various actors in the child's social environment, and the influences that are brought to bear on his or her behaviour and on the behaviour of others. Although the first symptom of an underlying problem may be the child's behaviour, it may be that the social worker will choose not to work with a child but may be with the parents or some school staff whose behaviour has a direct influence on that of the child.

The following are the elements on which a school social worker could focus (these relate to the descriptions of problems described earlier in the chapter).

(a) *The child:* Behaviour at home and at school, relationships with parents, adults, other than teachers, siblings and peers.

(b) *The family:* Marital relationship, levels of functioning, economic pressures and crises, relationships with other families, attitudes to school and the child's problem, any significant events in family history, nature and use of authority within the family.

(c) *The school:* Nature of key relationships between child and staff, attitudes towards child's problem, staff responses to child and parents, staff explanations of problems, previous attempts to deal with the problem.

(d) *The community:* Relationships with peer groups, other adults, play opportunities and habits, prevalence of delinquency, poor housing, unemployment, etc., within the community.

As previously stated the social worker assesses the interaction between the elements in a situation defined as a problem in relation to a particular child and works at understanding the origins of the problem and the strength of the forces to which the child is subject, both emotional and social. Based on this assessment the social worker, wherever possible with the client, works out and carries out a plan of action to achieve the necessary changes.

This approach can be illustrated by the two case examples given so far. In the first the social worker examined the relationship between the child and the mother, and then the relationship between the child and the teacher. She concluded it was the child–teacher relationship which was problematic, not the mother–child relationship. In the second example the children's behaviour was symptomatic of their mother's own fear of communicating. This was the source of the problem which expressed itself in the marital relationship. No work was done with the children, the primary client was the mother. As a result of this work, and the increasing confidence of the mother, the children began to speak again and acted normally in school.

Social work diagnosis, now more commonly called assessment, has moved from the aetiological/clinical to the dynamic/interactionist approach. The style of assessment used depends on the agency setting and the nature of the problem. In each referral the worker attempts to divine the best form of intervention in the client's life, having answered the question 'Is it appropriate to intervene at all?' The assessment is made against a background of various social expectations of how the client ought to behave, together with what the client can realistically be expected to achieve in the light of his or her life history, personal resources and immediate environment.

Conclusions

Social work services are overwhelmingly crisis-oriented and consequently rarely become involved in processes of trying to identify problems at an early stage. However, the need to change emphasis is recognised and some initiatives have taken place. This chapter has focused upon probably the major development in this area — the involvement of school social workers with teachers to identify social and emotional problems, to try to provide help and support and indeed to prevent further problems developing.

School social workers are a new and rare breed, and they are thriving successfully in certain parts of the country. As yet there is very little descriptive or research material about the functioning of school social workers in the literature, let alone a write-up of a full-scale project in which a social worker based in a school has been a member of an interdisciplinary team operating formal screening procedure.

Evidence from Sheffield so far suggests that the advantages of attaching social workers to schools are as follows:

(1) Because social services departments are at present crisis-oriented and have a 'worst first' policy of deciding case priorities, social workers attached to schools cater for a large number of unmet needs which would not have received attention from the social services department. The non-stigmatising availability and accessibility of a school social worker in the normal institution of the school is a positive

encouragement for parents, children and staff to seek help at an earlier stage and thus prevent the escalation of problems.

(2) Having undergone the sometimes painful task of gaining acceptance for their professional stance and skills, and having demonstrated that they are of value in the school setting, school social workers have been able to help school staff gain a better knowledge and understanding of the social and emotional problems of parents and children at an early stage in the child's school career. This has been accompanied by changes in attitude and sometimes policy and procedure within schools. This has been a significant and important effect.

(3) In every case the contribution of the social worker to dealing with the problem of children and families has meshed effectively with the education and health staffs' approaches and resources, to improve the effectiveness and co-ordination of services for children and families. The attachment of social workers to schools has stimulated the creation of inter-disciplinary teams.

The attachment of social workers to schools is preventative in two aspects. First, social work service is accessible to a range of individuals and families who are able to seek help at a stage before the problem reaches a crisis. Therefore problems can be dealt with by social workers before they deteriorate and thus avoid the generic social worker at a later stage. Second, school social workers have been effective in changing the attitudes and practices within schools and are thereby contributing to the development of institutional environments which are more sensitive to the needs of individuals and which are, therefore, responsive to individual and family problems. As a result problems can be recognised earlier and either dealt with more sensitively on the spot, or children and parents can be signposted towards helping agencies at an earlier stage.

School work needs to take a higher profile through the writing up of projects and research reports and their publication before a readily identifiable body of knowledge and practice is developed and recognised as having validity within the teaching profession as a whole.

It is in fact the professional rivalry between teachers and social workers, largely based on ignorance and stereotype, which inhibits the development of future attachment of social workers to schools. When teachers and social workers meet as concerned people with specific commitment and skills to deal with social and emotional problems of parents and children and put aside their professional rivalries, effective communication and co-operation does take place.

9 THE 1981 EDUCATION ACT AND ITS IMPLICATIONS

Geoff Lindsay

On 1st April 1983 the 1981 Education Act became operative. Assessments of special educational needs are now subject to this legislation. Although the content of the Act was somewhat less than various groups would have liked, its importance is unquestionable. To take just one aspect, parents must now be intimately involved in the assessment process from start to finish and must have access to the statement (in draft form) which is written on their child.

This Act is also important in its effect on professions outside the education service. Although speech therapists and social workers, for example, are not employed by the LEA, they also have a significant contribution to make to the process of assessment in certain cases. Indeed the Act is relevant to all the professionals under consideration here and to the parents of any child with special educational needs.

The 1981 Education Act

The 1981 Education Act lays a duty on LEAs to ensure that special educational provision is made for pupils who have special educational needs. Section 4 (1) states:

> It shall be the duty of every local education authority to exercise their powers under this Act with a view to securing that of the children for whom they are responsible, those with special educational needs which call for the local education authority to determine the special educational provision that should be made for them are identified by the authority.

The LEA has a duty to perform an assessment on a child to discover these educational needs. Before so doing, the parents must be informed of this proposal, of the procedure to be followed, the name of an officer of the authority from whom further information may be obtained, and their right to make representations and submit written

153

evidence to the authority within a period of not less than 29 days from the time when the notice is served (Section 5).

Where an assessment has been made under this section, and the child is deemed to have special educational needs, the LEA shall make a statement of these special needs. Parents have the right to see a copy of the statement, which they may challenge. If this happens, the LEA must arrange meetings with appropriate officers to discuss differences of opinion, but if the problem is still not resolved, the parents may appeal against the statement to an Appeals Committee constituted in accordance with paragraph 1 of Part 1 of Schedule 2 of the 1980 Education Act. Finally a parent may appeal to the Secretary of State. In addition, parents have a right to request that an assessment of their child's educational needs is carried out by the LEA and this must be done, unless it is considered unreasonable.

The Regulations accompanying the Act (DES, 1983a) specify the professionals who must contribute to the assessment procedure. These comprise a medical officer, a teacher and an educational psychologist. With very young children, particularly, other professionals are appropriate (e.g. health visitors, speech therapists).

The Act makes it clear that the LEA are responsible for all children in their area — not only for those who are attending school, but also for those who are aged two and over (but not over 16 years) who are not at school. In addition, with the consent of the parent, the LEA may assess a child under two years and must do so if the parent requests it. Thus pre-school children, and even those below two years, can be assessed under the Act and hence have a statement made of their needs.

In the context of the present discussion it is necessary to note that this system, which pertains to an Act of Parliament, is of necessity rather formal. The Circular (Assessments and Statements of Special Educational Needs, DES 1983b) does give useful advice on how this formality may be reduced, but the degree to which this can be done will be limited. Parents now have a right to request an assessment, and the LEA has to justify if it refuses. On the other hand, parents can challenge proposed statements about their child. Furthermore, they will be given copies of the statement which contains the reports of the professionals involved.

Each school must ensure that it has an appropriate system of identifying needs and involving outside professionals. Indeed there is a duty under the Act on the school itself, through the governing body:

It shall be the duty of the governors, in the case of a county or voluntary school, and of the local education authority by whom the school is maintained, in the case of a maintained nursery school –

a) to use their best endeavours in exercising their functions in relation to the school, to secure that if any registered pupil has special educational needs the special educational provision that is required for him is made;

b) to secure that, where the responsible person has been informed by the local education authority that a registered pupil has special educational needs, those needs are made known to all who are likely to teach him; and

c) to secure that the teachers in the school are aware of the importance of identifying and providing for those registered pupils who have special educational needs.

                                                    1981 Education Act, Section 2 (5)

This places responsibility directly on the school to identify needs, and to ensure that these needs are communicated to relevant teachers in order that they might be provided for.

The District Health Authority is specifically charged with informing the parents and the LEA of children whom it suspects to have special educational needs. If a child is thought to have special educational needs the DHA must inform the parents of its opinion and of its duty under Section 10 of the Act to inform the LEA. 'After giving the parent an opportunity to discuss that opinion with an officer of the Authority, [the DHA shall] bring it to the attention of the appropriate local education authority' (1981 Education Act, Section 10 (1)(b)).

Many children, particularly those with severe handicaps, will be identified by the medical services before school age. There is, therefore, clearly a need for good collaboration between medical and educational personnel, and with the parents.

Process of Assessment

It has been shown in other chapters that the assessment of young children is a delicate and complex task. It is not sufficient to have merely one person to complete a single, simple assessment when the subject of that assessment is a child with complex learning difficulties. Many professionals will, and must, be involved if that assessment is to be both comprehensive and worthwhile. In some places this requirement has been formalised with a team of people working in collaboration, usually in a hospital setting. This has the benefits of economy of time and effort (e.g. the child can see several professionals on one visit) but its very comprehensive nature can lead to problems. For example, a child may tire after seeing several people for examination. Also, hospital-based assessments are not appropriate for major aspects of the child's development, particularly educational and psychological development. Assessment of a child's cognitive abilities in an alien, clinical setting may not reveal a true picture. Accordingly, a combination of hospital-based and community-based assessments is required in order to obtain a comprehensive view of the child.

The Regulations (DES, 1983a) which accompany the Act specify the people who must be involved in the assessment process. For all children there should be a report from a teacher (even, it seems, with pre-school children), an educational psychologist and a medical practitioner. In the case of children with sensory handicaps, the educational advice must include a report from a qualified teacher of the deaf or blind (depending on the case). When other psychologists are involved with the child (normally clinical psychologists), educational psychologists are responsible for incorporating the advice of those colleagues into the report they will write themselves.

Unlike the previous system, which made use of so-called SE (Special Education) forms, the new system specifies no forms which the professionals must complete. Rather, a checklist of areas is suggested as a framework to help the writing of the advice.

Parents are also involved in the assessment stage. They must be given the opportunity to submit their own report on their child. This may be limited to their own views and opinions but may include reports commissioned by themselves from other professionals.

Good practice, it is envisaged, will follow the suggestions of the Warnock Report (DES, 1978) with the assessment process being spread over a period of time. The extent and degree of assessment will be increased, until a point is reached when it is decided the child is likely to have special educational needs and so requires an assessment under the Act. Thus, although the assessment process itself must, of necessity, have various formal components (e.g. specific time intervals during which things must be done) it is hoped that this can be offset by a preparation of the child and parents over a longer period of time prior to that formal process. Also, such an extended period will allow assessment over time, and facilitate more thorough and comprehensive investigations.

The Statement

The form and content of the statement are prescribed in the Education (Special Educational Needs) Regulations 1983 (DES, 1983a) although the design and production of the statement document will be a matter for individual LEAs. It will comprise an Introduction (Section I) and four main sections.

Special Educational Needs (Section II). The LEA must take into consideration any representations and evidence submitted by the child's parent, the advice the LEA has obtained from professional advisers, and any relevant information provided by the District Health Authority (DHA) or Social Services Department (SSD). Copies of these documents must be appended to the statement, and if the LEA accepts the advice of its advisers (which must take account of the views of parents) it can simply say so in this section.

Special Educational Provision (Section III). The LEA may discuss the provision to be made for the child with some or all of the professional advisers who reported in Section II. It must specify the special educational provision to be made for the child in terms of facilities and equipment, staffing arrangements, curriculum and other arrangements to be made to meet the child's special needs.

Appropriate School or Other Arrangements (Section IV). The LEA must describe the type of school they consider appropriate for the child and name the particular school if known. If the child is to be educated otherwise than at school (an apparently growing trend with parents of a broad range of children) this provision must be described. Also, if the parents are meeting the cost of schooling, the name of the school is not required on the statement.

Additional and Non-Educational Provision (Section V). In this Section the LEA must specify the details of provision which would be available for the child by a DHA or some other body in addition to the child's special educational provision. For example, the support of a speech therapist or psychiatrist would be stated here.

In addition to these Sections, it is expected that full copies of relevant documents be attached as appendices. A suggested format is provided in Appendix 2 of Circular 1/83. If this is followed a statement will also have the following additions:

Appendix A: Parental Representations. This will include both written representations (in full) and a summary of any oral recommendations made, which the parent agrees is accurate.

Appendix B: Parental Evidence. This might include additional evidence provided by the parent on the child's behalf, for example by a professional in private practice, or a worker from a voluntary body who is supporting the child and/or parent.

Appendix C: Educational Advice. In almost all cases of children of school age this will be provided by the headteacher, in consultation with teachers who have actually taught the youngster. In addition, if the pupil is deaf or partially hearing or blind or otherwise visually handicapped, the educational advice must be given following consultation with a person qualified as a teacher of the deaf or blind respectively.

In the case of pre-school children, educational advice might be provided by an advisory teacher of the pre-school handicapped, as they are called in Sheffield. Such people are experienced teachers who have specialised in work with the young pre-school child with special educational needs. In other authorities the titles and roles of such teachers may differ, and in some there may be no directly comparable person.

Appendix D: Medical Advice. This must be given by a registered medical practitioner who is designated by the DHA or nominated by them in the individual case.

In Sheffield the system has been developed whereby all relevant medical advice is co-ordinated by one of a specific number of senior clinical medical officers, who will be responsible for producing the medical advice which will be submitted. This advice might include assessments from clinical medical officers, paediatricians, psychiatrists and other medical practitioners. Other authorities might produce different systems; indeed Appendix G is designed to include reports from various professions in the DHA or Social Services Authority.

Appendix E: Psychological Advice. This must be provided by an educational psychologist either regularly employed by the LEA, or employed for the case in question. If another psychologist is involved, normally a clinical psychologist, the educational psychologist must consult with that colleague before providing the advice.

Appendix F: Other advice obtained by Education Authority. This might include advice from a previous LEA, or any other educational advice considered helpful.

Appendix G: Information furnished by the District Health Authority or Social Services Authority. In this section reports by, for example, a psychiatrist, social worker, speech therapist or probation officer might be included.

There are two important aspects of the statement. The first is that it makes a clear distinction between the assessment of needs and the allocation of resources to meet those needs. The reasons for this are given in Circular 1/83. Assessment should not simply be conducted with a view to available provision, although that knowledge is useful to the professional concerned.

The effects of this distinction remain to be seen. Not only is there a tidier arrangement at an intellectual level, there is possibly a better basis for parents who may wish to take issue with the LEA. For example, a statement may say, in Section II that the child's needs require that certain facilities be provided. If the LEA does not have these and so fails to match Section II with Section III the parents can use this evidence in their appeal.

The second point to make is that the procedure and the documentation must be more carefully considered than before. The procedure is derived from an Act, and the statement and accompanying reports can be viewed by an Appeals Committee in cases of dispute. What teachers and other professionals write, therefore, could become open to much greater scrutiny.

Parents

The issue of the involvement of parents is a crucial one under the Act. For the first time they have a statutory basis both for demanding an assessment of their child and for seeing the reports making up the statement. The Appeals machinery is a further positive element in their favour, although its powers under the 1980 Education Act will be more limited than the comparable machinery for children in ordinary schools. On the other hand, critics of the Act point to the ultimate legal sanction of forcing children to be assessed even against their parents' wishes. Also Tomlinson (1982) argues that the Appeals Committee, and recourse to the Secretary of State, will rarely be used: 'Parental rights, under the 1944 and the 1980 and 1981 Education Acts, amount to a grudging appeals system to which few parents will actually have recourse' (p. 108).

The issue of parental involvement actually incorporates several different components, each of which is contentious, and the several issues are often confounded.

Rights of the Parent

Here the issue is legal in nature and incorporates concerns such as access to information and provision. It is certainly the case that the Act does extend parents' rights, at least in theory. Whether this extension is sufficient can be questioned. There is also the separate issue of whether parents are aware of their rights, and will fight accordingly. Hannon (1982) argues that, before this Act, challenges in the courts were rare. However, it is possible that parents will become more aware of their rights and make use of the appeals and other machinery if they are dissatisfied. This was once largely a middle-class phenomenon and could be exemplified by appeals of parents against placement of children in ESN(M) schools, which rarely happened with working-class parents. However, recent events have shown a greater, and increasing political awareness of working-class parents. School closures are now being fought in working-class as well as middle-class areas. For example, parents of children at Croxteth School, Liverpool, refused to accept closure and occupied the premises during the Summer of 1982, leading to a reversal of the closure decision by the new Labour administration which gained control of the council in May 1983.

Children's Rights

It is often very difficult to separate discussions of children's and parents' rights. However, this is an area which has come to recent prominence, and clarification of some of the basic issues, at a legal level, has been made (e.g. see King, 1981; Morris, Geller, Szwed and Geach, 1980). Within the field of special education, children's rights have gradually improved. Severely mentally handicapped children, for example, were excluded from the education system until the passing of the 1970 Education (Handicapped Children) Act. Under the present Act, one of the main benefits will be from an extension of the LEA's responsibility to assess children even below the age of two years, if the parents request this.

Within the group of children under consideration here the main benefits in terms of rights are those which follow from a more complete and thorough system of assessment and — assuming this happens — provision. Thus the parents of pupils who are deemed to have special needs, as specified in the statement, will have a more sound basis for demanding better provision.

Access to Reports

When the White Paper Special Needs in Education (DES, 1980), on which the 1981 Education Act was based, was being discussed there was much debate on access to reports. Some professionals argued strongly against this, while other organisations, particularly pressure groups, argued for greater access. This debate can be seen within the wider context of access to school reports (e.g. Newell, 1982) and indeed to reports in general (e.g. Cohen, 1982). The Data Protection Bill which was published in 1983 sought to improve access to data on computers, but some argued that it did not go far enough and should include all types of records. The Warnock Report (DES, 1978) argued that 'parents too should be treated as partners in this process [of exchange and information] whenever possible . . . they should be able to see most of the factual information about their child' (p. 298). Under the 1981 Act parents must have a copy of the statement and so have copies of the professionals' reports.

All professionals involved, therefore, must be aware that what they write will be seen by the parents. This applies equally to medical officers and educational psychologists, and to the other professionals who may contribute to particular statements. For many professionals this is a cause of concern, and some practice in the writing of reports will clearly be required. There are two main issues here. One relates to usefulness and is discussed in more detail below. The second concerns defensibility. Professionals often make assumptions about the capacity of other professionals to understand their arguments, and so do not justify all their comments in a report. This practice will need to be re-examined. Furthermore, some of the basic assumptions underlying ways of thinking, and recommendations, may need to be reconsidered as they could be challenged (e.g. see Sutton, 1981).

Working Together

A discussion of legal rights of parents and children, and even access to reports, often assumes a confrontationist attitude. There is an assumption that the parents and child are fighting a system which is trying to impose its will on an unwilling victim. Tomlinson's (1982) perspective on special education is very much of this kind and her analysis of the failing of the system to some extent justifies this. There is some validity in the argument that the special education system is designed to solve the problems of the main system, rather than to help the children concerned. The past research on the effectiveness of special education has not been encouraging, particularly with the deaf (Conrad, 1979) and the ESN(M) (Galloway and Goodwin, 1979; Ghodsian and Calnan, 1977). Also, Tomlinson's study of children referred to ESN(M) schools indicates worrying aspects of the system (Tomlinson, 1981).

However, these arguments do not necessarily justify a view that assessing a child as having special educational needs is sinister and negative in its nature. Most parents, in my experience, are quite aware when their child has problems and, even if this is not the case initially, sensitive discussions and presentations of evidence can reveal this. At times this can be traumatic (e.g. in the diagnosis of profound deafness or severe intellectual impairment), but parents are rarely unaware that there is a problem and, almost invariably, are keen for something to be done to alleviate or solve it. Indeed a common complaint is that their justifiable concerns were 'ignored' by professionals. Thus, while rights are important, the issue of collaboration is also a major factor.

In the present case this must demand several components. First, parents must feel that they are treated as partners in the process. This requires early discussions when a professional worker has a concern, or alternatively a sympathetic and positive response if the parent is worried. Second, they must be kept fully informed of what is happening and what the possibilities are. This may not always be possible, particularly when several hypotheses are being tested or when very sensitive issues are being explored, but these should be the rare exceptions and do not detract from the general principle.

Third, reports and information given to parents must be understood by them. Thus, in addition to concerns about the defensibility of statements in reports (see above) professionals must also be aware of the need to avoid jargon, explain their meaning, and to provide useful advice. Similarly the parents' own views should be listened to and taken into account. Fourth, discussions of options must be held. If this includes admission to a special school, the implications of this must be explored. A visit to the proposed school should also be arranged before a decision is made by the parents. It is rarely appropriate for this to be left to an administrator who has no contact with the family. Rather this task would normally be undertaken by a professional who has worked with the family, or a person from a relevant Voluntary Body, often a parent of a child with special needs.

Finally, professionals must be sensitive to the effects of their style of working. Are the parents being guided and helped to learn of the nature of their child's special needs and the possibilities for assistance, or are they being manipulated into accepting the professionals' view of things? This is a very difficult issue as it strikes at the heart of each professional's self-awareness.

Provision

In some cases, an assessment will reveal no special needs and so no extra provision will be required. In other cases however the LEA must state how it will meet the needs identified, in Section III of the statement.

Circular 1/83 suggests that:

> Formal procedures should be initiated where there are prima facie grounds to suggest that a child's needs are such as to require provision additional to, or otherwise different from, the facilities and resources generally available in ordinary schools in the area under normal circumstances (para. 13).

It goes on to suggest that these pupils will have: 'severe or complex learning difficulties which require the provision of extra resources in ordinary schools' (para. 14) in addition to those youngsters in special schools and units. However, the Circular specifically exempts pupils for whom 'schools provide special educational provision from their own resources in the form of additional tuition and remedial provision, or, in normal circumstances, where the child attends a reading centre or unit for disruptive children' (para. 15).

It is clear that the intention is to restrict statements to a very small number of pupils, and these sound suspiciously like those that presently attend special provision. It must be remembered that the Circular does not have the force of law — interpretation of the Act is for the Courts — but what will this mean in practice? If schools successfully integrate pupils, with the help of their own remedial provision, will that render those pupils ineligible for a statement? Surely the Circular cannot be reinforcing the old idea of medically-defined conditions? What of pupils with specific learning difficulties — will they be excluded from the benefits of a statement? Are statements to be confined to the 2 per cent or all the 20 per cent suggested by the Warnock Committee?

There is clearly a difficulty here. At the conceptual level, there is some confusion over who has special needs, and whether there are, or are not, different groups of children. At the practical level, there is the issue of which children should be the subject of statements. The Act and accompanying Circular clearly have in mind a small number — i.e. about 2 per cent — who represent those children presently within the special education system. There is, therefore, a danger of simply perpetuating a system whereby special education is seen as a segregated system. Avoidance of this will depend on the policies of LEAs in making provision to meet the needs identified, and on the results of appeals by parents against LEAs who, they believe, are not making the appropriate provision. Pressure will almost certainly come from a number of groups: first, parents who want their child integrated into the ordinary school system, and demand extra resources to enable this to happen. This is clearly happening but in a random way, resulting in individual children being integrated in odd schools and little overall planning of resource allocation.

Section 2(2) of the Act specifies that the child must be 'educated in an ordinary school' but, under Section 2(3) there are three let-out clauses. This education must be compatible with:

(a) his receiving the special educational provision that he requires;
(b) the provision of efficient education for the children with whom he will be educated; and
(c) the efficient use of resources.

Second, parents of children in the so-called 18 per cent, who are regarded as having special needs, but about whom the LEA may be reluctant to make a statement. The main population here will be those pupils with reading difficulties, particularly those who may be called 'dyslexic'. Given the problem of definitions (see Tansley and Panckhurst, 1981; Cornwall, Pumfrey and Hedderley, 1983), it is questionable whether it is possible to decide on psycho-educational grounds whether many such children should be the subject of statements or not. It remains to be seen whether LEAs adopt loose or rigid approaches to this issue.

Third, there are pressure groups, whether of parents or combinations of parents and others, who object to the type of provision made. In the 1970s the West Indian community particularly took great exception to the apparent over-representation of their children in ESN(M) schools (the Rampton Report, Cmmd 8273, 1981). Recently concern had been expressed about the growth of units for children considered to have behavioural problems. Again, the West Indian community had been particularly affected. The argument here, therefore, is not whether provision should be made, but its type. Unlike the pressure groups discussed above who *want* their children recognised as having special needs, the groups under consideration here would challenge this concept, arguing that their children are normal, but are subjected to inappropriate curricula, and in the case of some ethnic minority groups, racism. The problems of assessing young children are compounded when English is a second language and the difficulties of teasing out what is a 'real' problem and what an artefact are great. Given these difficulties and the issues discussed above, it is essential that parents of these children are given help to fully understand the professionals' views and for the professionals to understand theirs. Interpreters will often be necessary, but this provides no panacea as there are potential problems in translating difficult concepts.

Conclusions

The 1981 Education Act has been seen by different people in quite different ways. Some argue that it perpetuates a legal framework which is against the interests of children. Others would suggest that it does not go far enough in protecting children. There are many issues to be resolved, which can only be worked out in practice. There are ambiguities, but that is in the nature of the issue. Once it is accepted that children cannot be easily and justly classified, it becomes very difficult to produce a precise framework which applies only to a defined population.

It is important, therefore, to return to the issue of motivation. If the ideas behind the Warnock Report are accepted then we should be producing a system which aims to identify needs and then make suitable provision to meet those needs. Parents are seen as partners and the process is viewed as a collaborative venture to ensure the best outcome for the child. This will depend on the needs specified and may range from appliances to help the child in the ordinary classroom to transfer to a separate school.

However, this view can be said to be too rosy. At a time of stringent cutbacks in the education service, resources are being reduced. Provision, therefore, may be made which is a very loose approximation to a 'good fit'. Similarly schools, under increasing pressure, may be more keen to define a pupil as having special educational needs resulting from patterns of behaviour, more for the sake of the school than the benefit of the individual child.

Clearly these issues range beyond the educational, into the legal and political arenas. Professionals must be aware of these perspectives, as must parents. However, I would contend that it is important to discriminate between the legal–political and educational issues, and this should be possible under the Act. If professionals really are working with parents, for the children, the assessment part of the process is the place to make a clear statement of the young person's needs. The provision to meet those needs is, as has been stated above, a quite different issue. It is here that the main debates should be held and battles fought.

10 OVERVIEW
Geoff Lindsay

Screening – Is it Possible?

Issues

In the preceding chapters we have discussed the various ways in which a variety of professionals who deal with young children set about identifying their special needs. It is obvious that an accurate and efficient system of identification is desirable because until the child's needs are recognised no clearly directed help can be available. Instead, the child will receive a mixture of an input of resources normally available to children combined with certain modifications resulting from guesses, or feelings of uneasiness. For example, a parent of a child with a hearing loss may not appreciate this fact but may have learned, without realising it, to speak more loudly to the child, and even to ensure that the child is able to lip read by unconsciously adopting the best position when talking.

Unfortunately, many children's needs are not recognised to even this limited degree. It is not uncommon for children with even severe problems to 'fall through the net' for some considerable time. The National Deaf Children's Society, for example, argues that many children with a significant hearing loss are recognised far too late in their early childhood.

It is because of this kind of problem that the various services whose business it is to help parents care for their children have been keen to try to identify special needs at the earliest time possible. The rationale is simple: the earlier the better. This rationale is, of course, built on several assumptions which are held to be true with varying degrees of firmness.

(1) Children's needs are related to their assessed abilities and disabilities. A child with, say, a major intellectual deficit will have different needs compared with a child of normal or exceptionally high general cognitive ability.

(2) Difficulties should be identified as soon as they appear: the sooner a fault is spotted, the better. An analogy here could be with a

motor car – if the oil warning light comes on, stop the car and rectify the fault (i.e. fill up with oil). To ignore the fault will lead to worse problems.

(3) If possible, identify problems before they exist as such. Some difficulties are thought to have precursers; behaviours or attributes predictive of later problems might be seen at an earlier age. If these can be identified help can be provided even before the problem itself appears.

(4) The identification of difficulties can be accurately made at both the concurrent and predictive ('at risk') stages. Unless identification is possible nothing directly related to the child's special needs can be done. If accurate identification is possible at the 'at risk' stage, so much the better.

(5) Screening, as opposed to detailed assessment, is a useful technique as it is economical on resources.

These five issues underlie the area of identification of special needs. The question is, to what degree do they hold true? Is screening possible? Can children's problems be identified before they actually develop but when the children are 'at risk' of their developing?

The Use of Screening Procedures

We have seen that the use of screening procedures varies both with respect to the problem at hand, and to the resources or philosophy of an authority. For example, screening for PKU is now universal in this country, screening for educational problems is common, but screening for vision before school appears infrequent. It is only recently that all authorities implemented health-visitor screening of hearing; general developmental screening by health visitors, however, is not universal. Some screening tests are in the process of development (e.g. for alpha-fetoprotein) while others are possibly on their way out owing to critical evaluation.

Evaluation of Screening

In earlier chapters we have considered how different types of problems are identified by screening. For example, hearing difficulties may be identified by set screening procedures at one of two ages. It is apparent that the use of screening varies between professionals, as does the success of its application. Note also that while the type of a problem to be identified is linked to one professional more than others, there are significant overlaps. In some cases this may be the result of deliberate collaboration, as with health visitors screening hearing, and then passing children through the audiology clinic system; in other cases the linkages are less formal. For example, a teacher who uses a screening test for educational attainments may identify, say, a speech problem which calls for a referral to another professional. Often such linkages are not built into the system.

There are several points that can be made about the use of screening procedures by the professionals who deal with young children.

Extent of Evaluation. There is a general lack of evaluative studies of the usefulness of screening of some problems. Educational screening, for example, has been criticised for being introduced without clear evidence for its usefulness. This applies to work which originates from teachers, psychologists and educational advisers. Often 'good ideas' become Authority policy and practice. When these comprise home-grown instruments with no real evaluation a very worrying state of affairs exists. It is clearly elementary scientific method to ensure that measuring instruments are reliable and valid. Why is it that so often in the area of screening it is assumed that an untried product can be safely used? Compare this with the extensive evaluation that was conducted on the use of the Eleven Plus, and on IQ tests. Given the debate surrounding these two procedures, and the concern for their effects, owing to less than complete accuracy of measurement and prediction, how can we justify using screening instruments which are unproven?

But this state of affairs is not limited to educational and psychological screening procedures. We have also seen how health-visitor screening of hearing, vision and general development is largely unevaluated. This state of affairs must give cause for concern especially as, in common with psychological and educational screening, the few studies which have been carried out have raised doubts about the effectiveness of the screening procedures.

Results of Evaluation

There are, however, a number of studies which allow us to make an assessment of the usefulness of the various types of screening procedures used. These have largely been reviewed in the preceding chapters. A number of common patterns emerge when these studies are considered together.

Medical Screening

Neonatal. Medical screening in fact covers a large number of different areas, and the results of evaluation studies differ with respect to the area in question.

The screening for phenylketonuria (PKU) has been shown to be a good example of effective screening. However, the screening of mothers for children with neural tube defects (e.g. spina bifida) using alpha-fetoprotein has not proven so straight-forward. Holtzman (1983) and Roberts *et al* (1983) have both reported poor efficacy. Not only was the test itself less accurate than earlier studies suggested, but many women did not undergo screening, and there could be problems if the necessary ultra-sound examinations were not available for follow-up of those women found to be positive.

The use of perinatal neurological screening has also been found to be problematic. The evaluation of 'at risk' registers as proposed by Sheridan in the early 1960s has shown them to be ineffective. Knox and Mahon (1970) for example conclude that 'none of these determinants were sufficient to justify the continuation of selective 'At Risk' registers whose purpose is defined in terms of prediction'.

This view was echoed by Rogers (1971) who suggested that many registers were too large, having 60 per cent of births on them, yet even so these included only 70 per cent of 'cases'. Although there is evidence that some children are especially high-risk — e.g. those whose mothers had rubella during pregnancy — the general use of 'at risk' registers as then carried out was dismissed.

Subsequent work has shown that the main correlates with later educational and psychological criteria are social class factors (e.g. Neligan, Prudham and Steiner, 1974; Neligan, Kolvin, Scott and Garside, 1976) although there is evidence that children of low birth weight, especially those 'born too small' (i.e. of normal gestational age, but low weight) do have a greater chance of later problems (Neligan *et al*, 1976). However, these results may be out of date as paediatric procedures have improved greatly during the past decade. Bennett, Robinson and Sells (1983) for example report that their sample of very low birth weight babies (< 800g) who survived (80 per cent died at birth) showed generally good development. Of the survivors, 81 per cent were without major central nervous system impairment and were developing normally at 6 months and 3 years, when mean IQ was 106. Although other studies have shown less successful outcomes, there is a trend of decreasing prevalence of disability among survivors of low birth weight (< 1500g).

Neurodevelopmental screening has been found to be less successful as a predictor. The Neligan study, discussed above, found that such examinations at birth showed a lower relationship with later perform-ance than social economic status or birth weight. A study by Touwen, Biermann-van Eedenburg and Jurgens-van de Zee (1977) found that a screening procedure, developed by Prechtl, identified a rate of 50 per cent false positives at one day old compared with the full neurological examination. Bierman-van Eedenburg, Jurgens-van der Zee, Olinga, Huises and Touwen (1981) report the results of a follow-up of the 79 babies found to be neurologically abnormal at birth. Of these only 13 (16 per cent) were classified such at 18 months.

These results suggest that the use of screening of babies in the first four weeks of life is far from effective, apart from a few conditions such as PKU. In general, a large proportion of false positives is identi- fied — i.e. babies who have symptoms shared by those with severe developmental impairment but who later show normal development.

Pre-school. In the subsequent three to five years screening becomes the province of the health visitor rather than medical practitioners. As we have seen, the prevalence of health visitor screening is unknown, apart from that for hearing which is now universal. Evaluation studies are sparse. However, those that do exist are generally critical.

The use of screening tests of general development, for example, appears to be growing with little evaluation. The Denver Develop-mental Screening Test has been widely used in the United States, but has been found to falsely identify many children. A study in Israel by Jaffe, Marel, Goldberg, Rudolph-Schnitzer and Winter (1980) produced a similar finding. Of 134 infants identified by the first screening for questionable or abnormal results, only 68 were confirmed at the second examination. This number dropped to 44 at the third examination (when the Stycar Test was used). Hence two-thirds of the children first identified were false positives. However, these results were considered better than the normal system of unstructured observations currently operating in that area.

Screening of hearing is now universal but has recently been criticised for its accuracy (e.g. Nietupska and Harding, 1982, p. 124). Apart from the actual problem of administering the tests — some young children will not co-operate — there is the further problem of take-up. Nietupska and Harding found that many children had missed screening tests for hearing (over 50 per cent of their sample). This echoes the finding of a survey of developmental screening of babies by the Central Birmingham

Community Health Council (1981) in a similar social priority area. They conclude: 'we would be surprised if more than 40 per cent turned out to be fully immunised and fully screened by the time they were a year old.'

Screening for Language Difficulties

Screening for language difficulties is not routinely carried out by speech therapists. When it does occur it will be part of the health-visitor screening of general development (see page 91). Yet the need for early identification of difficulties has been demonstrated by the studies of Silva (1980) and Fundudis *et al* (1980). These authors suggest very simple screening tests for language development: at the age of 36 months the child should use 'three or more words strung together to make some sort of sense' (Fundudis *et al*, 1980) or 'speak in sentences of four or more words' (Silva, 1980). Their remarks show, however, that such criteria would result in large numbers of false positives – children who will not later have speech and language difficulties. However, speech therapists prefer to check on such children who may cause concern rather than to let them go unnoticed. Similarly many schools and nurseries are now screening children for speech and language difficulties, and again the number of false positives can be high, but this may be acceptable.

Screening for Social Problems

Social work services are primarily crisis-oriented, as has been shown in Chapter 8. Screening is rare, although social workers have collaborated with medical staff in screening for children at risk of non-accidental injury. There is also the possibility of social workers being involved in the identification of problems of social and emotional development among school children, if a school social worker service develops. Otherwise, individual social workers may take their own action to try to identify problems at an early stage, rather than use screening procedures. For example, the social worker attached to the provision for the hearing-impaired in Sheffield will also make himself known to the parents of babies shortly after diagnosis and so be in a position to identify other problems at an early stage.

The phenomenon of non-accidental injury of children (or 'baby-battering' as it often known) is closely related to social stress (Lealman, Haigh, Phillips, Stone and Ord-Smith, 1983). However, while it is possible to predict that families under stress are more likely to abuse their children, the prediction is far from perfect. In Lealman *et al*'s study, two-thirds of all recognised abuse occurred in the 18 per cent predicted at risk — but that leaves one-third which occurred in the rest of their sample. Also, the percentage of the at risk group who actually suffered abuse was relatively small, and the rate of serious injury (about 2 per cent) was similar in both the 'at risk' and the 'not at risk' groups.

Psychological and Educational Screening

The review of evidence on psychological and educational screening reveals that such measures are far from perfect, in the early school years. There has been an increase in the number of LEAs conducting screening in the 5-7 year age range (e.g. Lindsay and Wedell, 1982; Potton, 1983), yet evaluative studies have questioned the use of 'at risk' screening at this age. A consistent finding has been that children who will later perform satisfactorily are identified as such, but the prediction of children who will later have problems is a much more difficult proposition.

As a result of such findings, it is argued that the emphasis should switch from LEA screening to a school-based monitoring system comprising the careful use of good instruments and enhanced record-keeping systems, backed by in-service education of teachers (Lindsay, 1981c; Lindsay and Wedell, 1982; Trickey and Kosky, 1983).

Screening – Some Conclusions

A common thread running through the preceding discussion is that of the probabilistic nature of the relationship between the results of the screening test and the actual existence of a problem, either in the present or future. When judging the efficiency of screening procedures, therefore, it is important to weigh up the relative cost of the inaccuracy inherent in the procedure.

Table 10.1 presents a hypothetical result of a screening programme. In this a screening test was given to 1,000 children, and they were later assessed to check whether they actually had the problem for which the screening was conducted.

In this example, the overall accuracy of the screening was good as the correct result was achieved for 875 of the children (correct positives and correct negatives). Thus the 'hit' rate was 87.5 per cent, and the 'miss' rate 12.5 per cent. However, of the 125 children who were deemed at risk as a result of the screening test, only 75 actually had the problem: a 40 per cent 'miss' rate. Also, 75 of the 875 children who passed the screening test did have the problem: an 8.6 per cent 'miss' rate. Looking at the results another way, only 75 of the 150 who were

Table 10.1: The Accuracy of a Screening Test's Prediction of the Existence of a Specified Problem (based on 1,000 children)

| | | Outcome | |
		Positive (child has problem)	Negative (child does not have problem)
Result of Screening	Not at risk	False negatives 75	Correct negatives 800
	At risk	Correct positives 75	False positives 50
		Total positives: 150	Total negatives: 850

found to have the problem had been positively identified by the screening test: a 'miss' rate of 50 per cent.

These results are not atypical; evaluation of some screening procedures has produced far worse levels of accuracy. However, we must go beyond bald statistics to look at real problems. In some cases we might be satisfied with a screening test which over-identified large numbers of children as 'at risk' — particularly where serious damage might result. All such children could then be given full assessments. However, we must be aware of the dangers inherent in this. Bodegard, Fyro and Larsson (1983), for example, report that the false positive results of a screening programme for hypothyroidism produced strong emotional reactions in about three-quarters of the parents, and that 18 per cent of parents continued to have feelings of insecurity about the baby's health which they linked with this screening, six to twelve months after the child had been cleared. Similarly, parents wrongly suspected of being potential child abuses are likely to react badly — and sometimes their parenting ability might even be affected adversely by such misplaced suspicion. (Keeping such classifications from parents reduces these problems but raises others).

Alternatively, such high rates of inaccuracy might result in an unacceptably inefficient system. This is the case, for example, with much educational screening. The decision on the usefulness of a screening procedure must take into account these factors, together with the others mentioned in Chapter 1, and a decision must be made on the overall assessment of cost benefits.

Prediction

Alan Clarke, in his Presidential address to the British Psychological Society, called prediction 'the most obvious hallmark of a successful science' (Clarke, 1978). He then went on to show how limited our ability to predict human development really is. Yet, like the Holy Grail, it is something we continually seek. The reasons are obvious. If we can predict children's development we could possibly intervene earlier to avert the predicted outcome, e.g. with a handicapped child; conversely, we might encourage a predicted outcome. What we are concerned with here is control.

One of the problems with prediction is that it is best conceived when we are talking about stability. For example, if a child's intelligence is fixed at birth, barring head injuries and the like, then prediction is merely a question of finding an accurate measure of intelligence at that time, or any other time. For example we could test a child's IQ at 5 years and, if the test is well constructed, we should be able to predict attainments. Unfortunately, as we know, this is far from being the case. A major study by Hindley and Owen (1978) illustrates this (see Table 10.2). Here we see, from a study of 84 children followed from 6 months to 17 years, how variable intelligence test scores are when comparisons of IQ measured at different ages are made. Changes were particularly common in the pre-school range. For example, when comparisons were made with quotients at 6 months and 5 years, half the sample altered by at least 19 points, over one standard deviation. But, as the table shows, these changes, though largest at this age, are not limited to early development.

What is apparent is that human development is not stable. Children not only develop at different rates, they change position relative to each other on different dimensions, and also their own profiles of abilities vary over time. Work with severely deprived children has shown how even those who appear mentally handicapped can improve

Table 10.2: Variation of IQ over Time

Age	Amount of Variation
6 months and 5 years	50% changed by ⩾ 19 points
	25% changed by ⩾ 30 points
5 and 11 years	25% changed by ⩾ 16 points
	3% changed by ⩾ 30 points
11 and 17 years	25% changed by ⩾ 19 points

Source: Hindley and Owen, 1978.

to normality under certain conditions (e.g. Koluchova, 1976; Douglas and Sutton, 1978).

When making an assessment of children, either individually or by a screening procedure, these factors must be kept in mind. Thus it is very difficult to predict a child's later behaviour, status or attainments from the results of examinations in the early years. Children must be seen as changing, active individuals who develop in a way which is related not only to their own constitutional abilities and disabilities, and to their learning environment, but also to their own way of using the combination of these two domains.

Compensatory Interaction

This formulation brings us on to a model of human development which takes note of these various factors. It is presented in Wedell and Lindsay (1980) under the title 'Compensatory Interaction' (see Figure 10.1).

Under this formulation a child's status at any time is seen to be a result of the interaction between intrinsic and extrinsic strengths and weaknesses. In addition, there is a third dimension of time: the pattern may change from month to month, or even more quickly. There is evidence to suggest that, in general, children at the extremes of good or poor influence are more predictable, but even here this evidence is found in groups of children: individuals with such characteristics may be very variable (as Clarke, 1978, described); but the large mass of children, who are subject to less extreme influences, are more variable. For example, educational screening tests which try to identify, say, 15-20% of children have been found to be of little value (Lichtenstein, 1982). The children around the borderline of pass/fail are easily misclassified, so leading to a test of low predictive power. Lichtenstein (1982) has argued against

> the common practice of investing excessive resources to definitely identify and diagnose these children in the 'borderline' area (i.e. children with mild problems or deficits), a task that borders on the impossible. Given the evidence, it appears that extensive assessment of young children at a single point in time is a poor investment of system resources (p. 72).

Conclusions

The results of these and other studies suggest that in almost all areas of child development one-off assessments and screenings are of little use.

Figure 10.1: Compensatory Interaction

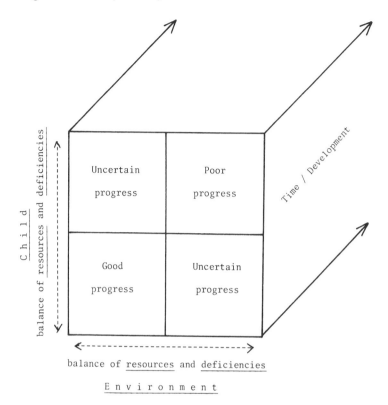

Source: Wedell and Lindsay, 1980.

Worse, they may be positively misleading by giving those concerned a false sense of security. What will be proposed is a coherent system of monitoring children's development. But before this is described it is necessary to consider the relationship of the professionals involved.

Inter-personal Relationships

Most children will receive attention at some stage from several professionals. These include the health visitor who makes the visits to the child in the early months, the clinical medical officer who sees the child at the well-baby clinic, the general practitioner and the teacher.

In addition, those children who are born in hospital will have some contact with the paediatrician. Even among these professionals contact will vary from child to child. Some parents rarely take their children to the family doctor; incidence of attendance at baby clinics drops off quickly and in some, relatively few cases, access by a health visitor is actually discouraged or prevented by the parents.

Some children with special needs are seen by a further range of professionals depending on their problems. These include the speech therapist, social worker, educational or clinical psychologist, clinical medical officer working in schools and other medical personnel. Children with one difficulty often in fact have two or more difficulties (e.g. behaviour in addition to an intellectual problem) as has been shown by studies such as Rutter, Tizard and Whitmore (1970) and Chazan, Laing, Shackleton-Bailey and Jones (1980). In these cases the child, and the parents, might need to come into contact with perhaps a dozen or more professionals. If to these are added the additional workers such as administrators in the health and education services, it is readily apparent that a potentially chaotic system could prevail. In this section we will consider how inter-professional working can be improved. The issue of work with parents is so important that it is considered in a separate section.

In order for these people to work in the best interests of the child, it is essential that certain preconditions exist.

First, each professional should have an appreciation of the limits of his or her own expertise.

Second, they should be aware of the help which is available from other services. This book is an attempt to meet part of that need by providing basic information about the various services and considering some of the relevant issues.

Third, there must be easy access between professionals. That is, in fact, far from easy. I know, for example, that most people who try to phone me must make several attempts – professionals who work in the community, by definition, are rarely in their office to talk by phone to colleagues.

Fourth, there must be trust and respect. These attributes unfortunately, are often missing. It is too easy to scapegoat other professions and attribute blame. This process, although unhealthy in some ways, is seen as a part of life by some professionals and may be a necessary response by professionals (and parents) under stress. Teachers commonly blame the Head, the 'office' or other professionals (particularly advisers and psychologists) for what are really faults in the system, particularly lack of resources. Professionals must be aware of these tendencies and be willing to explore the true nature of the problem. But ultimately it is by engendering trust and mutual respect that good collaborative working develops.

Working Together for Children in Sheffield

In 1980 the DES and DHSS conducted a study in an area of Sheffield to examine how collaboration between professionals could be encouraged. This was based on similar premises to those outlined above. For example, it was thought that teachers and social workers often failed to work together because they held stereotype views of each other – the social worker being seen by the teacher as soft, liberal, woolly-thinking and anti-school; the teacher being seen by the social worker as authoritarian, didactic, constraining and against autonomy.

The project encouraged professionals to identify areas for discussion and work, one of which was the early identification of difficulties, the working group which I was asked to lead. Relevant professionals from different agencies were brought together to consider each other's perspectives on a common problem and produce a way forward.

What was immediately apparent was the lack of knowledge we had of each other's work and the system within which it was carried out. Discussion soon helped to identify the frustrations we each felt (Why doesn't the social worker take the child into care? Why isn't this teacher giving the child more attention?). Gradually we came to understand the constraints under which we all worked and to appreciate each other's positive attributes. At this point it was possible to suggest ways in which a better system of collaboration could be produced.

Power Struggles

The project described had as its aim the improvement of understanding between professionals, with an ultimate goal of better service delivery for the public. Some success was reported. But we must acknowledge that the picture is not always so positive. Professionals do argue among themselves and engage in power struggles. These have been the subject of several studies by sociologists, a recent one being Sally Tomlinson's (1981) study of children who were being assessed for admission to schools for children with moderate learning difficulties (ESN(M) in the terminology of the time). She is highly critical of the way in which, in her view, professional infighting and power struggles get in the way of helping the child. She has put this conflict in an historical context, tracing the gradual change in special education from a pervasive medical influence to the present psycho-educational domin-ance. This change is clearly seen in the 1981 Education Act which now removes the responsibility for ascertaining children as needing special educational treatment (1944 Act) from medical officers and makes it clearly the responsibility of the education service.

Conflict can be seen as a 'good thing': an irritant in a stable system resulting in exciting change and innovation. It can also be a thorough nuisance: reducing effectiveness and impairing service delivery. Circular 3/74 on Child Guidance Services (DES, 1974) recognised these prob-lems, and the changing inter-professional relationships, and argued for a 'network' approach to services. This is a useful idea which we favour. Under this, professionals are seen as autonomous (i.e. not answerable to colleagues from different professions). Colleagues from different disciplines contribute to discussion of, and decisions about, children without an inevitable hierarchical relationship. In some cases − for example, medical supervision − some hierarchical relationships are inevitable, but with most children different professionals must take the lead at different times. For example, decisions on drug treatment, educational need, social work support, speech therapy and other issues must be taken by the most relevant professional.

'Professionalisation' is an important, but complex, issue. Several writers have criticised professionals for mystification. An Open University Test which forms part of Course 241, 'Special Needs in Education' (Potts, 1982) provides a useful summary of these criticisms. How can professionals really be both caring and maintain (and even enhance) their own status? Does not the history of the professions in this field reflect issues of control rather than care? Do professionals seek to make a mystique of their work by not entering into discussion with other colleagues, e.g. teachers, and especially parents? Is a veil of secrecy erected in the name of a generally applied principle of confiden-tiality? (Fitzherbert, quoted in Potts (1982) reports that even 'a letter from a child guidance clinic with travel instructions was headed "Con-fidential" because the printed stationary of the clinic automatically bears that heading'.)

We hope we are aware of our own failings in these areas. We are committed to the ideal of engendering purposeful teamwork for the benefit of children, rather than professional self-aggrandisement. But we would be naïve if we ignored our own failings or expected that the failings of others, largely produced by the historical development of the professions, would easily be eliminated.

A System of Monitoring and Identification

We have argued that a simplistic notion of screening children for most problems of development is naïve. The evidence available suggests that, apart from some very specific physical disorders with a high 1 to 1 correspondence with a developmental disability (e.g. PKU), we are talking in terms of probabilities rather than certainties. The degree of variation from high to low probability is related to many factors including nature of the problem, age and what the problem is thought to be predicting.

We have argued for a model of Compensatory Interaction as a description of child development in this area. Following from this we would argue that, in terms of action, what is required is a coherent, co-ordinated system of monitoring children's development.

In some respects this occurs. In Chapter 2 we saw how the medical service has a system of surveillance, while in Chapter 6 we saw how teachers are also trying to improve their monitoring procedures. But in order that this system works well the following elements must be incorporated:

(1) *The system within each specialist area must be comprehensive and well-conceived*. Teachers, for example, should have a carefully constructed system of record-keeping about their children. These records must be comprehensive in the areas they cover, accurate and non-ambiguous in the information they contain, and useful. Teachers' records vary greatly as the Schools Council Project by Clift *et al* (1981) has shown. In this study, official LEA school records were found to vary even on such basic requirements as date of birth and address of child (demanded by only 98% and 93% of the sample, respectively). When records are examined by subject area the range was even more remarkable. In written language, for example, records were kept by only 45% of the sample. Some teachers refused to keep anything other than minimal records, believing this to be in children's best interests. The situation with younger children is probably even more variable with many nursery teachers being highly reluctant even to keep records, let alone pass them on to the infant or first school. It is true that teachers often differentiate the exceptional children and would consider keeping and passing on more detailed accounts about them. But, as we have argued throughout this book, we are, in agreement with the Warnock Report, discussing a significant proportion of children, about a fifth, and not the odd one or two per cent.

(2) *Each service's monitoring system must mesh efficiently with those of other services.* Teachers and speech therapists, for example, must endeavour to ensure that the information they each discover which is relevant to the other's work should be shared. To this must also be added, as appropriate, information from the audiologist, educational psychologist and other professionals. As a child develops, the monitoring system must ensure maximum use of all available information for the sake of the child.

Clearly this aim demands several prerequisite conditions. There must be good, trusting working relationships, no unhealthy power struggles and none of the obfuscation criticised earlier. But there must also be an efficient means of sharing information. One of the results of the project in Sheffield described above was a highlighting of the fact that understanding each other, and feeling better about our own roles and those of others is not enough. It helps to appreciate the reasons why I can't contact a colleague, but that alone doesn't help the child.

Some simple administrative modifications can help here. Booklets which contain relevant names and addresses of workers are useful, if up-to-date. With micro-technology, such datafiles can be easily modified to give accurate information. Notification that a request for intervention has been received can avoid the common situation of wondering whether lack of action means the request was never received. Workers' areas can be drawn to overlap to a greater degree, and the workers themselves could move about less frequently. In addition, lunch clubs and the like can provide a useful 'drop-in' session when people can meet face-to-face.

(3) *Confidentiality* will be a major issue if such developments occur. Will easier access result in too much sharing of information, to the point of gossip? The increased access to microcomputers increases concern in this area. In 1983 a Data Protection Bill was introduced into Parliament which had unknown implications for professionals. It was lost with the calling of a General Election, but has reappeared with the new government.

But these developments do not affect the essential aspects of confidentiality, only issues of degree. Considerations of privacy, access and accuracy must be present anyway: the rise of the micro has simply brought these issues into greater focus. We would contend, also, that it is important to distinguish aspects of privacy in this debate. Professionals have traditionally maintained a cloak of secrecy around their work and especially their reports (see above) but there is now an accelerating movement towards access by the person about whom a report is written. The 1981 Education Act gives access to the statement, by right, to parents (and probably to youngsters themselves). The Advisory Centre for Education has campaigned for some time to 'open up' school records. In general we see moves to greater access as both inevitable and desirable.

But the issue is not simple. For example, a child's parents might each individually give delicate information to, say, a psychologist on the understanding that this is not reported to the other parent. Such delicate situations are not uncommon in work with children, particularly in cases of child neglect, abuse or arguments over custody. The interests of the child must be the guiding principle but, unless the matter goes to law and the professional must comply with, say, a judge's decision, the professional is still left to make his or her own decision on what is right for the child.

'Confidentiality' can be a cop-out, a smokescreen for increasing spurious professionalisation. But privacy for the individual and the sharing of helpful information are both essential for good practice, as we conceive it.

(4) *Screening and Monitoring*. In the formulation presented here, screening and assessment are seen as part of a continuous monitoring system. Children in school, for example, might be screened shortly after entry on various dimensions, and again a year later. Some will be assessed in more detail as a result. But all should have their progress monitored, with varying degrees of intensity. Unless this happens effectively, children can 'slip through the net'.

Take for example hearing problems. We have seen, in Chapters 3 and 4, how early screening is not foolproof, and also that there is at least a five-year gap between that done before 1 year and that conducted in the infant school. The National Deaf Children's Society have argued recently that many children are not identified early enough. Access to children pre-school is difficult, if they are not taken to clinics. But once a child enters a nursery, or later an infant or first school, the teachers can play an important part in monitoring a child's reaction to sound. This can supplement the audiological screening.

A second example concerns children's learning ability. Screening tests at, say, 3 to 5 years have only limited usefulness as many children would be wrongly classified. However, if a well constructed instrument is used the teacher can be alerted to possible problems. This information, together with that derived from continuous monitoring can give a much fuller picture of the child's rate of development in relevant areas. This does not mean 'testing' necessarily, but checking a child's response to learning and social situations. Targets can be set, and their attainment or otherwise, can be judged. 'Continuous' does not mean watching a child every minute of the day, but sampling his or her behaviour, and recording it as appropriate. In some cases this might be daily, in others weekly.

Some might argue that this idea is unworkable, demanding too much attention to detail, too frequently. We would dispute this. Careful monitoring and assessment is time-consuming, but by efficient use of resources and some modification of practice it can be achieved. For example, Chazan *et al* (1980) report a number of comments made by teachers who cared for handicapped children in special schools and nurseries which suggest that more frequent access and discussion with other professionals was desired but, in this sample, rarely achieved. Regular visits to schools by an educational psychologist, clinical medical officer and speech therapist, for example, would, if done on an informal basis, allow teachers to discuss their concerns about their children. More importantly, our experience has been that such practice engenders a greater awareness of the need to identify problems early and allows this to be done more effectively. First, because the teacher knows the other professional is available, there is some point in bothering to identify the problem. Second, if the other professionals are seen to be helpful, the teacher is again encouraged to act.

Such initiatives are certainly easier when children are in school (i.e. nursery age upwards) as the school provides a natural community focus. But similar systems can be established at the pre-school stage based on Mother and Toddler groups, GP surgeries, well-baby clinics (provided these are run as welcoming community resources) and other community centres.

Parents

We consider parents to be of crucial importance in this discussion, and so a separate discussion of their role is necessary. Our views are shaped by our experience of working with children over many years. In short, unless we are able to work with parents the child will not benefit to the extent possible. But these may be just fine words. Remember that the critics of professionals have argued that parents have been ignored, patronised and coerced. Their position may be seen as at the wrong end of a power struggle. As Sutton (1982) points out:

> In the face of massive and mysterious panoply of local and central

government, the child's parents, who have to represent this family to outside authority, will probably be as helpless and powerless as are most individuals whose lives are in part in the hands of bureaucracies (p. 14).

It is very difficult for many professionals to appreciate what it is like to be in the position of parents of a child with special needs. The stress suffered by such parents takes different forms at various times. First, there is the shock and trauma when hearing that your child has a problem. This is most acute in the case of a profound handicap. Many parents of children known to be handicapped from birth report that they couldn't take in what the paediatrician was saying. Those of us who have had a profoundly handicapped child can empathise more easily but most professionals are not in this position. In the case of children with less severe problems the stress is perhaps milder but gradually builds up. Parents see their child progressing more slowly than friends' children. This can also be the case for children with severe problems not recognised at birth.

Coming to terms with the problem is difficult enough, but then parents must also come to terms with the treatment. Children with developmental problems often have difficulties in several areas of functioning, and such children could visit several different professionals. From the parents' point of view stress here takes several forms. There are the practical problems of taking a child to several specialists, often in different locations. At each visit there might be a long wait, with an increasingly impatient child, or children. By the time the professional is seen, the parent (let alone the child) may be in a far from ideal state to consider advice or discuss the child dispassionately. Anyone who has sat in a hospital out-patients waiting room with a child will know how difficult a time this can be. In fact, I always recommend to the medical students I teach that this should be a compulsory part of their training.

Screening and assessment of pre-school children are usually best done with a parent present; this makes the child feel more secure and consequently more relaxed. Parents also are major sources of information about the child and in the pre-school years are usually *the* major source. But discussion should be two-way. We should not expect parents to give us information without our giving in return. Do we explain why we are conducting the tests we give? What the child's responses indicate? Or what our concerns are? If we entered into a real dialogue our knowledge of the child would increase. When we see the point of something we tend to think more about it and so produce more meaningful responses.

In addition we must be prepared to accept the validity of parents' views and not dismiss them as 'fussy'. Freeman, Carbin and Boese (1981) for example, report that parents of hearing-impaired children often realised there was a problem before the professionals – indeed they report a study in Vancouver where one half of family physicians consulted by the parents of children later found to be deaf did not agree that the child was deaf, and more than a third refused referral to a specialist!

If parents are fully involved at the assessment stage they are more likely to be willing to involve themselves in helping their child when questions of appropriate intervention arise. The important role of parents in helping their children is now extensively documented and it is therefore incumbent upon professionals to learn how to maximise the resources that parents can provide. A number of examples with handicapped children are given by Pugh (1981) in her book *Parents as Partners*. Recent work in London (Tizard *et al*, 1982) and in Rochdale (Jackson and Hannon, 1982) has shown how parents can help their children to develop reading. These initiatives and those of Bushell, Miller and Robson (1982) on 'paired reading' have been extended in Sheffield where hundreds of parents have been helping their children develop reading, working in collaboration with teachers and educational psychologists (Gallivan, personal communication).

Conclusions

In this book we have tried to describe the ways of working of the major professionals who deal with children with special needs. We have concentrated on the area of identifying problems, although we have referred to treatment and provision. We have tried to show that the identification of problems in young children is far from easy and that a coherent system of monitoring children, which includes screening as appropriate, is required. We have also argued that the role of parents as partners is central to the optimal provision of help to the child.

What of the future? At the time of writing, Sheffield, like other areas, is in a state of change. A new District Health Authority has just been formed. The implications of the 1981 Education Act are being considered and the Education Department, District Health Authority and Family and Community Services are trying to produce a coherent and comprehensive system in line with the Act's requirements.

In the next few years the impact of this legislation will be a major issue, particularly in terms of provision. Parents are likely to demand more provision in normal settings. This may mean more integrated nurseries and first schools for children with special needs. The city already has three such nurseries which are being evaluated. In their first three years of operation two-thirds of their children have moved on to placements in normal schools. There is also likely to be a further re-examination of the role of parents. Given the increasing recognition of the importance of this, ways of increasing the effectiveness will be explored. This will include a variety of professionals, advising and guiding parents, and also the development of more self-help groups by parents. Voluntary bodies will continue to be of importance in this area.

It is also likely that increased effectiveness of preventative methods will reduce the number of children with severe handicapping conditions. The incidence of some conditions such as Downs Syndrome and sensory handicap has already decreased. Improved methods of screening the embryo for severely handicapped conditions are likely to be developed. But much will depend on finance. Research and provision cost money and unless the Government is prepared to provide the money, chances will be lost.

The early years of a child's life are of the utmost importance. It is then that major developmental changes occur which provide the basis for the child's future. We professionals have a duty to ensure that we offer to children the best help that is available. As we have argued in this book, this requires the development of useful methods, tests and instruments, the optimal collaboration between professionals, and treating parents as partners.

BIBLIOGRAPHY

Ainscow, M. and Tweddle, D. (1979) *Preventing Classroom Failure: An Objectives Approach*, Chichester: J. Wiley

Algie, J. (1975) *Social Values, Objectives and Action*, London: Kogan Page

Arnold, H. (1982) *Listening to Children Reading*, London: Hodder and Stoughton

Bailey, T. and Rogers, C. (1979) 'Screening diagnosis and prescription: An infant reading check', *Association of Educational Psychologists Journal, 5* (1), 47-56

Bax, M. (1982) 'Editorial', *Developmental Medicine and Child Neurology, 24*, 139-40

Bax, M. and Whitmore, K. (1973) 'Neurodevelopmental screening, in the school entrant medical examination', *Lancet, ii*, 368

Becker, W.C., Engelmann, S., Carnine, D.W. and Rhine, W.R. (1981) 'Direct Instruction Model' in W.R. Rhine (ed), *Making Schools More Effective*, London: Academic Press

Bennett, F.C., Robinson, N.M. and Sells, C.J. (1983) 'Growth and development of infants weighing less than 800g at birth', *Paediatrics, 71*, 319-23

Berry, H.K., O'Grady, D.J., Perlmutter, L.J. and Bofinger, M.K. (1979) 'Intellectual development and academic achievement of children treated early for phenylketonuria', *Developmental Medicine and Child Neurology, 21*, 311-20

Bierman-van Eedenburg, M.E., Jurgens-van der Zee, A.D., Olinga, A.A., Huisses, H.H. and Touwen, B.C.L. (1981) 'Predictive value of neonatal examination: a follow-up study at 18 months', *Developmental Medicine and Child Neurology, 23*, 296-305

Blatchford, P., Battle, S. and Mays, J. (1982) *The First Transition: Home to Pre-school*, Windsor: NFER-Nelson

Bodegard, G., Fyro, K. and Larsson, A. (1983) 'Psychological reactions in 102 families with a newborn who has a false positive screening test for congenital hypothyroidism', *Acta Paediatrica Scandinavica*, Supplement 304

British Association of Teachers of the Deaf, National Executive Committee (1981) 'Audiological definitions and forms for recording audiometric information', *Journal of British Association of Teachers of the Deaf, 5*, 83-7

Bryant, G.M., Davies, K.J. and Newcombe, R.G. (1974) 'The Denver Developmental Screening Test: Achievement of test items in the first year of life by Denver and Cardiff infants', *Developmental Medicine and Child Neurology, 16*, 475-84

——, Davies, K.J. and Newcombe, R.G. (1979) 'Standardisation of the Denver Developmental Screening Test for Cardiff children', *Developmental Medicine and Child Neurology, 21*, 353-64

Burns, E.C. (1982) 'Essential investigations in children of short stature', *Maternal and Child Health*, April, 140-2

Burstall, C. (1978) 'The Matthew effect in the classroom', *Educational Research, 21*, 19-25

Bushell, R., Miller, A. and Robson, D. (1982) 'Parents as remedial teachers', *Association of Educational Psychologists Journal, 5* (9), 7-13

Central Birmingham Community Health Council (1981) '6/10 should do better: A report on parents' perceptions of child health services in central Birmingham'

Chazan, M., Laing, A., Shackleton-Bailey, M. and Jones, G. (1980) *Some of Our Children*, London: Open Books

Clark, A.D.B. (1978) 'Predicting human development: Problems, evidence and implications', *Bulletin of British Psychological Society, 31*, 249-258

Clark, J. (1973) *A Family Visitor*, London: Royal College of Nursing

—— (1974) *The Role of the Health Visitor*, London: BBC Publications

Cleave, S., Jowett, S. and Bate, M. (1982) *And So to School: A Study of Continuity from Pre-School to Infant School*, Windsor: NFER-Nelson

Clift, P., Weiner, G. and Wilson, E. (1981) *Record-Keeping in Primary Schools*, Basingstoke: Macmillan Educational

Cohen, R.N. (1982) *Whose file is it anyway?* London: National Council for Civil Liberties

Conrad, R. (1979) *The Deaf School Child*, London: Harper and Row

Cooper, J., Moodley, M. and Reynell, J. (1979) 'The developmental language programme: Results from a five year study', *British Journal of Disorders of Communication, 14*, 57-69

Cornwall, K. (1979) 'The development of a screening technique: Some reflections on four years' experience in one local authority', *Occasional Papers of the Division of Educational and Child Psychology, 3*(1), 3-10

——, Pumfrey, P. and Hedderley, R. (1983) 'Enquiry into pupils with specific reading difficulties', *Occasional Papers of the Division of Educational and Child Psychology, 7* (3)

—— and Spicer, J. (1982) 'DECP enquiry: The role of the educational psychologist in the discovery and assessment of children requiring special education', *Occasional Papers of the Division of Educational and Child Psychology, 6* (2), 3-30

Crystal, D. (1980) *Introduction to Language Pathology*, London: Edward Arnold

Daniels, J.C. and Diack, H. (1958) *The Standard Reading Tests*, London: Chatto and Windus

David, T.J., Parris, M.R., Poynor, M.V., Hawnaur, J.M., Simm, S.A., Rigg, E.A. and McCrae, F.C. (1983) 'Reasons for late detection of hip dislocation in childhood', *Lancet*, July 16, 147-8

Dean, J.G., MacQueen, I.A.G., Ross, R.G. and Kempe, C.H. (1978) 'The health visitor's role in the prediction of early childhood injuries and failure to thrive', *Child Abuse and Neglect, 2*, 1-17

Department of Education and Science (1968) *Psychologists in the Education Services*, London: HMSO

—— (1972) *Speech Therapy Services* (The Quirk Report), London: HMSO

—— (1974) *Circular 3/74: Child Guidance*, London: HMSO

—— (1975) *A Language for Life* (The Bullock Report), London: HMSO

—— (1978) *Special Educational Needs* (The Warnock Report), London: HMSO

—— (1980) *Special Needs in Education*, London: HMSO, Cmmd 7996

—— (1983a) *Education (Special Educational Needs) Regulations 1983*, Statutory Instrument 1983 No. 29, London: HMSO

—— (1983b) *Circular 1/83: Assessments and Statements of Special Educational Needs*, London: HMSO

Department of Health and Social Security (1956) *An Enquiry into Health Visiting* (The Jameson Report), London: HMSO

—— (1976a) *Fit for the Future* (The Court Report), London: HMSO

—— (1976b) *Prevention and Health: Everybody's Business*, London: HMSO

—— (1980) *Research into Services for Children and Adolescents*, London: HMSO

—— (1981) *Care in Action*, London: HMSO

Dickson, R.A. (1983) 'Scoliosis in the community', *British Medical*

Journal, 286, 615-17

Dodge, J.A. and Riley, H.C. (1982) 'Screening for cystic fibrosis', *Archives of Disease in Childhood, 57*, 774-80

Douglas, J.E. and Sutton, A. (1978) 'The development of speech and mental processes in a pair of twins: a case study', *Journal of Child Psychology and Psychiatry, 19*, 49-56

Earle, E. (1981) 'Stress after amniocentesis for high maternal AFP measurements', *Maternal and Child Health, 6*, 347-50

Education Act (1981) London: HMSO

Egan, D.F., Illingworth, R.S. and MacKeith, R.C. (1969) *Developmental Screening 0-5 Years*, London: Spastics International Medical Publications

Evans, P. (1980) 'Measuring deafness in newborn babies' (letter) in *Bulletin of British Psychological Society, 33*, 46

Evans, R., Davies, P., Ferguson, N. and Williams, P. (1979) *Swansea Evaluation Profiles for School Entrants*, Windsor: NFER-Nelson

Forfar, J.O. (1968) 'At Risk Registers', *Developmental Medicine and Child Neurology, 10*, 384

Frankenburg, W.K., Fandal, A.W., Sciarillo, W. and Burgess, D. (1981) 'The newly abbreviated and revised Denver Developmental Screening Test', *Journal of Paediatrics, 99*, 995-99

———, Goldstein, A.D. and Camp, B.W. (1971) 'The revised Denver Developmental Screening Test: its accuracy as a screening instrument', *Journal of Paediatrics, 79*, 988-95

Freeman, R.D., Carbin, C.F. and Boese, R.J. (1981) *Can't your Child Hear?*, London: Croom Helm

Frude, N. (1980) *Psychological Approaches to Child Abuse*, London: Batsford

Fundudis, T., Kolvin, I. and Garside, R.F. (1980) 'A follow-up of speech retarded children' in L.A. Hersov, M. Berger and A.R. Nicol (eds.), *Language and Language Disorders in Childhood*, Oxford: Pergamon Press

Galloway, D. and Goodwin, C. (1979) *Educating Slow Learning and Maladjusted Children – Integration or Segregation?*, London: Longman

Ghodsian, M. and Calnan, M. (1977) 'A comparative longitudinal analysis of special education groups', *British Journal of Educational Psychology, 47*, 162-74

Gill, C. (1982) 'Integration for the deaf: a most restrictive environment?', Unpublished MSc dissertation, University of Sheffield, Institute of Education

Gordon, R.R. (1979) 'An attempt to reduce incidence of N.A.I. in Sheffield', *Journal of Abuse and Neglect, 3*, 795-801

Gray, D. and Reeve, J. (1978) 'Ordinary schools: Some special help', *Special Education, 5*, 25-7

Hannon, V. (1982) 'The Education Act 1981: New rights and duties in special education', *Journal of Social Welfare Law*, September

Harlen, W. (1977) *Match and Mismatch: Raising Questions*, London: Oliver and Boyd

Hart, H., Bax, M. and Jenkins, S. (1981) 'Use of Child Health Clinics', *Archives of Disease in Childhood, 56*, 440-5

Hegarty, S. and Pocklington, K. (1981) *Educating Pupils with Special Needs in the Ordinary School*, Windsor: NFER-Nelson

—— (1982) *Integration in Action*, Windsor: NFER-Nelson.

Hendrickse, W.A. (1982) 'How effective are our child health clinics?', *British Medical Journal, 284*, 575-7

Heron, A. and Myers, M. (1983) *Intellectual Impairment: The Battle Against Handicap*, London: Academic Press

Hindley, C.B. and Owen, C.F. (1978) 'The extent of individual changes in IQ for ages between 6 months and 17 years in a British longitudinal sample', *Journal of Child Psychology and Psychiatry, 19*, 329-50

De Hirsch, K., Jansky, J.J. and Langford, W.S. (1967) *Predicting Reading Failure*, London: Harper Row

Hobbs, P. (1973) *Aptitude or Environment*, London: Royal College of Nursing

Hodges, M. (1983) 'Screening secondary school children', *Nursing Times*, 31 August, 53-5

Hogben, D. (1972) 'The behavioural objectives approach: Some problems and some dangers', *Journal of Curriculum Studies, 4*, 42-50

Holtzman, N.A. (1983) 'Prenatal screening for neural tube defects', *Paediatrics, 71*, 658-60

Howells, J.G. (1974) *Remember Maria*, London: Butterworth

Humberside Education Authority (1981) *Infant Screening*, London: Macmillan Education

Illingworth, R.S. (1979) 'Some experience in an Area Health Authority child health clinic', *British Medical Journal, 1*, 866-9

—— (1982) *Basic Developmental Screening 0-4 Years*, 3rd edn., Oxford: Blackwell Scientific

Irwin, D.M. and Bushnell, M.M. (1980) *Observational Studies for Child Study*, London: Holt, Rinehart and Winston

Ives, L.A. and Morris, T. (1978) 'The creation and subsequent development of a diagnostic and advisory centre for hearing-impaired pupils with particular reference to the multiple handicapped', *Journal of British Association of Teachers of the Deaf, 2*, 61-4

Jackson, A. and Hannon, P. (1981) *The Belfield Reading Project*, Rochdale: Bellfield Community Council

Jacobs, D. and Lynas, W. (1982) 'The size of the educational problem of deafness', *Journal of British Association of Teachers of the Deaf, 6*, 102-5

Jaffe, M., Marel, J., Goldberg, A., Rudolph-Schnitzer, M. and Winter, S.T. (1980) 'The use of the Denver Developmental Screening Test in infant welfare clinics', *Developmental Medicine and Child Neurology, 22*, 55-60

Jones, J. (1983) 'HVA hearing screening survey (No. 2)', *Health Visitor, 56*, 191

Kempe, R.S. and Kempe, C.H. (1978) *Child Abuse*, London: Fontana/Open Books

King, M. (ed.) (1981) *Childhood, Welfare and Justice*, London: Batsford

Knox, E.G. and Mahon, D.F. (1970) 'Evaluation of 'Infant Risk' registers', *Archives of Diseases in Childhood, 45*, 634-9

Koluchova, J. (1976) 'The further study of twins after severe prolonged deprivation: a second report', *Journal of Child Psychology and Psychiatry, 17*, 181-9

Lawrence, D. and Blagg, N. (1977) *The Somerset Developmental Checklist*, Harlow: Good Reading

Lealman, G.T., Haigh, D., Phillips, J.M., Stone, J. and Ord-Smith, C. (1983) 'Prediction and prevention of child abuse — an empty hope?', *Lancet*, 25 June, *8339*, 1423-4

Lichtenstein, R. (1981) 'Comparative validity of two pre-school screening tests: correlational and classificational approaches', *Journal of Learning Disabilities, 14*, 68-73

—— (1982) 'New Instrument, Old Problem for Early Identification', *Exceptional Children, 48*, 70-2

Lindsay, G. (1979a) 'The early identification of learning difficulties and the monitoring of children's progress', Unpublished PhD thesis, University of Birmingham

—— (1979b) 'The Infant Rating Scale: some evidence of its validity from a selected sample of children', *Occasional Papers of the Division of Educational and Child Psychology, 3* (2), 27-41

—— (1980) 'Monitoring Children's Learning: an In-service approach',

British Journal of In-Service Education, 6, 189-191

――― (1981a) *Infant Rating Scale Manual*, Sevenoaks: Hodder and Stoughton

――― (1981b) 'The Infant Rating Scale', *British Journal of Educational Psychology, 50*, 97-104

――― (1983) (ed.) *Problems of Adolescence in the Secondary School*, London: Croom Helm

―― and Wedell, K. (1982) 'The early identification of educationally 'at risk' children: Revisited', *Journal of Learning Disabilities, 15*, 212-17

McCandless, B. (1972) 'Review of the Boehm Test of Basic Concepts' in O.K. Buros (ed.), *Seventh Mental Measurements Yearbook*, New York: Gryphon

McConkey, R. and O'Connor, M. (1982) 'A new approach to parental involvement in language interaction programmes', *Child Care, Health and Development, 8*, 163-76

Manning, K. and Sharp, A. (1977) *Structuring Play in the Early Years at School*, London: Ward Lock Educational/Drake Educational Associates

Margolis, H. (1976) 'The Kindergarten Auditory Screening Test as a predictor of reading disability', *Psychology in the Schools, 13*, 399-403

―――, Doherty, M., Sheridan, R. and Lemanowicz, J. (1981) 'The efficiency of Myklebust's Pupil Rating Scale for detecting Reading and Arithmetic Difficulties', *Journal of Learning Disabilities, 14*, 267-8

Marshall, C. and Gilliland, J. (1976) 'Early identification of children in need', *Occasional Papers of the Division of Educational and Child Psychology, 9*, 392-400

Martin, J.A.M. (1982) 'Diagnosis and Communication ability in deaf children in European countries', *Audiology, 21*, 185-96

Meade, L.S., Nelson, R.O. and Clark, R.P. (1981) 'Concurrent and Construct Validity of the Slingerland screening tests for children with specific language disability', *Journal of Learning Disabilities, 14*, 264-6

Medical Research Council Steering Committee (1981) 'Routine neonatal screening for phenylketonuria in the United Kingdom 1964-1978', *British Medical Journal, 282*, 1680-4

Mellor, D., Hanks, A. and Griffiths, S. (1981) 'Child abuse and the role of the school nurse', *Health Visitor, 54*, 283-5

Merriman, P. (1981) in D. Smith (ed.), *Sending Young Adults Down*,

Lancaster University: Centre of Youth, Crime and Community

Merritt, J. (1981) *Curriculum in Action*, Milton Keynes: Open University

Millham, S., Bullock, R. and Hosie, K. (1978) *Locking Up Children*, London: Saxon House

Mitchell, R.G. (1975) 'Editorial: changing concepts of risk', *Developmental Medicine and Child Neurology, 17*, 227-8

Morris, A., Geller, H., Szwed, E. and Geach, H. (1980) *Justice for Children*, London: Macmillan

Muller, D.J., Munro, S.M. and Code, C. (1981) *Language Assessment for Remediation*, London: Croom Helm

National Deaf Children's Society (1983) *Discovering Deafness*, London: National Deaf Children's Society

National Institute of Social Work (1982) *Social Workers: Their Role and Tasks* (The Barclay Report), London: Bedford Square Press

Neligan, G., Prudham, D. and Steiner, H. (1974) *'The Formative Years': Birth, family and development in Newcastle-upon-Tyne*, Oxford: University Press

————, Kolvin, I., Scott, D.M. and Garside, R.F. (1976) *Born too soon, or born too small*, London: Spastics International

Newell, P. (1982) 'Private Lives?', *Times Educational Supplement*, 23 April

Newton, M.J. and Thomson, M.E. (1976) *The Aston Index*, Wisbech: Learning Development Aids

————, Thomson, M.E. and Richards, I.L. (1979) *Readings in Dyslexia*, Wisbech: LDA

Nietupska, O. and Harding, N. (1982) 'Auditory Screening of school children: Fact or Fallacy', *British Medical Journal, 284*, 717-20

Nolan, M. and Tucker, I. (1981) *The Hearing-Impaired Child and the Family*, London: Souvenir Press

Oakland, T. (1978) 'Predictive validity of readiness tests for middle and lower socioeconomic status Anglo, Black and Mexican American children', *Journal of Educational Psychology, 70*, 574-82

Potton, A. (1983) *Screening*, London: Macmillan Education

Potts, P. (1982) *The Professionals*, Unit 7 of Course 241, 'Special Needs in Education', Milton Keynes: Open University Press

Povey, R.M., Latham, D. and Cliff, S.M. (1983) 'Inter-rater reliability and the IRS', *British Journal of Educational Psychology, 53*, 247-8

Professional Affairs Board (1981) *Psychological Services for Children in England and Wales*, Leicester: British Psychological Society

Pugh, G. (1981) *Parents as Partners*, London: National Children's Bureau

Reichmann, J. and Healey, W.C. (1983) 'Learning disabilities and conductive hearing loss involving otitis media', *Journal of Learning Disabilities, 16*, 272-8

Rennie, E. (1980) 'The West Riding Screening Six Years On', *Educational Research, 23*, 47-50

Rigby, M.J. (1981) 'Child health – a time for better understanding', *Health Trends, 13*, 97-99

Rist, R.C. (1975) 'Student social class and teacher expectation: the self-fulfilling prophecy in Ghetto education' in Insel, P.M. and Jacobson, L.F. (eds.), *What Do You Expect?*, Menlo Park: Cummings

Roberts, C.J., Hibbard, B.M., Elder, G.H., Evans, K.T., Laurence, K.M., Roberts, A., Woodhead, J.S., Robertson, I.B. and Hoole, M. (1983) 'The efficacy of a serum screening service for neural tube defects: The South Wales experience', *Lancet*, 11 June, 1315-18

Robertson, C. (1981a) 'Measuring the effectiveness of health visitors', *Health Visitor, 54*, 20-1

—— (1981b) 'Review of vision screening in pre-school children', *Health Visitor, 54*, 52-7

—— (1981c) 'Monitoring pre-school screening of visual acuity by Health Visitors – a feasibility study', *Health Visitor, 54*, 104-5

Rogers, M.G.H. (1971) 'Early Recognition of handicapping disorders in children', *Developmental Medicine and Child Neurology, 13*, 88-101

Rosenthal, R. and Jacobson, L.F. (1968) *Pygmalion in the Classroom*, London: Holt, Rinehart and Winston

Rutter, M. (1975) *Helping Troubled Children*, Harmondsworth: Penguin

——, Maughan, B., Mortimore, P. and Ouston, J. (1979) *Fifteen Thousand Hours*, London: Open Books

——, Tizard, J. and Whitmore, K. (1970) *Education, Health and Behaviour*, London: Longmans

Sainsbury, E. (1970) *Social Diagnosis in Casework*, London: Routledge and Kegan Paul

Satz, P. and Fletcher, J. (1979) 'Early screening tests: some uses and abuses', *Journal of Learning Disabilities, 12*, 56-9

Sheridan, M. (1962) 'Infants at risk of handicapping conditions', *Monthly Bulletin, Ministry of Health Laboratory Service, 21*, 238

—— (1968) *Manual for the Stycar Hearing Test* (Revised Edition), Windsor: NFER

—— (1973) *Manual for the Stycar Vision Tests*, Windsor: NFER-Nelson

—— (1975) *Children's Developmental Progress from Birth to Five Years*, Windsor: NFER-Nelson

Silva, P.A. (1980) 'The prevalence, stability and significance of developmental language delay in pre-school children', *Developmental Medicine and Child Neurology, 22*, 768-77

Stenhouse, L. (1975) *An Introduction to Curriculum Research and Development*, London: Heinemann

Sutton, A. (1981) 'Science in Court' in King, M. (ed.), *Childhood, Welfare and Justice*, London: Batsford

—— (1982) *The Powers That Be*, Unit 8 of Course 241, 'Special Needs in Education', Milton Keynes: Open University Press

Sylva, K., Roy, C. and Painter, M. (1980) *Childwatching at Playgroup and Nursery School*, London: Grant McIntyre

Tansley, A.E. (1976) 'Special educational treatment in infants schools: A 6½ year screening' in Wedell, K. and Raybould, E.C. (eds.), *The Early Identification of Educationally 'At Risk' Children*, University of Birmingham: Educational Review Occasional Publications, No. 6

Tansley, P. and Panckhurst, J. (1981) *Children with Specific Learning Difficulties*, Windsor: NFER-Nelson

Taylor, E.M. and Emery, J.L. (1982) 'Two year study of the causes of post-perinatal deaths classified in terms of preventability', *Archives of Disease in Childhood, 57*, 668-73

Thorndike, R.L. (1968) 'Review: "Pygmalion in the Classroom" ', *American Educational Research Journal, 5*, 708-11

Tibbenham, A.D., Peckham, C.S. and Gardiner, P.A. (1978) 'Vision screening in children tested at 7, 11 and 16 years', *British Medical Journal*, 1312-14

Tizard, J., Schofield, W.N. and Hewison, J. (1982) 'Collaboration between teachers and parents in assisting children's reading', *British Journal of Educational Psychology, 52*, 1-15

Tomlinson, S. (1981) *Educational Subnormality – A Study in Decision-making*, London: Routledge and Kegan Paul

—— (1982) *A Sociology of Special Education*, London: Routledge and Kegan Paul

Tough, J. (1976) *Listening to Children Talking*, London: Schools Council, Ward Lock Educational

—— (1977) *The Development of Meaning*, London: Allen and Unwin

Touwen, B., Bierman-van Eedenburg, M. and Jurgens-van der Zee, A. (1977) 'Neurological screening of full-term new born babies', *Developmental Medicine and Child Neurology, 19*, 739-47

Trickey, G. and Kosky, R. (1983) 'The Barking Project: Organising for diversity', *Remedial Education, 18,* 53-8

Tyler, S. (1980) *Keele Pre-School Assessment Guide,* Windsor: NFER-Nelson

Walker, V., Clayton, B.E. and Ersser, R.S. (1981) 'Hyperphenylalaninaemia of various types among three quarters of a million neonates in a screening programme', *Archives of Disease in Childhood, 56,* 759-64

Weatherall, J.A.C. (1982) 'A review of some effects of recent medical practices in reducing the numbers of children born with congenital abnormalities', *Health Trends, 14,* 85-8

Wedell, K. and Lambourne, R. (1980) 'Psychological Services for Children in England and Wales', *Occasional Papers of the Division of Educational and Child Psychology, 4* (1 and 2)

―――― and Lindsay, G. (1980) 'Early identification procedures: what have we learned', *Remedial Education, 15,* 130-5

Williams, P. (1971) *Swansea Test of Phonic Skills,* Oxford: Basil Blackwell

Wilson, J.A. (1982) 'Child Health Services after re-organisation', *Archives of Disease in Children, 67,* 1-2

Wilson, J.M.G. and Junger, G. (1968) *The Principles and Practice of Screening for Disease,* Geneva: World Health Organisation

Wolfendale, S. (1976) 'Screening and early identification of reading and learning difficulties ― a description of the Croydon Screening Procedures' in Wedell, K. and Raybould, E.C. (eds.), *The Early Identification of Educationally 'At Risk' Children,* Birmingham University: Educational Review Occasional Publications, No. 6

Woods, J. (1981) 'A practical guide to preventing child abuse', *Health Visitor, 54,* 281-3

World Health Organisation (1980) *Early Detection of Handicap in Children,* Geneva: World Health Organisation

Zinkin, P. and Cox, C. (1975) 'A study of the allocation of resources in the detection of children under 3 years with developmental delay. Description and preliminary results' in Wedell, K. and Raybould, E.C. (eds.), *Early Identification of Educationally 'At Risk' Children,* University of Birmingham: Educational Review, Occasional Publications, No. 6

―――― (1976) 'Child Health Clinics and inverse care laws', *British Medical Journal, 2,* 411-13

NOTES ON CONTRIBUTORS

Judith Connell, Chief Technician in Paediatric Audiology, Audiology Department, The Children's Hospital, Sheffield.

Bryan Craig, Chief Assistant (Education Liaison), Family and Community Services, Sheffield.

Mary Jane Drummond, Headteacher, Holt House Infant School, Sheffield LEA.

Kathleen Jennings, Formerly State Registered Nurse, State Certified Midwife and Health Visitor, Sheffield Area Health Authority; currently Educational Psychologist, Kirklees LEA.

Geoff Lindsay, Senior Educational Psychologist, Psychological Service, Sheffield LEA; Honorary Lecturer, Division of Education, Sheffield University; Visiting Professor, Instituto Superior Psicologia Aplicada, Lisbon.

Anna MacCarthy, Principal Clinical Medical Officer (Audiology – Preschool and School Children), Sheffield DHA.

Ruth M. Powell, Principal Medical Officer (Child Health), Sheffield DHA and the Ryegate Centre, The Children's Hospital, Sheffield.

Kath Thompson, Formerly Chief Speech Therapist, Department of Communication, Children's Hospital, Sheffield DHA; currently District Speech Therapist, Sheffield DHA.

INDEX

abortion 19–20
amniocentesis 18
Aston Index 124–7, 130–1
    evaluation 126–7
audiogram 77–8
audiological assessment 77–82
    evoked response audiometry
        81–2
    impedance audiometry 79–80
    pure tone audiometry 77–9
    speech tests of hearing 80–1
audiological screening 50–2, 71–7
    evaluation 51–2, 83, 171
    perinatal 71–2
    pre-school 50–1, 74–7; distraction
        test 50–1, 74–5; subjective
        tests 75; toy discrimination
        75–6; sweep test 76
    school age 27
    secondary school 73
audiological technician 68
audiologist 65–6
audiology service 65–9

birth weight 25
    as predictor 170–1

child abuse
    register 37–8
    risk factors 59–61, 142; evalua-
        tion 61, 172–3
    see also health visitor, screening,
        registers in childhood
clinical medical officers 13–14
clinical medical officers (audiology)
    66
clinical psychologists 118–19
community assessment clinics 31–4
community health councils 14
compensatory interaction 176–7, 181
confidentiality 160–1, 182–3
cot deaths 40–1
counselling
    genetic 41
    need for 20, 41
Croydon Checklist 124, 130, 146–7
    evaluation 131

Data Protection Bill 161, 182
Denver Developmental Screening
    Test 59
    evaluation 59, 171
district handicap team 31–4
doctors *see* clinical medical officers,
    clinical medical officers – audio-
    logy, medical practitioners
Downs Syndrome 5, 18, 187
Duchenne muscular dystrophy 18–19

early identification
    evaluation 15, 80
    need for 80, 85, 90–1
    rationale 5, 90, 121, 141
    see also screening
educational psychologist 67, 117–19,
    132
    numbers of 117–18
    training 118–19
educational screening 106, 119–33,
    168
    evaluation 126–7, 128–9, 129–32
    examples 122–9
    prediction 123, 131
    timing 121–2
educational testing 112

glue ear 27, 79–80

health visitor 23, 31, 43–62
    development of the profession
        43–5
    notification of births 48
    screening: general development
        55–9, 168; hearing 50–2, 72,
        168; non-accidental injury
        59–61; vision 52–5
    surveillance 44, 48, 50, 62, 147
    see also 'audiological screening'
    training 45–6
hearing loss
    educational implication 82–5
    types of impairment: conductive
        loss 69–70; glue ear 27, 79–
        80; sensori-neural loss 70–1
    see also audiological assessment,
        audiological screening

height, measurement of 3, 25
hips, congenital dislocation of 24–5

Infant Rating Scale 92–3, 127–9
    evaluation 128–9
integration 84–5, 163

Keele Pre-School Assessment Guide
    92, 102–3, 123
Kendall Toy Test 81

language problems
    assessment 94–7
    screening 90–1, 172; pre-school
        91–2, 172; school 92–3
Linco–Bennett Auditory Response
    Cradle 71–2

Manchester Picture Test 81
medical practitioners 12–14
medical screening
    antenatal: alphafetoprotein 17,
        168, 170; amniocentesis
        17–19; blood tests 15; blood
        group incompatibility 16–17,
        19; fetoscopy 19–20; radio-
        logy 20; rubella 16; ultrasound
        17, 19–20, 170
    neonatal: cystic fibrosis 22–3;
        phenylketonuria 21
    post-natal 23–5
    school entry 26; neurodevelop-
        mental 28–30, 170–1
    see also phenylketonuria
medical surveillance 10, 23–5, 41–2
    evaluation 34–5, 42
monitoring children's development
    132–3, 173, 181–4
    see also school records

National Deaf Children's Society 64,
    72, 83, 167, 183
1981 Education Act 64, 153–66,
    180, 182
    assessments 153–6
    children's rights 160, 182–3
    parents' rights 154, 156, 159–60,
        182–3
    statement 6, 154, 157–9, 163–4;
        parental access 161, 182
non-accidental injury *see* child abuse

observation 113–15
otitis media *see* glue ear

parents
    as partners 11, 63–4, 161–2,
        184–6
    case conferences 33
    contact with school 101–2
    rights 154, 156, 159–60, 182–3
phenylketonuria 21, 181
    screening 21–2, 168; effectiveness
        of 1, 3, 170–1; problems with
        4
prediction
    problems of 142–3, 170
    self-fulfilling prophecy 98
professionals
    collaboration between 65, 84,
        120, 152, 169
    communication between 84, 96
    knowledge of 10
    networks 180
    stereotypes 10, 134, 179
pure tone audiometry 76–9

Quirk Report 88–9

referral procedures
    audiologists 51, 72–4
    educational psychologists 133
    health visitors 31, 51, 54, 58
    medical practitioners 30–1
    school social workers 144–5
    speech therapists 87, 93–4
    teachers 113
registers in childhood
    at risk 36–7, 170
    at risk of sudden death in infancy
        40–1
    congenital malformations 38–9
    handicapped 39–40
    non-accidental injury 37–8

school-based social work
    approaches 137–41, 151
    prevalence 136, 151
    screening 141–3, 146–7
    Sheffield project 143–7; origin
        143–4; screening 146–7;
        welfare network 144–5
school records 84
    basic skills 109, 181
    checklists 102–3, 108
    children's work 110
    informal 111
    interpretation 112
    learning processes 104–5

objectives 103–4
parents' information 101–2, 109
profile sheet 107–8
see also monitoring children's
   development
schools
   age of entry 99–100
   classroom organisation 100–1
   special 8–9, 163
   transition to 101–2
Schools Council 113–15
scoliosis 30
screening
   acceptibility 3, 15, 61
   accuracy 4, 15, 170–4
   at risk 5, 36–8, 40–1, 55
   cost effectiveness 4, 15, 41, 51,
      173
   lack of evaluation 62, 129–30,
      169
social work, assessment 147–51
social workers
   education 136
   for hearing impaired 67
   generic 137
   prevalence 135

training 135–6
special needs
   definition 7
   incidence 7–10, 98
   provision 163–5
speech audiometry 81
speech therapist 67, 86–9, 178
   role 87, 93–4
   staffing and workloads 88–9
   training 88
squint 53–4
Stycar hearing test 50–1
Stycar vision test 53–5
survey 2

Tay–Sach disease 19
teachers 158, 169
   of hearing impaired children
      64–5, 82, 158

vision
   deterioration with age 5, 28
   screening: colour 28; evaluation
      54–5, 168; pre-school 53–4;
      school entry 27–8; squint
      28, 53–4